BOOTSTRAP DREAMS

BOOTSTRAP DREAMS

U.S. MICROENTERPRISE DEVELOPMENT IN AN ERA OF WELFARE REFORM

NANCY C. JURIK

ILR PRESS

AN IMPRINT OF
CORNELL UNIVERSITY PRESS
ITHACA AND LONDON

First published 2005 by Cornell University Press
First printing, Cornell Paperbacks, 2005

Printed in the United States of America

Design by Scott Levine

Library of Congress Cataloging-in-Publication Data
Jurik, Nancy C.
    Bootstrap dreams : U.S. microenterprise development in an era of welfare reform / Nancy C. Jurik.
        p. cm.
    Includes bibliographical references and index.
    ISBN 0-8014-4299-0 (cloth : alk. paper)—ISBN 0-8014-8997-0 (pbk : alk. paper)
    1. Microfinance--United States.   2. Informal sector (Economics)--United States.   3. Marginality, Social--United States.   I. Title.
    HG178.33.U6J87 2005
    338.6′42′0973--dc22
                                            2004018924

Cornell University Press strives to use environmentally responsible suppliers and materials to the fullest extent possible in the publishing of its books. Such materials include vegetable-based, low-VOC inks and acid-free papers that are recycled, totally chlorine-free, or partly composed of nonwood fibers. For further information, visit our website at www.cornellpress.cornell.edu.

Cloth printing   10 9 8 7 6 5 4 3 2 1
Paperback printing   10 9 8 7 6 5 4 3 2 1

To Gray Cavender

CONTENTS

I was born into a family of small farmers. They were the kind of small-business people who needed loans to survive and expand. My parents often borrowed money to plant crops in the spring that would be harvested in the fall; when the crops came in, they repaid the loan. Our hometown bank loaned them the money without collateral. They secured the loans with their good reputation in the small Texas community where we lived.

For 48 years, my uncle worked at the bank that provided my parents with these loans. When he began, the bank was a small, family-owned concern. During the early 1970s, it was sold to a larger holding company based in a neighboring town, and later in the 1970s, it was sold again, this time to a larger corporation based in the metropolitan area nearest us. At the time, I asked my uncle how these dramatic shifts in ownership had changed his job. He answered that it had made banking a lot less personal: "It used to be that when farmers like your parents asked to borrow money to make their crop, I could loan them the money on their good name," he said. "People in town knew your mom and daddy, and knew they would pay back that loan. Now, if people like your parents come into the bank to ask for a loan, I have to ask them for collateral. They have to guarantee that loan with property or savings accounts. That makes it harder for folks just starting out in business and trying to establish themselves."

During the 1980s, a merger between our banking conglomerate and another formed the largest banking concern in the state. Shortly after that, Texas entered an economic recession and the corporation that contained our hometown bank became part of the largest federal bank bailout in U.S. history (at least at that time). One afternoon, I asked my uncle what had happened to the bank and why it went under. He said it had made too many risky loans to speculators. I reminded him of our earlier conversation in which he said that the bank required collateral to secure its loans. "Can't they simply seize those assets?" I asked. He explained, "No, there wasn't enough collateral to seize. It's true that small businesspeople have to provide collateral for a bank loan these days, but that was not true of the businesses who borrowed money from our officers out of Dallas. The owners of those companies received very large loans based on their business ideas and connections to the banking community."

This book is a story of programmatic attempts to restore lending opportunities to individuals in small businesses so that, like the large businessmen and speculators in my banking bailout story, small entrepreneurs would be able to borrow money on their word and business ideas. Although such lending programs have been described as revolutionary, it is important to remember that there were times in the past when lending to small businesses was just something that regular banks did.

■ ■ ■ ■

This project began late in 1992 and has spanned more than a decade. Thus, there are many people to thank for its completion. My understanding of microenterprise development has been informed by the struggles and achievements of program founders, practitioners, and clients. I thank all those individuals who were willing to share their experiences and include me in the work of microenterprise development. I hope this book is helpful to them.

I also thank the graduate research assistants who helped with various phases of the project. They include Diego Castro, Mako Fitts, Joyce Longfellow, Yvonne Luna, Phoebe Morgan, and Jennifer Murray. Belinda Herrera and April Crosoli worked as undergraduate research apprentices on small parts of the research. Julie Cowgill was my research assistant throughout most of the project. She conducted interviews with practitioners and participants and spent hours observing training sessions. She coauthored the two chapters with which she was most integrally involved, and it has been a pleasure to work with her.

Funding support came in the form of a number of grants from programs at Arizona State University. I received support from ASU's Faculty-Grant-In-Aid Program, College of Public Program's Dean's Incentive Grant Fund, Motorola Great Societies Program, and Women's Studies Program. During a bout of carpal tunnel syndrome while I was completing this manuscript, the School of Justice Studies and the director, Marie Provine, provided extra funding for typing assistance.

My colleagues at ASU and other universities were important at all stages of this research. The late Rita Kelly first introduced me to microenterprise development work. A number of colleagues including Madelaine Adelman, Laura Enriquez, Helen Ingram, Gale Miller, Anne Schneider, and Marjorie Zatz read chapters of my manuscript in progress and provided helpful comments and suggestions. Conference panel discussants including Luis Fernandez, Joanne Miller, Patricia Yancey Martin, and David Smith provided insights that also shaped the development of my analysis. Discussions with Jane Aiken, Mary Bernstein, Mona Danner, Jo Dixon, Betsy Grey, Cecilia Menjivar, James Messerschmidt, Mary Romero, Candace West, Nancy Wonders, and Joel Nomkin offered ideas and encouragement to complete and publish the project. Valerie Jenness and Elizabeth Segal read the entire manuscript on quite short notice. Despite the short time frame, they both provided insights that strengthened not only the analysis but my confidence in it.

Through Cornell University Press, I was fortunate to encounter two additional reviewers whose suggestions helped me to greatly tighten and improve the analysis and its relevance for life in today's world. Marjorie DeVault has read the entire manuscript at least twice and provided detailed and invaluable guidance for completing the project. Christopher Gunn also provided both support and critical suggestions. Working with Cornell's senior editor Fran Benson has been a true pleasure. Her encouragement and critical feedback were very helpful in turning this project into a book. Julie Nemer put a great deal of time and care into copyediting my manuscript.

Several individuals helped with the final preparation of the manuscript. Janelle Sotello helped bring the figure in chapter 6 to life on the computer. Naomi Bellot helped with proofing, Belinda Herrera helped with typing and editing, and Joanna Pearson helped with web citations. Mary Fran Draisker at ASU's Publication Assistance Center formatted the final manuscript and prepared the references. I know she was especially glad to see the tables leave her hands.

I am most fortunate of all to have a wonderfully supportive family both by birth and by marriage. My mother, Carolyn Jurik, and father, Willie Jurik, are a constant source of encouragement and support. Even though my dad passed away over twenty years ago, his voice of encouragement remains strong. My aunt and uncle, Florence and Joe Vitovsky, were like a second set of parents. My uncle let me hang around with him at the bank where he worked, perhaps planting the seeds for my interest in small-business development and lending. My sister and brother-in-law, Joyce and Ed

Plasek, provided support and constant reminders of the difficulties of operating a small business. My nieces and nephews, Kelly, David, Jeff, Kara, Scott, and Julia, were sources of affection and good times. Miriam Longino, Tom High, Catherine Cavender, and Doc Pace listened many hours to the perils of working in and writing about microenterprise development.

Last of all and most of all, I must thank my mate, colleague, and friend, Gray Cavender, for all the time, intellectual support, and love that he provided before, during, and after this project. He carefully listened to my ideas at every stage and provided suggestions that often times saved the day. He read and reread all chapters of this manuscript, offering vital editorial and substantive suggestions for improvement. He lights up my life and my work, and I lovingly dedicate this book to him.

ABBREVIATIONS

ACCION Americans for Community Cooperation in Other Nations

AEO Association for Enterprise Opportunity

AFDC Aid to Families with Dependent Children

ALA Accelerated Lending Assistance Workshop (ME)

ARIES Assistance to Resources Institutions for Enterprise Support Project

CAA Community action agency

CAP Community action program

CBDO Community-based development organization

CDB Community development bank

CDBG Community development block grant

CDC Community development corporation

CDFI Community Development Financial Institution

CED Corporations for Enterprise Development

CRA Community Reinvestment Act

EAS Enterprise Allowance Scheme

FIELD Fund for Innovation, Effectiveness, Learning and Dissemination (Aspen Institute)

FINCA Foundation for International Community Assistance

HHS U.S. Department of Health and Human Services

HUD U.S. Department of Housing and Urban Development

IDA Individual development accounts

IE Institutional ethnography

ILP Individual lending program

IMF International Monetary Fund

JOBS Job Opportunities and Basic Skills

MDP Microenterprise development program

MESBIC Minority enterprise development company

MICRO Microbusiness and Housing Development Organization

NGO Nongovernmental organization

PISCES Program for Investment in the Small Capital Enterprise Sector

RISE Rivercities of Iowa/Illinois Self-Employment Program

ROSCA Rotating Savings and Credit Association

SBA U.S. Department of Small Business Administration

SBDC Small Business Development Center

SEAP Self-Employment Assistance Program

SEED Self-Employment and Enterprise Development Demonstration

SEID Self-Employment Investment Demonstration

SELP Self-Employment Learning Project (Aspen Institute)

SEWA Self-Employed Women's Association

SSBIC Specialized small business investment company

TA Technical assistance

TANF Temporary Assistance for Needy Families (replaced AFDC)

USAID U.S. Agency for International Development

WEDCO Women's Economic Development Corporation

WSEP Women's Self-Employment Project

BOOTSTRAP DREAMS

INTRODUCTION

We want to reach the women who are tucked away in
their homes making tamales to sell to the people whose houses they
clean. We want to offer them training and loans—the tools they need to
grow their businesses and provide a better life for their families.
—COMMITTEE MEMBER FOR MICROENTERPRISE DEVELOPMENT PROGRAM

Slightly more than a decade ago, I was invited to attend a meeting of individuals interested in forming a self-employment lending program in a
large western metropolitan area. The group hoped to make loans to poor
and low-income women operating very small businesses, or microenterprises. The steering committee charged with planning the program included community volunteers, civic leaders, social service workers, and
academics. Several of the committee leaders had heard about microenterprise lending at a national conference on hunger where speakers argued
that even very small loans to support self-employment projects among the
poor could promote self-sufficiency and significantly reduce world hunger.
Although such lending originated in southern hemisphere or developing
nations, the steering committee leaders had heard that these microenterprise development programs were successful in the United States as well.
One of the committee members even traveled to Bangladesh to visit the
most famous of these programs, the Grameen Bank. She was convinced
that important components of the Grameen model would work for a program in her locality. At the meeting I attended, she argued the need to provide both business training and loans to poor women in the area. The
quotation at the beginning of this chapter is her description of the early
guiding image of the program.

The steering committee agenda included lobbying state government
officials to lift asset limits so that women on welfare could start small

businesses and accumulate business capital without immediately losing their eligibility for social assistance.

The enthusiasm and commitment of the group was contagious, and I found myself agreeing to coordinate a needs-assessment study for a microenterprise development program (MDP). Our study included an analysis of the economic conditions in the region. We identified the sort of economic problems that have been associated with the postindustrial economic period. This era, popularly known as the "new economy," began in the late 1970s and is characterized by increased global competition for jobs, declining proportions of good-paying, unionized, assembly-line jobs, and increasing proportions of flexible production, service-sector, part-time, and temporary employment (e.g., Piore and Sabel 1984; Rubin 1996; Smith 2001). For example, our western region was troubled by continuing layoffs and persistent unemployment in a period widely proclaimed to be one of national economic recovery and local economic boom. Large numbers of undocumented immigrants and unemployed workers from other parts of the nation were moving into the area looking for work. The number of new jobs being created fell disproportionately in low-wage service-employment sectors and lacked health benefits, and wage levels failed to keep pace with rapid increases in the area's cost of living. The number of families living near and below the poverty line was increasing. Ironically, these conditions of economic insecurity were accompanied by national rhetoric demanding cuts in welfare spending, demands that enjoyed the firm support of citizenry and politicians in the area.

The needs-assessment study included interviews with social service workers and a review of existing lending and training programs in the area. Respondents perceived a strong need for basic and low-cost self-employment training and business loans under $60,000, especially to individuals who lacked traditional collateral or solid credit histories. The review indicated that there were no programs that offered basic self-employment training and small loans under $15,000 to poor and high-risk entrepreneurs. Accordingly, our study concluded that there was significant need for an MDP in the area.

A little more than two years later, the steering committee's work led to the establishment of an MDP that I will call MicroEnterprise, Incorporated (ME). ME has been in operation for more than eight years and has assisted more than 1,500 individuals starting and expanding microenterprises, primarily in the areas of small-scale sales, manufacturing, and personal and professional services. For example, Maria, whose parents were immigrants from Mexico, used her ME loan to expand her garage-based business of sewing low-cost clothing. Carlos, an immigrant from Mexico, came to the ME program when he decided to start an import business after being laid off from several other jobs. ME training and loans helped Tamara move her child-care business from her home to a separate, licensed facility.

Despite its many accomplishments, the program also underwent significant changes over the course of its operations. Although most of the changes were important for organizational survival, many of them contradicted the original vision (as stated at the beginning of the chapter) and the images of poverty alleviation advanced by MDP proponents more globally.

The promise of ME and of MDPs generally was that they would facilitate self-sufficiency and economic development in impoverished communities. Moreover, because of their business orientation, it was hoped that MDPs would emphasize businesslike standards in their operations and thereby avoid both heavy government involvement and the associated operational practices. Of course, whether MDPs can significantly alleviate poverty and meet such cost-effectiveness standards is an empirical question. Interestingly, most of the literature on MDPs to date has focused on programs in the southern hemisphere, and the relatively fewer studies of U.S. programs have emphasized advocacy through the documentation of successful outcomes and cost effectiveness.

During my years of work with the ME program, I became interested in more than outcome measures. I wanted to understand how MDPs emerged and became so popular, how they survived, and how they changed in the process. Accordingly, this book examines the emergence and institutionalization of microenterprise development in the United States. Relying on an institutional ethnography (IE) approach (see Smith 1987, 1990), I began with my own experiences in the microenterprise development field and explored the routine practices of the ME program staff and clients and of the staff at fifty other U.S. MDPs.

I worked with the ME program as a volunteer and researcher throughout its planning and institutionalization phases. My work included interviews with volunteers, staff, and clients, and observations of program training and lending activities. With the help of graduate research assistants, I also examined the history of microenterprise development, attended national conferences of MDP practitioners, and interviewed staff at a variety of other U.S. programs.

These experiences revealed a series of dilemmas that practitioners and clients confronted in trying to achieve successes in their programs. In particular, MDPs struggled to secure funding, produce positive outcomes such as high loan-repayment rates and successful businesses, and still address the needs of poor clients. Outlining the disjuncture between the U.S.

MDPs goals and actual program operations was the initial focus of my inquiry. I then explored the roots of this problematic, or contradiction, by examining the connections between U.S. MDPs and their larger national-international contexts. Accordingly, my analysis follows the IE agenda of beginning with everyday experiences and then mapping connections between local practices and the demands of their larger social historical context or extra-local institutional milieus (Smith 1987; P. Grahame 1998; Campbell and Gregor 2002).

I argue that the new economy, which has brought increasing insecurity to workers through industrial restructuring, government fiscal crises, global competition for cheap labor, layoffs, and the growth of contingent work, has encouraged the widespread identification of microenterprises as a viable avenue for boosting family income. Declining government investments in employment, social service, and safety net programs encourage the involvement of nongovernmental organizations (NGOs) in social welfare and economic development, and, indeed, NGOs have been a driving force in the worldwide growth of MDPs.

MDPs aim to address poverty and underemployment issues in a manner that comports with today's popular faith in market-driven solutions for social problems (Blau 1999). Many proponents argue that MDPs can cover most or all of their program costs with revenue from training and lending services (Daley-Harris 2002). Some even argue that on the right scale, MDPs can be profitable (Christen and Drake 2002). Yet this emphasis on poverty alleviation and businesslike program operation promotes contradictions in practice. Expectations that MDP practitioners can assist poor individuals develop successful businesses through services that recoup most or all of program expenses are out of touch with the barriers faced by disadvantaged entrepreneurs in the new economy. In order to understand the issues confronting MDPs and their significance, it is necessary to further consider the history, nature, and context of MDPs.

HISTORY AND VARIETY OF MDPs

Although it has become very popular over the past two and a half decades, microenterprise development is by no means entirely new. Poverty alleviation through the provision of subsidized loans was a key component of international development strategies dating back to the 1950s (Adams and Von Pishke 1992). Most of these experiments ended with poor loan repayments rates and the diversion of credit to well-off rather than poor entrepreneurs (Morduch 1999, 2000).

Microenterprise development was rediscovered and revamped in the late 1970s when Mohammed Yunus founded the Grameen, a nonprofit bank, to provide credit for poor, landless men and women in Bangladesh. Since then, MDPs have exploded in numbers, popularity, and reported successes (Otero and Rhyne 1994). For example, the Grameen has loaned money to buy livestock and thread for making fishing nets, for trading, and for home-based grocery stores. The Grameen Bank now serves over 2.4 million borrowers, operates in over 40,000 villages, and serves as a model for microenterprise development worldwide (Grameen Bank n.d.). Other well-known MDPs include programs such as Americans for Community Cooperation in Other Nations (ACCION) International and Foundation for International Community Assistance (FINCA), which were developed in Latin America, and the Self-Employed Women's Association (SEWA), which was begun in India as a women's trade union and later incorporated lending and savings components.

This new generation of MDPs targets poor entrepreneurs. In 1997, a Summit of microlending practitioners and advocates set a goal of getting credit to the "world's poorest families" (Microcredit Summit 1997). Pioneering MDPs have been financially supported and heavily influenced by international development organizations from northern, or developed, nations (e.g., U.S. Agency for International Development, USAID; the World Bank; and the Ford Foundation). Critics argue that this influence has sometimes thwarted the agendas of more grassroots, local economic development programs (Poster and Salime 2002).

Some of these organizations and foundations (e.g., the Ford, Charles Stewart Mott, and Ms. Foundations; and CalMeadow) also supported the diffusion of MDPs to northern hemisphere countries. During the 1980s, MDPs became popular in the United States, and now more than three hundred programs offer training, lending, and other support to U.S. microentrepreneurs (Walker and Blair 2002). Microenterprises are typically defined as very small businesses that are owner-operated, have fewer than five employees, and have minimal capital investments (e.g., less than $20,000 in the United States) (Clark and Kays 1995). MDPs offer varying combinations of small loans, training, and technical assistance to individuals starting or expanding microenterprises. Frequently noted MDP goals include (1) the alleviation of poverty through self-employment, (2) the promotion of economic development in impoverished regions; (3) the empowerment of individuals, and (4) collective empowerment through the mobilization of microentrepreneurs and their communities (Coyle et al. 1994).

As a group, MDPs fill a void left by commercial establishments and government lending programs. They lend to borrowers in very small businesses who have problematic credit histories and who need business loans smaller than those offered by banks. Many programs target women because they have been neglected by economic development projects in the past and tend to be more likely than men to repay loans and use the resulting income to support their families (Dignard and Havet 1995; Blumberg 2001).

Despite many commonalities, the characteristics of MDPs vary widely. Some offer lending to individuals and function much like regular banks, requiring collateral, credit checks, and solid business plans before issuing loans. However, even these more traditional lending programs typically make smaller business loans than do commercial banks.

The best-known MDPs such as the Grameen Bank and ACCION International, as well as the ME program in this study, use innovative lending methods. They waive collateral requirements and credit checks, lending on the basis of business plans or client character alone, even to clients with poor credit histories. Their most notable innovation is the peer-lending approach through which loans are made to groups of borrowers rather than to individuals. These borrowers' groups, or circles, review one another's business plans, decide which members may borrow, and set the size of the loan received. The entire group may be held accountable for a member's failure to repay. Accordingly, the circles monitor and pressure borrowers to repay loans in a timely fashion. Borrowers' circles also provide networking support for their members through information and problem sharing. Although the circles combine the contradictory functions of peer support and peer pressure, their popularity is heightened by reported repayment rates of 98 percent (Auwal and Singhal 1992; Anthony 1997; Woolcock 1998).

Many lending-oriented programs provide only minimal technical assistance and little or no training (M. Johnson 1998b). In contrast, training-oriented programs view lending as just one of an array of services they extend to microentrepreneurs. The ME program in this study, like a large number of U.S. programs, emphasizes training in basic business skills (Mondal and Tune 1993; M. Johnson 1998b; Taub 1998; Servon 1999a). Savings, checking, consumer lending, and insurance services for the poor are offered by a few U.S. programs, but are more often components of MDPs in southern nations (Solomon 1992). A few U.S. programs go beyond business and banking components to offer other services such as assistance in child care and transportation. A number of southern-nation MDPs also sponsor loans to build community infrastructure and programs to bolster community participation and labor organizing (see for example, Rose 1996).

CONTEXT OF MDP POPULARITY

The explosion of self-employment programs seems rather abrupt, both in northern hemisphere countries such as the United States that have typically relied on an array of government safety net and job development programs and in southern hemisphere nations that have been dominated by top-down, large-scale modernization planning and assistance. This widespread popularity of MDPs is integrally linked to global economic restructuring trends and the accompanying neoliberal social policies that justify them.

Over the past three decades, policymakers have grown pessimistic about the ability of governments and large businesses to produce sufficient numbers of jobs with livable wages for their citizenry. Several trends, including deindustrialization in northern hemisphere nations, the growth of high-technology industries and jobs, and the increasing globalization of production and consumption, have combined to produce a phenomenon that many refer to as the new economy (Rubin 1996; Smith 2001). Although some have applauded the opportunities associated with the new economy, researchers have also documented its contribution to a growing sense of insecurity for a large percentage (if not the majority) of individuals in the world today (Piore and Sabel 1984; Portes 1997; Korten 2001). The intensifying worldwide competition for jobs has greatly increased workplace and economic insecurity for most citizens. Technological developments and global competition among firms has encouraged the reorganization of production jobs and new national and international divisions of labor. Many formerly unionized, good-paying industrial jobs with benefits that were taken for granted in northern nations have been relocated to the south in an effort to reduce wages and other production costs. Remaining northern jobs have been reorganized and either downsized or redefined as contingent work: they have become subcontracted, part-time, and temporary positions. The growth of low-paid service-sector jobs has outpaced the development of higher-paying knowledge-intensive positions. Contingent work opportunities along with the underemployment associated with them have stimulated informal economic and self-employment activities (Portes and Sassen-Koob 1987). Employment security has declined and individuals must often piece together multiple jobs to support themselves and their families (Rubin 1996; Blau 1999).

In southern hemisphere nations, paid employment opportunities have increased, but wages and working conditions tend to be highly exploitative. Subsistence agriculture is being destroyed by export-oriented agriculture and cheap imported food (De Janvry 1981). These dynamics have exacerbated hunger and disease in these nations. In the face of growing national debts, international lending and trade associations have pressured nations to reduce protectionist trade practices and decrease state employment and social service expenditures. This fiscal austerity agenda, frequently referred to as structural adjustment, is part of a neoliberal orientation that stresses a minimalist state and unfettered market as the keys to national and global economic success. Within this worldview, the only acceptable role for the state is to assure that markets remain open (McMichael 2000).

Even wealthy northern nations are under pressure to cut social investment and safety net programs and to reduce industrial protections and regulations. In countries such as the United States, this has meant large cuts in welfare, educational, and health-care spending and increasing rates of underemployment, poverty, and child-care problems (Blau 1999). In 1996, President Bill Clinton signed the Personal Work and Responsibility Act, which is credited with ending welfare as we knew it. This law ended the federal entitlement to assistance that dated to the Social Security Act of 1935, instituted a program that limited the duration of welfare benefits, and incorporated mandatory work requirements even for mothers with small children (Blau 1999).

With the decline of safety net programs, policymakers stressed an increased reliance on informal economic sectors and small businesses to provide jobs and increase the economic well being of the citizenry. Microenterprise development has been offered as one avenue for incorporating the poor and economically marginalized into the market economy. MDPs are said to promote self-sufficiency and economic development in impoverished communities. These virtues are contrasted with welfare and other safety net programs that are derided for promoting dependency and lowered self-esteem among the poor (Microcredit Summit 1997; Clinton 1999; Portes 1997).

MDPs blend well with neoliberal agendas advocating the privatization of government functions. Traditionally, the term *privatization* refers to the sale of industries formerly owned and operated by government to private-sector firms and the subcontracting of services formerly performed by government to privately owned firms and nonprofits (Dantico and Jurik 1986). Because many MDPs are operated by nongovernmental, nonprofit, and, increasingly, even for-profit groups, they are praised for relying on market-based principles and eschewing heavy government involvement.[1]

Recently, privatization trends have escalated, and they now include proposals for the reconceptualization of government services. Jill Quadagno (1999, 3) a sociologist, has critically analyzed a trend toward what she calls the "capital investment welfare state," whereby public benefits are being restructured so that they better reflect the principles of the marketplace. This restructured state shifts collective responsibility for its citizens' well-being onto individuals through personal investing, savings, and asset accumulation programs (also see Naples 1997; Poster and Salime 2002). Calling for the alleviation of poverty through self-employment assistance rather than through more traditional welfare and safety net programs is quite consistent with the growing capital-investment welfare state described by Quadagno (1999; also see Cowgill and Jurik In press).

The market-based strategy for dealing with poverty has enhanced their popularity, but the widespread appeal of MDPs draws on fundamental values of social welfare that cross the political spectrum (Goodin et al. 1999). For economic conservatives on the political right, MDPs invoke sentiments of *individualism,* appealing to long-held values of faith in free enterprise, the entrepreneurial spirit, self-sufficiency, and pulling oneself up by one's bootstraps (Arnold 1941 [1937]; Auwal and Singhal 1992). MDPs offer to mediate the negative effects of global capitalism without large-scale permanent government safety net programs (e.g., welfare) (Solomon 1992).

Contemporary liberals and communitarians admire MDPs for their *integrative* functions (Ehlers and Main 1998). They offer disadvantaged people opportunities to participate more fully in the global economy and therein to be empowered as individuals (Anthony 1996, 1997; Balkin 1989).[2] To political populists, microlending promotes a greening of capitalism by fostering a vision of small-scale entrepreneurs to challenge or at least balance corporate domination (Light and Pham 1998; Herrold 2003). Because many MDPs target women, most of whom work in home-based businesses, these programs are praised by feminists and nonfeminist alike for helping mothers to combine paid work with child-care responsibilities (Servon 1999a; Creevey 1996).[3]

For those more left of center, MDPs offers a hope of community mobilization or *collective empowerment* (see Young 1994; Breton 1995). Borrower groups and other support networks are a strategy for bringing the poor and other disadvantaged groups together to share common problems (Anthony 1997). This sharing and networking may provide them with a heightened awareness and an organizational base from which to collectively confront structural inequalities emanating from global capitalism (Rose 1996; Woolcock 1998). In some southern nations, clients actually own and control MDPs, and, as noted, some MDPs grew out of efforts to organize informal sector workers (Counts 1996; Rogaly 1996; Rose 1996). Local control of MDPs leads proponents to suggest that the programs can help build viable community-controlled nonbureaucratic organizational forms (Anthony 1997).

RESEARCH ON MDP EFFECTIVENESS

The research on MDPs identifies both program strengths and weaknesses. Proponents draw on research to praise MDPs as an avenue for alleviating poverty without heavy governmental expenditures; other analysts question whether MDPs can or even should serve the poor. However, conclusions are weakened by methodological difficulties with study designs.

Much research on microenterprise development has focused on programs in southern hemisphere nations. There are many case studies of the origins and development of pioneering programs such as the Grameen and SEWA (Bhatt 1995; Counts 1996; Rose 1996; Bornstein 1996) and research documenting their successes and struggles (Wahid 1993b; Wood and Sharif 1997; Amin, Becker, and Bayes 1998; Remenyi and Quiñones 2000; Blumberg 2001). From these studies, researchers have identified techniques for program evaluation and advice for practitioners about the most successful operational models or best practice in the MDP field (e.g., Otero and Rhyne 1994; Gulli 1998; Daley-Harris 2002). Many impact evaluations have been positive, suggesting that MDP clients experience increased and more stable incomes, increased asset accumulation, higher consumption levels, and improved educational opportunities for their children (Berger and Buvinic 1989; Hulme and Mosley 1996).

The relatively fewer U.S. studies also report that MDPs promote business growth, create jobs, and increase client incomes, self-esteem, and community involvement (Balkin 1989; Auwal and Singhal 1992; Edgcomb, Klein, and Clark 1996; Anthony 1997; Himes and Servon 1998; Light and Pham 1998; Servon 1999a). One seven-year study by the U.S. nonprofit Aspen Institute reports that MDPs develop and stabilize businesses, create jobs, and alleviate poverty (Edgcomb, Klein, and Clark 1996). Other research (e.g., Clark et al. 1999) reports significant gains in household income, some large enough to move clients out of poverty. "The average change in household income was $8,484—rising from $13,889 to $22,374 over five years" (Clark et al. 1999, vii). A study of ACCION's U.S. programs reports that clients increased their net income by $450 or more per month (Himes and Servon 1998). Other evaluations report that MDPs move individuals from unemployment and welfare assistance to economic independence (Else and Raheim 1992; Raheim and Alter 1998).

Despite the many proclamations of MDP achievements, data on their long-term success are neither complete nor unequivocal. Evaluations in the United States and elsewhere are weakened by methodological problems, including a reliance on indirect measures of success (e.g., loan repayment rates), a lack of adequate comparison groups of nonclients, and lack of long-term follow-up. These components are essential in determining how much movement out of poverty occurs, how much the movement is actually due to MDP interventions, and whether the improved situations persist.

Poverty alleviation goals are especially challenging for U.S. programs. Research on pioneering U.S. MDPs suggests that these programs have even more difficulty in reaching poor entrepreneurs than do their southern hemisphere counterparts. A number of studies conclude that only approximately one-third or less of MDP clients are actually poor, and even those served by MDPs are not among the poorest: they rank significantly above national averages for the poor on assets, education, experience, and skills (see also Clark and Huston 1992; Edgcomb, Klein, and Clark 1996; Himes and Servon 1998; Bates and Servon 1996; Schreiner 1999c).[4] Critics charge that MDP program success relies on "creaming," wherein clients with the least likelihood of success are either discouraged by staff from continuation or choose to drop out of the program (Ehlers and Main 1998; Howells 2000).

Some researchers in the United States and elsewhere suggest that even if MDPs reach very poor clients the programs will not significantly alleviate poverty in the new economy; that is, they argue that although MDPs may offer valuable assistance to poor microentrepreneurs, the resulting very small businesses rarely grow enough to make significant contributions to the economic growth and employment of their regions (Grosh and Somolekae 1996; Hulme and Mosley 1996; Bates and Servon 1996; Ehlers and Main 1998). The type of business selected is also a key determinant of success (Servon and Bates 1998). "Traditional lines of business, such as personal services and small-scale retailing, tend to be favored by clients of microenterprise programs, yet these are the least profitable lines of small business" (Servon and Bates 1998, 421). This tendency is especially problematic for the many women MDP clients who are encouraged to start small-scale, traditionally female businesses (Ehlers and Main 1998); such ventures tend to be labor intensive, low profit, and highly unstable (Servon and Bates 1998; Ehlers and Main 1998). These findings lead U.S. researchers Lisa Servon and Timothy Bates (1998) to recommend the institutionalization of a two-track service system wherein MDP lending is offered only to individuals who are likely to develop businesses that can lead to economic self-sufficiency and, for individuals who do not have the skills for such growth businesses, MDP training concentrates on specific skills that "can serve as a basis for viable small firm creation and operation" (421).

A growing body of literature identifies recurrent problems confronting MDPs worldwide. On the one hand, the attraction of MDPs is their promise to alleviate poverty through self-help and without expensive government-funded safety net programs. Many program funds are allocated and specifically targeted for MDPs that serve poor and low-income populations. On the other hand, the future funding of MDPs is dependent on programs simultaneously showing successful client outcomes and prospects for long-term sustainability (i.e., low operating costs). Proponents argue that in order to significantly reduce poverty and remain institutionally viable, MDPs must maintain an economy of scale by reaching large populations of poor borrowers while minimizing programming expenditures (Gulli 1998; Bhatt, Painter, and Tang 2002; Simanowitz and Walter 2002). Accordingly, program and client successes are gauged by measures that include the number of clients served, volume of lending, ratio of clients served to program operating costs, rate of loan repayment, and client outcome such as growth in household income, business assets, and the number of new jobs created.

MY RESEARCH

My study of the origins, development, and institutionalization of U.S. MDPs reveals both the opportunities and problems in microenterprise development. I conceptualize microenterprise development as an embedded and emergent process. Economic sociology uses the concept of embeddedness to analyze the effects of social structures and dynamics on economic action (Portes and Sensenbrenner 1993; Guillen et al. 2002). However, economic sociology often aims to develop and test universal propositions about the impact of social, political and cultural phenomena on the market; it tends to avoid more critical analyses of capitalism and its contradictions (Krier 1999).

My use of IE provides a more grounded approach that facilitates an understanding of the complexities and contradictions of microenterprise development as well as its links to contemporary capitalism and its contradictions. IE begins with the concrete, everyday experiences of the setting participants. I began with my own MDP planning and work experiences and then examined those of other program planners, staff, and clients in ME and fifty other U.S. programs.[5] In my analysis, I refer to these experiences as MDP *practice*. Practice includes program-planning activities, routine daily operations, face-to-face interactions, and problem-solving strategies used by MDP actors (Miller 1989; K. Grahame 1998a, 1998b; Campbell and Gregor 2002).

The exploration of practice revealed contradictory demands on MDP practitioners and clients. IE seeks to investigate the source of such contradictions, or problematics, uncovered in research (Campbell and Gregor 2002). In the case of the ME program, I was puzzled by the expectation that programs could help poor women start businesses through such limited business training and lending services. Later, I was struck by the disjuncture between the program's stated goals of helping disadvantaged individuals start businesses and the evolving staff profiles for screening clients prior to lending stages. This gap between goals and operations created other dilemmas for both staff and clients in the program. I refer to these as the *contradictions* of MDP practice.

To understand the source of the contradictions encountered in everyday practice, IE encourages researchers to move beyond local routines and face-to-face interactions and ask the question: "Where did these experiences come from?" The aim behind this question is to uncover how extra-local contexts inform and shape local practices and contradictions. In IE, an extra-local context is the social organization, including the conditions and institutions, both national and global, that lie outside the immediate research setting. Through interviews with practitioners in fifty U.S. programs, I was able to examine the links across MDPs and the connections between MDPs and other organizations and institutions. The methods used in IE can be diverse and varied (K. Grahame 1998a). Drawing on websites, prior literature, program documents, and interviews, I trace the history of microenterprise development, as well as the links between its diffusion and the larger global economic, social, and political conditions. I refer to this component of my analysis as the *context* of U.S. microenterprise development.

IE and analyses of lived experiences (Smith 1987; Collins 1990; De-Vault 1999) are integrally linked to feminist and multiracial perspectives. Gender relations give rise to diverse experiences and standpoints for men and women in society, but race, ethnicity, and class also effect multiple standpoints within gender groups. Pioneer MDP practitioners reported problems with mixed-gender and mixed-racial/ethnic client groups. Women clients tended to be more passive in training and lending interactions that included men. Likewise, local and regional race and ethnic tensions sometimes disrupted client relations in racially or ethnically diverse training and lending groups (Coyle et al. 1994; Kidder 1998). Accordingly, my analysis of MDP practice, contradictions, and context is sensitive to the ways in which gender, race, and class relations were embedded in both local practices and extra-local contexts (Acker 1990; Omi and Winant 1994). These insights are crucial for understanding MDPs because they target assistance to poor women and minorities who, although they may share a sense of cultural and economic marginality, may also have diverse standpoints and conflicting interests as clients in social service programs.[6]

My study maps the ways in which MDP experiences emerge from extra-local as well as from internal organizational dynamics. Microenterprise development is an emerging process that is embedded within a larger context of the new economy and the welfare reform and new privatization that accompany it. This context simultaneously advances the popularity of MDPs as a solution to poverty and underemployment, but poses dilemmas that challenge their success. The tensions and strategies that emerge within these programs reflect, reinforce, and challenge social and economic inequalities and accompanying ideologies (Krier 1999).

The new economy and its associated policies promote a milieu in which MDPs become defined as a viable method for poverty alleviation and economic development. In turn, MDP poverty alleviation claims further justify the elimination of social investment and safety net programs (Rogaly 1996; Ehlers and Main 1998; Howells 2000). Ironically, programs that actually lend to large proportions of poor, low-income, and otherwise high-risk clients have an increased likelihood of loan defaults. Also, the greater amounts of staff time and services needed to assist those poorer clients add significantly to program operations costs. The businesses of highly disadvantaged clients are less likely to be as successful as those of clients with more resources. Accordingly, programs that serve lots of poor clients may appear less effective and efficient to funders than programs that serve better-off clients (Grosh and Somolekae 1996; Hulme and Mosley 1996; Gulli 1998). Yet much available funding is targeted for assistance to the poor. In this manner, extra-local opportunities produce conflicting demands for local MDP practitioners. Practitioner responses to contradictory goals and directives shaped MDP practice.

In addition to providing an example of a market-based solution to social problems, MDPs also illustrate the further extension of privatization processes. New privatization strategies move beyond the subcontracting and sale of government assets, and even beyond the reconstruction of government services as new personal investing programs. The new privatization promotes the reorganization of both governmental and nonprofit organizations to better reflect the operational principles of private firms (see Jurik 2004). Nonprofit and government organizations must *reinvent* themselves in a manner that is compatible with popular images of market-sector operations; they must demonstrate that they operate as efficiently and cost effectively as private firms. In keeping with these new privatization trends, modern MDPs promise to avoid government subsidies and operate in a more businesslike manner than either previous microloan or welfare programs (Morduch 2000).

I use the term *new privatization* to refer to the increasing adoption of market principles as standards for government sector and nonprofit organizations (Aronowitz 2000; Hammack and Young 1993). Along these lines, emerging MDP "best-practice" standards emphasize images of businesslike efficiency, cost-effectiveness, and quantitative success outcomes (Poster and Salime 2002; Christen and Drake 2002). In light of both social scientific study and recent media revelations about corporate practices, it is clear that these market efficiency standards are often more idealized values than a reflection of real business functioning (Sclar 2000; Fligstein 2002; Deutsch 20003).

PLAN OF THE BOOK

Chapters 1 and 2 of this book ask where MDPs came from. They describe the global and national contexts in which microenterprise development emerged as a plausible mechanism for addressing poverty and economic marginalization. When I was first asked to assess the need for a new MDP, I began by reading about the history of MDPs, their roots in southern hemisphere nations, and famous programs that ME founders wanted to emulate. I wondered how such programs had become so popular in what seemed like a rather short time. My search uncovered reports of both the strengths and weaknesses of these programs. Chapter 1 details the updated results of this search. It outlines the origins of microenterprise development and the structural context of the new economy and popular neoliberal philosophies that have fueled its popularity in southern hemisphere nations. Drawing on the large body of research on program histories and evaluations, I discuss several of the most prominent southern MDPs, identifying their major successes and ongoing problems. This chapter facilitates an understanding of the historical and global context of microenterprise development and of the relevance of southern hemisphere programs for U.S. MDPs.

Chapter 2 addresses the question of how MDPs came to the United States. It describes the experiences of the new economy in the United

States and the resource mobilization efforts that fueled the diffusion of southern hemisphere MDPs to northern nations. It also examines the influence of past U.S. economic development and social service traditions on U.S. MDPs. When I attended my first national MDP conference, one pioneering U.S. practitioner said: "I was doing microenterprise development here long before any of us knew about the Grameen Bank!" This interaction, as well as conversations with local economic development and social service providers, sensitized me to the important influence that these U.S. traditions have had on the microenterprise development field. Chapter 2 also details the history of a national association and self-proclaimed social movement of U.S. MDP providers. Drawing on information gleaned at national conferences of MDP providers and a review of association literature, the chapter identifies the ways in which this movement has disseminated information about MDP successes, developed national standards for MDP practice, and lobbied for favorable legislative and funding climates at the national, state, and local levels. Prevailing economic problems and associated cultural ideologies of privatization and welfare reform provided opportunities for MDP activists. Activists sought to frame their activities in ways that would garner support from the broad range of conservatives, liberals, and leftists (Snow et al. 1986; Williams 1995; Naples 1997). Practitioners adopted *and* adapted international MDP models so as to enhance their popular appeal and their compatibility with U.S. cultural ideologies and economic conditions.

Chapter 3 (coauthored with Julie Cowgill) focuses on a national sample of MDP programs. Based on interviews with practitioners, it describes program practice and attempts to map the ways in which practitioner experiences and strategies are informed by extra-local contexts of economic conditions, trends in nonprofit management, and funder demands. The programs varied considerably, having diverse goals, target populations, funding sources, organizational structures, and lending and training methodologies. Practitioners described an array of program accomplishments, but also identified common tensions in their microenterprise development work, including contradictions between program service goals and organizational maintenance demands. Staff identified strategies for balancing these competing demands.

Chapters 4 and 5 detail the history and transformation of the ME program[7] over a ten-year period. It is these chapters that best convey the emergence and dynamics of a local MDP. This case study analysis begins with the experiences of staff, board members, and clients in the program. Then it draws on the information developed in chapters 1, 2 and 3 to analyze the local and extra-local contexts that form the terrain in which these local program experiences occur. The contradictions of microenterprise development and the strategies designed to ease such conflicts are played out in the words and examples of daily life in the ME program.

Chapter 4 (coauthored with Julie Cowgill) details the planning and early operations of ME, including struggles among staff, board members, funding sources, and program clients in the first year of operation. Chapter 5 focuses on program changes over time. Despite funding pressures, the program struggled to maintain a low-income client base and protect its peer-lending and training components. Gradually, staff developed mechanisms for projecting a more businesslike image to clients and funders. They also developed methods to screen out more ill-prepared and troublesome clients and to increase control over lending and circle operations. Some clients actively resisted staff control strategies, whereas others worked to effect policy changes in more subtle ways. Race, class, and gender relations were often salient in staff and client interactions. Over time, the service population for this MDP included fewer poverty-level, low-income, and business start-up clients. These demographics raised questions when the board and staff reevaluated their initial program mission and identified future funding opportunities associated with services to low-income, poverty-level, and welfare-to-work clients.

Chapter 6 examines the significance of the microenterprise development story for life in the new economy. Drawing together portraits gleaned from case study and national sample data, this chapter summarizes the contradictions of the microenterprise development process and its connections with more fundamental contradictions in the new economy and the associated policies of welfare reform and privatization. MDPs help to legitimate the welfare reform agenda. Moreover, new privatization trends, wherein nonprofits and government organizations increasingly mimic idealized images of private firms, are well-exemplified in today's MDPs. These trends have important implications for the future of social services.

In contrast to previous studies that fix MDPs at one point in time, my findings elaborate microenterprise as an unfolding and embedded process. The IE approach facilitates an understanding of the ways in which practitioners negotiate conflicting organizational demands generated by the extra-local context, organizational maintenance requirements (e.g., funding), and client needs. Thus, IE provides a useful approach for researching the institutionalization and transformation of program innovations and social service delivery.

My findings challenge proponent and media images that frame MDPs as alternatives to state welfare and job-training programs. Over time, ME and other MDPs have found that it is difficult to serve poor and very-low-income clients and still record sufficient program successes to stay in business. Proponent rhetoric about self-help and client motivation also have often distracted from issues of structural disadvantage and reinforced images that poor and low-income people are responsible for their failures.

Given current trends toward a capital-investment welfare state, it is important to understand the contradictions surrounding microenterprise development. Can MDPs really alleviate poverty in the new economy? If they cannot, their claims to do so and associated efforts to use Temporary Assistance for Needy Families (TANF) dollars to fund MDP services only exacerbate and legitimate the state's failure to provide effective programming for the poor. Without deeper analysis, MDP success rhetoric may simply reinforce the hegemony of the market as a solution to all social problems. Understanding the embedded process of microenterprise development can improve MDP practice and framing so as to encourage the recognition of other viable policy alternatives.

CHAPTER 1

THE INTERNATIONAL ROOTS
OF MICROENTERPRISE DEVELOPMENT

Conventional banking institutions do not make loans to the poor,
especially to rural women. The bankers I met laughed at me.
—YUNUS (1997)

After the bank's eighteen years in business, one could estimate
that conservatively half a million families were able to throw off a life
of destitution and begin living with a modicum of honor and dignity
as a result of intervention from the Grameen Bank.
—COUNTS (1996)

[T]he development community is riding the microcredit
band-wagon given that it is consistent with the dominant paradigm
of self-help, decentralization . . . and given that structural adjustment
programs have forced the poor into self-employment.
—MCMICHAEL (2000)

A major source of the excitement surrounding microenterprise development has been the Grameen Bank in Bangladesh (Ryan 1997; Brill 1999).
The statement by Mohammed Yunus, the bank's founder, describes his
struggle to offer microcredit in the 1970s. The second statement captures
the popular acclaim surrounding the bank and the hopes for future microenterprise development. Many U.S. MDPs were modeled after famous
southern programs such as the Grameen (Wahid 1993a; Counts 1996).
Despite praise for these programs, MDPs also have serious critics; the
third statement expresses the concern that MDPs direct too much attention toward individual self-help and distract from structural economic
conditions that promote and perpetuate poverty.

This chapter addresses one of my first questions as a microenterprise
development volunteer: Where did all these U.S. programs come from?
The answer that I typically received to this question was that U.S. MDPs

were inspired by successful programs in developing countries. In other words, the northern industrialized world had imported them from the southern hemisphere—a unique turn of events given that development programs have usually moved in the opposite geographical direction. Only one U.S. provider told me that she started her program before she had even heard of the famous Grameen Bank.

When I took a more in-depth look at microenterprise development history, I found that this south-to-north importation thesis was not the whole story. The circumstances that led to the formation and spread of MDPs were far more complex: they entailed the importation of ideas from north to south as well as from south to north. Tracking the history and sources of MDP innovations locates microenterprise development squarely within the context of the conditions and policies of the new economy. An examination of the emergence and practice of southern MDPs reveals not only program successes, but also fundamental contradictions in microenterprise development.

CONTEXT OF MICROENTERPRISE DEVELOPMENT

MDPs were developed to extend business credit and training to the "poorest of the poor" in Africa, Bangladesh, and Latin America (Microcredit Summit 1997; Rogaly 1996). The decades of the 1970s and 1980s were times of worldwide economic recession and government fiscal shortfalls. In the 1980s and 1990s, modern MDPs became recognized as viable mechanisms for dealing with some of the human economic tragedies of the crises. MDP strategies were consistent with the neoliberal policy agendas of minimal government and market-based solutions that also came to predominate during this period. These programs were to address the growing problems of poverty and unemployment that continue to characterize life in the new economy.

From the 1970s on, southern nations were faced with increasing debts to industrialized countries that they could not repay. During the 1980s and 1990s, international financial concerns and global financial regulatory agencies—such as the International Monetary Fund (IMF) and The World Bank—pressured the governments of southern nations to sharply curtail spending, ease international trade regulations, and privatize nationally owned banking institutions and industries (Jonakin and Enriquez 1999; McMichael 2000). These requirements were consistent with a neoliberal economic ideology of smaller government and the elimination of trade restrictions. This neoliberal agenda, typically referred to as a structural adjustment policy, entailed massive layoffs of state workers and the curtailing of social investment spending for education, health care, and the like (Teeple 2000). The resulting withdrawal of many southern hemisphere governments from the public sector has encouraged an increased reliance on NGOs and community-based services for the poor (Desai 2002).[1]

Even before recent globalization and structural adjustment regimes, decades of export-oriented production had precipitated declines in small-scale family-level agriculture oriented toward local consumption needs (Roberts 1978; De Janvry 1981). Available credit and agricultural support programs were oriented to larger-scale agribusiness farms. Impoverished rural populations migrated to the cities in search of employment. Proponents of structural adjustment policies predicted that the liberalization of trade and financial markets and the expansion of private banking would eventually counter the ill effects of shrinking state expenditures and loss of jobs. However, continuing declines in agriculture and the resulting migration to urban areas outstripped the formal employment opportunities there.

The jobs that became available in these areas failed to offer either improved working conditions or economic security. Trade liberalization requirements demanded that government minimize labor, environmental regulations, local industry protections, and other barriers to international trade. These rules limited worker pay and safety protections and promoted barriers to collective organizing. Many new work opportunities entailed more informal subcontracting work arrangements rather than permanent employment. The constant global search for cheaper labor and the increased mobility of work sites meant that even those limited employment opportunities created by international trade might vanish at any time.

Although southern nations always maintained a large informal sector, structural adjustment policies and the increasing decentralization of production produced a population explosion of informal workers. Individuals engaged in the informal subcontracting of formal sector activities (e.g., in garment manufacturing) made up a large sector of this group, but many also turned to more autonomous informal entrepreneurial ventures (Portes and Sassen-Koob 1987; McMichael 2000; Agadjanian 2002).

Concerned about growing poverty and shrinking government resources, development specialists began to advocate the extension of credit to stimulate growth among small informal enterprises. They hoped that such assistance would stabilize impoverished communities, and encourage bottom-up economic development without expensive state-managed help and employment programs (Wahid 1994; Yunus 1997).

For-profit financial systems failed to deliver basic savings and credit to low-income customers, small farms and other small businesses, especially to women entrepreneurs (Light and Pham 1998). Banking services were inconvenient and costly due to hefty service charges, minimum balance requirements, and restricted withdrawal policies. Small consumer and business loans (e.g., less than $25,000)[2] were rarely offered because traditional banks claimed that these loans were too costly to administer (Yunus 1997). Individuals without sufficient collateral or with weak credit histories seldom received loans (Otero and Rhyne 1994). Thus, the poor typically relied on more costly informal financial services such as loan sharks.

Microfinance programs operated by nonprofit NGOs promised to fill the gap in financial services to the poor (Otero and Rhyne 1994; Jonakin and Enriquez 1999). Microfinance proponents argued that the failure of the commercial banks to serve poverty-level clients prevented the poor from accumulating assets. They associated the lack of assets with chronic poverty and a sedimentation of disadvantage (Oliver and Shapiro 1995; Yunus 1997). Microfinance services offered flexible checking, savings, and lending options tailored to poor clientele. These services allowed smaller minimum required balances, minimal service charges, and flexible withdrawal options. Loans were typically for smaller amounts, offered more flexible repayment options, and minimized collateral requirements. Some programs were partially or completely owned by individual clients or by their communities.

With their focus on training and lending to very small businesses, MDPs can best be considered a subset of microfinance organizations. However, some microfinance programs include MDP components and some MDPs include savings and consumer-lending services. Unlike many modern MDPs, especially those emerging in the United States, early microfinance organizations were more focused on lending and savings activities than on business training, technical assistance, or collective empowerment functions. Thus, microenterprise development activities are distinctive but still related to other microfinance and development services. Several innovations associated with modern MDPs were actually inspired by the practices of earlier microfinance groups.

EARLY MICROFINANCE ORGANIZATIONAL FORMS

Although the past two decades have seen a rapid growth in microfinance and microenterprise development services, such efforts are not entirely new. Many modern MDPs resemble microlending and credit cooperatives developed in nineteenth-century Europe for small farmers, entrepreneurs, and traders (Hollis and Sweetman 1998a, 1998b). Some programs were charitable concerns; others operated for profit. There is also an extensive history of lending programs aimed at small farmers in southern countries that date to the early 1900s. These programs included direct loans, credit cooperatives, specialized rural development banks, and regulations that required banks to lend a portion of their loan portfolio to small farmers, either directly or indirectly through development banks (Adams and Von Pischke 1992). The loans made by development lending programs from the 1950 through the 1980s were often subsidized by government agencies or other NGOs. These loans were regarded as failures because many ended in default and often ended up in the hands of prosperous rather than poor farmers (Jonakin and Enriquez 1999). Defaults were blamed on generous subsidies provided to lending organizations, subsidies that led them to operate in an inefficient and unbusinesslike manner (Morduch 1999).

Many of these earlier lending programs have disappeared, but two early forms of microfinance organizations remain popular around the world. First, the most informal and perhaps longest lasting microfinance organization form is the rotating savings and credit association (ROSCA). ROSCAs are widespread in the southern hemisphere and popular among some immigrant groups in industrialized nations (Laguerre 1998; Light and Pham 1998). ROSCA members contribute a regular amount each week or month, and group members take turns borrowing the money at no interest. Because they are known and trusted by each other, ROSCA members also provide social support for one another in consumption and business pursuits. Their informality and resource requirements mean that ROSCAs serve people with dependable incomes and social ties; they are unlikely to serve the very poor or destitute.

A second traditional form of low-cost lending and savings services is the credit union. Credit unions are cooperative financial institutions that began in southern hemisphere countries in the 1950s and are popular in industrialized nations (see Magill 1994). Credit unions are legally constituted financial institutions that are, for the most part, chartered and supervised under national cooperative legislation. They provide savings and credit services to their members. Membership has traditionally been defined in terms of some affiliation shared by all members (e.g., employment or geography). Credit unions are organized and operated as cooperatives. There are no external shareholders; the members are the owners of the institution, and each member has a vote in the organization. The policymaking leadership is drawn from members and, in new or small credit unions, these positions are unpaid. Individual credit unions may be affiliated with a national league, and there are regional associations of leagues called confederations. The apex organization for the credit union system is the World Council of Credit Unions (Magill 1994).

Although both ROSCAs and credit unions have been significant in offering savings and lending services to those who might not otherwise have access, they tend to serve the poor who are better off. The ROSCA form is limited in its scale and longevity of services. Although far less limited in scale and longevity, credit unions have not played a large role in microenterprise lending because their lending practices tend to be conservative and they do not offer training and technical assistance. Nevertheless, the modern MDP movement has built on the experiences of these past microfinance programs to nurture a grassroots dimension that enhances its popularity as a poverty-alleviation and economic development strategy.

MODERN MDPs AS A STRATEGY FOR ECONOMIC DEVELOPMENT

Microenterprise development is an important component in the reframing of international development discourse (McMichael 2000; Poster and Salime 2002). Throughout much of the twentieth century, development policies were focused on large-scale, centrally planned ventures that usually served the better-off people in southern countries (Visvanthan et al. 1997). Many programs provided goods and services, especially modern technology, to advance the development of poor countries. Historically, although this development discourse adopted a gender-neutral stance, producers were assumed to be men. Men received the direct benefits of development programs, and women's productive roles were largely ignored. Programs slowly integrated women into development concerns, but they were still viewed as secondary (Escobar 1995; Parpart 1995).

During the 1970s, researchers and policymakers effectively challenged the traditional development discourses of centralization and state-managed interventions (Escobar 1995). These challenges were fueled by the reported inefficiencies and failures of the top-down, or state-controlled, development initiatives. Although some challenges came from leftist-oriented groups, these attacks on government-provided development services were compatible with neoliberal policies that aimed to shrink the size of government and rely on a market-based production of all goods and services. Such privatization ideologies were consistent with the identification of the informal sector as an arena for low-cost and localized job creation (McMichael 2000).

The value of supporting self-employment as an economic development strategy was first publicized in a 1972 study by the International Labor Organization (ILO) in Nairobi, Kenya (Berger 1989; Raheim 1997). The study analyzed the problem of unemployment among low-income urban dwellers in southern countries. Findings indicated that although millions of urban dwellers did not have formal employment, many of them—especially women—were engaged in productive self-employment in the informal or unregulated, and often unrecorded, sector of the economy (Tinker 1989). Subsequently, this ILO discovery of the informal sector emphasized self-employment and women's role in it as a viable economic development strategy. After the ILO report, multilateral and bilateral assistance agencies devoted increasing attention to assisting women's enterprises in the informal economic sectors (Berger 1989; Portes and Sassen-Koob 1987; Portes 1997). Experts (e.g., Ashe 1985; Auwal and Singhal 1996) argued that giving credit to the self-employed poor would stimulate economic growth and ameliorate the unequal distribution of assets (i.e., wealth).

Over the past two decades, the promotion of self-employment has become the dominant model for assisting women in the southern hemisphere (Poster and Salime 2002). Again, consistent with the structural adjustment ideology, attention moved away from structural economic problems and toward the privatization of public services and the development of women as individuals. The discourse shifted from a focus on "development as charity" to a view of "development as business" (McMichael 2000, 295).

Microenterprise development is applauded as a southern hemisphere invention that was later copied or borrowed by programs in northern hemisphere countries (Coyle et al. 1994). However, such characterizations lose sight of the extent to which northern hemisphere–dominated governmental and nongovernmental organizations shaped the form and popularity of many of these programs. Organizations such as the Ford Foundation, United Nations Development Program, and, more recently, World Bank have been instrumental in defining the standards and funding parameters for southern MDPs (Prugl 1996; Alvarez 1999; McMichael 2000).

U.S. Agency for International Development Programs

In 1978, USAID sponsored the Program for Investment in the Small Capital Enterprise Sector (PISCES) in sixteen countries in Africa, Asia, and Latin American (Ashe 1985). PISCES analyzed the factors that shaped the success of microenterprises operated by the urban poor in these countries and also conducted demonstration projects to provide technical and financial assistance to microenterprises in four countries: Costa Rica,

Dominican Republic, Egypt, and Kenya (Ashe 1985). PISCES concluded that, by allowing the poor to develop their own plans for business, microenterprise offers significant social welfare and economic development benefits. The final report recommended a more decentralized approach that funded local intermediary organizations to support and assist microenterprises.

USAID next created the Assistance to Resources Institutions for Enterprise Support Project (ARIES) in 1985. ARIES provided management and technical assistance to intermediary agencies to enhance their capacity to serve microenterprises. These intermediaries included government agencies, private voluntary organizations, banks, business associations, and cooperatives (Balkin 1989).

More recently, USAID has hosted conferences aimed at the global dissemination of information about microenterprise development. For example, in 1999 USAID hosted the Second Annual International Women's Business Conference in Chicago. The conference was part of the USAID's Lessons without Borders, a project aimed at promoting the international exchange between policy planners and community activists about successful development strategies. The keynote presentations emphasized that restricted access to credit was a significant problem for third-world women and microcredit was portrayed as the best modern development strategy for empowering women (Poster and Salime 2002, 198–201).

In addition to USAID, other United Nations agencies as well as the Inter-American Development Bank and other donor groups sponsored pioneering lending programs in Latin American, Indonesia, India, and Bangladesh (Berger 1989). These lending programs began making loans and other assistance to microenterprises in the mid-1970s. Although initially resistant to the microenterprise development concept (see Yunus 1997), the World Bank began to sign on to MDP projects by the mid-1990s (Buckley 2002). In 1995, the World Bank established the Consultative Group to Assist the Poorest (CGAP), an organization dedicated to expanding the funding and outreach for microfinance organizations. Consistent with the neoliberal orientation of the World Bank, this group's mandate was to fund programs to aid the poor who are or can become financially self-sufficient (Buckley 2002, 113–14).

In 1997, the first Microcredit Summit convened in Washington D.C. The Summit's Declaration and Plan of Action defines the group as an assembly whose purpose is "to launch a global movement to reach 100 million of the world's poorest families, especially the women of those families, with credit for self-employment and other financial and business services, by the year 2005" (MICRO Loan Fund n.d.).

A second Microcredit Summit was held in New York City in fall 2002; delegates from one hundred countries attended. The United Nations has declared 2005 to be the International Year of Microcredit. The resolution requests that the observance of the year be a special occasion for encouraging microcredit programs throughout the world. The Microcredit Summit Campaign is meeting with UN officials to help coordinate events for 2005 (MICRO Loan Fund n.d.).

The innovations associated with pioneering MDP programs have been integral to framing the need for microenterprise development today. Specific program practices vary, but these innovations are common enough across programs to merit review.

INNOVATIVE MICROENTERPRISE DEVELOPMENT PROGRAM METHODS

The historical economic context just described is important for understanding the process of microenterprise development. Modern MDPs developed innovative methods for extending credit to the poor. Some of these innovations were modifications of predecessor programs described above. Modern innovations attempt to remedy problems that plagued past economic development and microfinance programs.

1. Focus on women clients. In the past two decades, most MDPs in southern countries have targeted women, and anywhere from 50 to 100 percent of their clients are women. This trend has occurred for several reasons. Feminists have criticized past development practices for excluding women or ignoring their economic responsibilities. This neglect of women is especially problematic because of a worldwide trend toward the feminization of poverty—70 percent of the world's poor are women. Women are disadvantaged economically because of their limited access to education, formal jobs, and resources such as land and credit, and in many nations women are deprived of fundamental economic, political, and human rights (see Desai 2002). Moreover, most victims of poverty are children who reside in mother-headed households, a situation that is of an even greater concern because a growing percentage of households are female-headed. Microenterprise development is seen as a possible corrective to the situation.

Working women in southern nations are disproportionately located in self-employment activities in informal sectors (Creevey 1996). A number of studies suggest that women invest more of their income in their families—for food, school, and shelter—than do men (Amin, Becker, and

Bayes 1998; Auwal and Singhal 1992), and some studies report that women repay their loans more reliably than men (Pitt and Khandker 1998; Blumberg 1995, 2001). Programs such as the Grameen Bank even incorporate explicitly antipatriarchal and pro-development ideologies.

2. Peer lending model. The peer-lending model (also referred to as borrowers' circles or solidarity groups) is a method of microenterprise development that adapts elements of the ROSCA model. As with ROSCAs, group cooperation and support are integral to success. In peer lending, three to ten microentrepreneurs join together to receive a loan or related services such as business training, social services, and organization building. Group members collectively guarantee loan repayment, and access to subsequent loans is dependent on successful repayment by all members. Loans are determined by borrower need, loan size, purpose, and terms. The peer group serves as a mechanism for loan administration, social support, community building, information exchange, and pressure for loan repayment. It is credited with increasing the repayment rate of very poor individuals with little or no collateral and weak credit histories (Berenbach and Guzman 1994). Peer lending is also praised for building networks, that is social capital, among the poor (Woolcock 1998).

3. Step lending. Another program innovation is graduated or step lending. Individuals starting new businesses or those with poor credit and a lack of collateral may build up to larger loans by establishing a good repayment history on small loans. Savings requirements may be a component of the step-lending process. This innovation allows MDPs to minimize their losses on high-risk loans. It also allows entrepreneurs time to develop their businesses and establish a pattern of savings before assuming larger loans (Himes and Servon 1998).

4. Local relevance. MDPs try to be responsive to their local situation. This innovation is a direct response to large-scale economic development programs of the past that were designed by and often for some other population and simply transplanted to a locality without concern for the uniqueness of that setting (Tinker 1999; Prugl and Tinker 1997; Visvanthan et al. 1997). Many MDPs are locally based NGOs. NGO forms have been praised as a type of third-way alternative to private- and state-sector solutions to social and economic problems. They promise to be less bureaucratic than government, more socially conscious than for-profit firms, and more responsive to local community needs (Giddens 1998; Schreiner and Morduch 2002).

5. Collective Organization and Empowerment. Although the sheer provision of microfinance services and microenterprise development to the poor is viewed as a path to the economic and social empowerment of *individuals,* many MDPs in southern countries adopt far more comprehensive agendas. They include extensive educational, health-care, or community economic development projects such as water or irrigation systems (see Self-Employed Women's Association [SEWA] n.d.). Several programs are client-owned and controlled (e.g., FINCA), and some actively organize clients at the occupational or community levels (e.g., into unions or collective buying and marketing groups). Collective organizing is responsive to the demands for local relevance because programs that are locally controlled are more likely to be locally relevant.

6. The Village Bank Model. Village banks are another innovative method for delivering microfinance services and microenterprise development. Village banks are community-managed credit and savings associations (see Hatch and Hatch 1989; Holt 1994). The concept borrows from the credit union model described earlier, but village banks aim for a greater presence in microenterprise development and community investment strategies. The village bank model may include any or all of the program innovations previously described—peer lending, a focus on women clients, stepped lending, and community organization. The financial operation of village banks begins when sponsoring agencies lend seed capital to newly established village banks, which then lend to their members. All members sign the loan agreement as a collective guarantee. First loans are typically small and short-term. The bank charges a commercial rate of interest. At the end of sixteen weeks, the bank repays the sponsoring agency with interest. When members repay their first loan on time, they can get a second loan, the amount of which is determined by the savings a member has accumulated through weekly contributions during the first loan period. Members' savings stay in the village bank and are used to finance new loans or collective income-generating activities. No interest is paid on savings; instead, members receive a share of profits from the village bank's relending activities and other investments.

7. Bridge Lending. Recently, some MDPs have developed mechanisms to aid the transformation of larger microenterprises into small businesses through training and longer-term loans of $3,000 or more (Reed and Befus 1994). Bridge lending responds to microenterprises that are too large for most MDP loans but too small to meet minimum loan amounts or collateral requirements in traditional banks. The loans assist the enterprise in hiring employees, increasing production, or moving into markets with higher-technology requirements.

PROMINENT MICROENTERPRISE DEVELOPMENT PROGRAMS

The MDPs that have been the most influential in U.S. microenterprise development have tended to be the older and larger programs such as AC-CION International and, most prominent of all, the Grameen Bank. ACCION International is an umbrella organization for affiliated microlending organizations and banks around the world. The Grameen Bank is a lending institution with numerous branches. It pioneered many elements of the village bank methodology. FINCA was established later than other programs, but has applied the village bank model around the world. Perhaps less well known in the United States, but nevertheless an important inspiration for many feminist-oriented U.S. MDPs, is SEWA. This program was developed by women and offered some of the earliest southern MDP services. It is distinguished by its direct organizing and comprehensive collective empowerment agenda. The next sections move from the most holistic to the more narrow models of southern MDP development.

Self-Employed Women's Association

SEWA (India) describes itself as an organization developed "by women for women" (SEWA n.d.). It has a comprehensive focus on women's social and economic development and collective empowerment. Although credit is an important SEWA goal, the organization's concerns extend well beyond business training or credit. The organization was founded by a charismatic leader, Ela Bhatt, a lawyer and labor organizer in India. Through its organizations, SEWA aims to empower the growing sector of contingent workers that characterize the new economy.

SEWA was established in 1972 as a trade union for women engaged in informal-sector enterprises. Most of these women were home-based and, as informal-sector workers, were not allowed to affiliate with established trade unions. Women in India were typically denied access to formal-sector employment and were highly exploited by the middlemen who subcontracted work to them or marketed their goods. Bhatt found some of these women living in the street without shelter. Their enterprises included work as street vendors, home textile workers, dairy farmers, and cart pullers. SEWA workers' cooperatives, or unions, help members negotiate with the middlemen, contractors, and merchants who use their services.

SEWA cooperatives represent many different occupational groups and boast over 2 million members (Desai 2002).

SEWA addresses members' credit needs through a village bank model. After serving as a financial intermediary between its members and lending institutions for several years, it established its own cooperative bank in 1974. The bank's membership is restricted to poor women, and it aims to help them become financially independent in their own enterprises. Self-employed women as shareholders own the bank, and their elected board makes the policies. The board hires professional managers to run the bank. As of 1999, SEWA Bank had approximately 93,000 active depositors, and over 33,000 loans outstanding. It has disbursed the equivalent of over $13 million in loans. The bank borrows and lends at market rates of interest (approximately 4 percent) and provides loans with a repayment period of three years. Loans under the equivalent of $55 require one guarantor; those above this amount require two. The maximum loan amount is the equivalent of approximately $700. Most loans are made directly to individuals, but SEWA uses the peer-lending model in rural areas. Loans are made for working capital, that is, for buying tools or for capital investments, such as a house, store, or work space. All borrowers are required to save. The bank reports that it is fully self-supporting and is not subsidized. It reports an average loan repayment rate of 95 percent.

SEWA Bank works closely with the SEWA trade union to provide additional services to members, include training in banking procedures, housing loans, and insurance. SEWA actively promotes collective empowerment through its labor cooperatives, which are involved in the provision of health care, child care, literacy, video technology, and community leadership training (SEWA n.d.). It is similar to the Working Women's Forum (WWF), an organization developed in Madras, India (Working Women's Forum [WWF] n.d.). Both SEWA and the WWF organize women informal-sector workers. Both have inspired some U.S. practitioners to design MDPs especially geared toward the needs of women.

Grameen Bank

The Grameen Bank is the prototype for the global MDP movement. It has been the subject of books, films, and television coverage and its founder has assumed an almost cultlike status as a leader of the field (Counts 1996; Brill 1999). The program has inspired numerous replications around the world including several U.S. programs. Like SEWA, the Grameen Bank was founded by a charismatic leader indigenous to the area that the program served. Also like SEWA, the Grameen Bank has a fairly holistic development agenda. However, this agenda does not entail union organizing.

Mohammed Yunus was a native of Bangladesh and professor of Economics at the University of Chittagong. His concern with rural poverty alleviation was heightened by the 1973–1974 Bangladeshi famine that killed several hundred thousand Bangladeshis (Auwal and Singhal 1992). The bank began as an experimental project in 1976 and turned into a formal nonprofit financial institution in 1983. Its purpose was to provide credit to poor, landless men and women. Yunus defined the poor as those who cultivated less than one-half acre of land or possessed assets worth less than the value of one acre of medium-quality cultivated land (Counts 1996, 46). Grameen loans were targeted to poor rural women because Yunus believed that women were more responsible savers and investors in family needs than were men (Auwal and Singhal 1992; Mizan 1993).

Yunus's targeting of women was especially significant because women's rights were so limited in Bangladesh: they faced Muslim rules of seclusion for women and were typically denied access to formal-sector wage labor (Creevey 1996). Yunus described their only borrowing options as loan sharks who charged exorbitant rates of interest. He argued that credit was a "fundamental human right" and that it could provide the poor with access to other human rights such as food, shelter, and health care (Counts 1996; Bornstein 1996).

The Grameen Bank operates by setting up a bank unit (or branch) with a field manager and several staff to cover fifteen to twenty-two villages. The manager and workers visit villages to recruit clientele and learn about the local milieu. Groups of prospective borrowers are formed, and, in this first stage, two members are eligible to borrow. The group is observed for a month to see if its members are conforming to bank rules. If after five weeks the two members have repaid their loans with interest, other members may borrow. The average loan size is $160 and the interest is approximately 20 percent. Five percent of each loan is paid into the Group Fund. Members must also make weekly payments of 1 taka (or approximately 3 cents) into the Group Fund. This fund belongs to the group, which determines how it will be used. In addition, members pay approximately 25 percent of their total interest payment into an Emergency Fund, which serves as life and accident insurance for members (Grameen Bank n.d.).

The groups meet weekly in the village with their bank assistant to discuss loan requests and any other matter of interest. Grameen staff provide comprehensive investment counseling and close supervision over borrowers' entrepreneurial activities to help improve their productivity and profitability. The peer-lending process aims to create a collective identity for the group. Each group elects officers and the branch elects a chief and deputy chief. The officers serve for one year and may not be reelected until others who are eligible have had the opportunity to serve in a leadership position. The Grameen Bank also requires that its borrowers generate savings in order to buy the bank's shares. This gives members ownership in the bank. Members elect representatives to serve on nine of the twelve available seats on the Grameen's board of directors (Auwal and Singhal 1992; Bornstein 1996).

Grameen leaders hope that the very existence of the organized borrowers' groups and centers will help members acquire the self-confidence, skills, and awareness to undertake other community actions (Wahid 1994; Bornstein 1996). Borrowers participate in decision making about the Grameen's practices during annual national workshops. For example, in one workshop, participants helped to formulate the Sixteen Decisions, a social contract that all members now recite at their meetings. The slogans include vows to eat nutritious food, educate children, and drink safe water; members also disavow domestic abuse and the practice of dowry (Solomon 1992). Through this contract, the bank seeks to undermine gender inequities and promote economic development. Accordingly, the Grameen Bank and this contract have stirred hostility among religious fundamentalist groups in Bangladesh, who resent what they regard as a Western influence (Goetz and Gupta 1996).

Because it became a formal bank, the Grameen Bank has made nearly 16 million loans, totaling over $3 billion. In 2002, the Grameen Bank had over 1,000 branches, had over 2 million members, employed 11,000 staff and worked in 41,000 villages of Bangladesh. There have been more than 170 Grameen Bank replications in more than forty countries (Grameen Bank n.d.).

The Grameen Bank reports a repayment rate of 98 percent, which is higher than the repayment rate of most traditional institutions in Bangladesh (Wahid 1994). The Grameen Bank attributes its high repayment record to its peer-lending model and to the use of the group's emergency fund to cover members' missed payments (Grameen Bank n.d.).

The Grameen Bank now operates as a for-profit institution. However, the bank is actually part of a family of institutions that includes other for-profit concerns and several nonprofit programs. With assistance from private donations, branch banks sponsor workshops for members to increase their knowledge of and commitment to improved health, contraceptive, and educational practices (Holcombe 1995). The bank family of programs also includes research and development projects that experiment with new technologies for increasing production, collective marketing of local products, and building infrastructure support for local businesses and communities (e.g., sanitation and water purification). These programs typically require additional funding from outside sources (Grameen Bank n.d.).

Foundation for International Community Assistance

FINCA is a nonprofit agency that began in Costa Rica in 1984. FINCA aims to alleviate poverty by developing banks in small communities that offer small loans and savings opportunities to low-income families. FINCA groups lend primarily to women.

Like women in Bangladesh and India, women in Costa Rica and other parts of Latin America are disproportionately relegated to work in the informal sectors. Although not facing the degree of religious-based restrictions encountered by Indian and Bangladeshi women, Latin American women still suffer from educational and economic disadvantages vis-à-vis men. Moreover, many Latin American men and women live in countries damaged by civil war, paramilitary rule, and an extreme polarization of wealth.

The FINCA organization pioneered the village bank method and is considered a leader in the microfinance field. FINCA coordinates a network of affiliates serving nineteen countries in Africa, Asia, and the Americas, including MDPs in the United States (Foundation for International Community Assistance [FINCA] n.d.).

The origins of FINCA are more directly linked to the United States than those of SEWA and the Grameen Bank. FINCA was founded by a U.S. economist, John Hatch, who had twenty years of experience in the international development field. Much of its funding comes from USAID (FINCA n.d.). Although its approach is less comprehensive than that of SEWA and the Grameen Bank, FINCA gives its participants the responsibility for running their bank and reinvesting its assets in their communities (Holt 1994). FINCA is also noted for encouraging savings, a microfinance service that is often underemphasized in other programs (Holt 1994). Its programs serve over 150,000 borrowers in over 8,000 groups.

FINCA Village Banks are support groups of ten to thirty-five members, mostly women, who meet weekly or biweekly to access small self-employment loans to start or expand their businesses. These groups provide structured savings programs and a community-based support system. FINCA borrowers receive loans so that they can buy rice in bulk at wholesale prices and resell it at retail prices; buy a used refrigerator to keep produce fresh; or purchase a sewing machine instead of stitching by hand. The aim of these loans is to make borrowers more productive so that they can increase their income and accumulate savings for other investments and emergencies. The groups guarantee one another's loans ranging from $50 to $500. Group loan guarantees substitute for traditional collateral. Like the Grameen Bank, meetings are participatory; members elect leaders, design bylaws, and manage funds and loans, including enforcing penalties for noncompliance. FINCA also provides technical assistance to groups. FINCA reports an overall loan repayment rate of 96 percent. Interest is approximately 3–4 percent per month. Sixty-five percent of FINCA's funding comes from the USAID, and the rest is from private foundations, corporations, and individual donors. The organization aims to help all FINCA country programs to become self-sufficient; some programs claim to be nearly self-sufficient, covering almost 91 percent of their in-country operating costs (FINCA n.d.).

Americans for Community Cooperation in Other Nations

ACCION International is a private, nonprofit organization that serves as an umbrella agency for a network of microfinance institutions in fifteen countries in Latin America, the Caribbean, Africa, and the United States. The organization was founded in 1961 in Caracas, Venezuela, by a group of U.S. students and volunteers. Their aim was to help poor communities to address pressing needs. At the outset, U.S.-based multinational corporations funded ACCION projects to improve the neighborhoods near their corporate offices. Later, ACCION leaders decided that the best mechanism for fostering political and economic development in Latin America was through assistance to informal sector workers. In 1973, ACCION shifted its attention to individual businesses and began to provide credit and training to the self-employed poor. It developed a peer-lending approach called solidarity lending (Servon 1999a; Himes and Servon 1998; ACCION International 2003). ACCION is the most narrowly focused of the four programs discussed here; it concentrates on lending to microentrepreneurs, and only minimal training and technical assistance accompany its loans.

ACCION targets borrowers who are self-employed and who rely on microenterprise as their main income source. ACCION reports that its clients are among the nation's poor at the time of their first loan, usually have no collateral, may not be able to read or write, and may not have enough collateral to open for business every day. They include market vendors, sandalmakers, and seamstresses. Women are 65 percent of ACCION's southern hemisphere clients (Himes and Servon 1998; ACCION International 2003).

The ACCION network provides small short-term loans at interest rates that reflect the cost of lending. Borrowers may apply for loans individually, but, if they lack physical collateral or a cosigner, they join with other borrowers to form solidarity groups (i.e., borrowers' circles). The first loans are small, as low as $100. Borrowers who repay on time are eligible for increasingly larger step loans. As of 2002, ACCION's average loan ranged from approximately $300 to $500 in Latin America and Africa, to almost $6,000 in the United States. It serves approximately 2.7 million clients and has disbursed the equivalent of $4.6 billion dollars with a reported repayment rate of 97 percent (ACCION International 2003).

ACCION prioritizes program self-sufficiency, and this goal, at least in part, explains its more narrowly focused strategies. Programs control operation costs by keeping training costs low. Required training is minimal, including only ten hours of classes that are structured through training notebooks and focused on lending groups and the lending process. A second, optional tier of training responds to requests from group members and includes management techniques appropriate to microenterprises (e.g., marketing and increasing profits). Technical assistance in the form of one-on-one counseling follows training sessions (Berenbach and Guzman 1994). ACCION's self-sufficiency goals necessitate that fees be attached to all program services. The organization argues that these prices provide a good indirect measure of training success by indicating the value of ACCION training to clients (ACCION International 2003).

Although funding comes from both public and private sources (e.g., grants from Citicorp Foundation, Ford Foundation, and the U.S. Department of Treasury), ACCION leaders doubt that there will ever be enough charitable monies for MDPs to have a significant impact on poverty. Thus, ACCION has designed its program in a manner consistent with new privatization trends; it attempts to model itself as a business. ACCION aims to become self-supporting and eventually to become commercial by increasing its loan volume, borrower interest, and associated loan and technical assistance fees. ACCION leaders believe efficiently managed MDPs can generate more income than they spend. Once commercially viable, these programs can become financial institutions and can access the international capital markets by issuing their own debt instruments, most typically as certificates of deposit or as bonds. ACCION publishes reports on best practices in an effort to help microlenders worldwide move toward financial sustainability (ACCION International 2003).

Some ACCION affiliates have reached commercial viability, been incorporated into their country's financial system as regulated institutions, and offer savings and other financial services to microenterprise clients

(Christen and Drake 2002). ACCION played a key role in the creation of commercial microfinance institutions such as BancoSol in Bolivia, Mibanco in Peru, and Finamerica in Columbia (ACCION International 2003; Rhyne 2001). BancoSol was the world's first commercial bank dedicated to microenterprise lending (Gonzales-Vega et al. 1997). ACCION has inspired the design of several U.S. MDPs and, beginning in 1991, formed affiliates in more than thirty U.S. cities.

European Programs

Although the inspiration for microenterprise development is typically associated with the poverty and economic crises of southern hemisphere nations, some European programs have also served to inform the microenterprise field. However, in contrast to southern nation MDPs, these programs have focused more narrowly on assistance to the unemployed. In 1980, the Chomeurs Createurs (Unemployed Entrepreneurs) enabled French citizens entitled to unemployment compensation to collect benefits in a lump sum to finance creating a small business (Balkin 1989). If the business failed, the individual could receive benefits again, but was required to repay the loss through higher unemployment insurance once he or she secured another job. In 1983, Britain introduced the Enterprise Allowance Scheme (EAS), a program wherein unemployed people were eligible for technical assistance to start their own businesses. Recipients received allowances, roughly equivalent to unemployment benefit amounts, that extended for up to one year (Balkin 1989).

SOUTHERN MDP SUCCESSES

The positive evaluations of pioneering MDPs encouraged the spread of these program innovations to other southern regions and to northern hemisphere countries (Gibbs 1990; Katz 1991; Schuman 1993). Evaluations reported significant successes in the areas of (1) poverty alleviation through self-subsistence, (2) economic development, (3) individual empowerment, and (4) collective empowerment through community organization. Many programs also reported successes in achieving or moving toward program sustainability.

In terms of poverty alleviation and economic development, many researchers associate MDPs with increased participant incomes and increased numbers of jobs in regions where programs operate. For example, one study of the Grameen Bank compared wage levels in villages served by the bank with a control group of villages that lacked a Grameen center. The researchers found a significantly higher wage level in the bank villages and concluded that economic activity fueled by Grameen credit had tightened the labor market and increased labor income (Khandker, Khalily, and Khan 1995). An interview study with 380 FINCA Village Bank borrowers in El Salvador revealed that their weekly incomes increased an average of 145 percent (Hahn and Ganuzza n.d.). Participant savings also increased significantly over time. One ACCION study found that family income increased at an average rate of 30 percent after a series of small loans (Himes and Servon 1998). Proponents rely on such research to associate microlending activities with job creation and client improvements in agricultural productivity, housing quality, income, and nutrition (Microcredit Summit 1997).

Some researchers emphasize the role of MDPs in empowering clients as individuals. Participation in peer-lending groups is associated with increases in confidence and self-esteem. Microenterprise development also may *indirectly* promote empowerment through inclusion in the economic system, improved health, education, greater input into household decision making, and less dependency on wealthy landlords or loan sharks (Naidoo 1994; Auwal and Singhal 1992; Rahman 1994; Rahman and Wahid 1992). The Grameen Bank's pro-development stance and its requirement that members must accept the Sixteen Decisions are cited as an important source of empowerment for women (e.g., vows to educate children and to disavow domestic abuse and the practice of dowry) (Auwal and Singhal 1992).

MDPs claim significant success in the realm of collective empowerment (i.e., community organizing) (Desai 2002). Union-focused organizations such as SEWA report a direct impact on women's income and working conditions through collective bargaining (Bhatt 1995; Rose 1996). Involvement in village banking or borrowers' circles is also associated with increasing women's awareness, participation in community organization, and community action (Naidoo 1994; Creevey 1996).

Some MDPs emphasize their potential to be self-sufficient programs. SEWA, ACCION, and the Grameen Bank cite low default rates and significant participant savings accumulation as important steps in their move toward institutional self-sufficiency. Others argue that microfinance is becoming more commercialized in the southern hemisphere, most notably in Latin American countries (Christen and Drake 2002). This trend is exemplified by NGOs that are transforming into licensed banks in order to access public funds or small savings deposits. In addition, banks and finance companies are exploring methods for offering microlending and savings services to the poor (Christen and Drake 2002). Consistent with a neoliberal emphasis on market-based solutions to social problems, a number of proponents argue that commercialization is an essential and viable step for MDP institutionalization and growth.

CRITICISMS OF MICROENTERPRISE DEVELOPMENT PROGRAMS

Evaluations—Methodological Concerns

Although positive evaluations support MDP success claims and funding requests, such reports are not without critics. The debates about MDP evaluations also provide insights into the dilemmas surrounding diffusion and further development in the MDP organizational field.

Many evaluations rely only on indirect measures of program success (i.e., proxies) to avoid costly client follow-ups. Proxies include the number of clients served, number of loans made, and rates of loan repayment as success indicators. More direct measures of success would include increases in client incomes, number of clients' business employees, and value of business assets after program involvement (Berger 1989). The duration of client follow-ups and the representativeness of follow-up samples are also important issues. A brief follow-up cannot assess the longevity of client businesses or long-term improvements in client incomes. On the other hand, longer follow-ups heighten the risk of sample bias as clients drop out or lose touch with programs over time. Such sample mortality is problematic because the least successful clients are those most likely to lose touch with the program.

Even studies that include direct measures and long-term follow-ups often fail to incorporate an adequate comparison group of non-MDP clients (Gulli 1998). Without good comparison groups, it is uncertain whether observed improvements are the result of MDP participation. Observed client outcomes might be the result of other unmeasured factors such as a general improvement in the economy or client resources that are unrelated to MDPs. Studies that examine the regional impact of MDPs are especially vulnerable to this type of error (Schreiner 1999b).

Research that addresses these methodological concerns is needed to inform future funding and diffusion of MDPs (Morduch 1999, 2000). However, strong evaluation designs are difficult to achieve. The introduction of proper comparison groups (who would be eligible for but do not receive services) can raise ethical concerns. Sound evaluations can be expensive and divert funds from important program services. Moreover, funders seem more interested in analyzing programs' potential for self-sufficiency than in rigorous assessments of impacts on poverty alleviation (Morduch 2000; Buckley 2002).

Other Issues

In addition to these methodological concerns, experts challenge the international MDP movement on other grounds. Some argue that MDPs legitimate structural adjustment policies that increase unemployment and restrict state responsibilities for social investment in the poor (S. Johnson 1998; Desai 2002). They challenge claims that individuals can lift themselves out of poverty with hard work and a little MDP credit or training (Rogaly 1996). Critics question the capability of most microenterprises to provide a livable income for families; the businesses are typically in sectors that are vulnerable to large-scale corporate competitors and cheap import policies (e.g., food production) (Grosh and Somolekae 1996). Some research suggests that MDP loans are used to meet daily consumption rather than commercial needs (Goetz and Gupta 1996; Singh and Wysham 1997). Many argue that in the absence of structural economic changes to promote a positive regulatory and economic environment for microenterprises, MDPs may simply increase indebtedness among the poor (Berger 1989; Adams and Von Pische 1992; Carr 1995). "It is only a short leap in argument from reports of a very large number of women borrowers and high repayment rates to promotion of financial services as an answer to poverty and the needs of the very poorest. . . . [Q]uite clearly, financial services are not always the most appropriate intervention. There may be much more urgent requirements, such as health and education services" (Rogaly 1996, 105).

Critics argue that despite expressed aims, MDPs fail to reach a sufficient number of poor people (Hulme and Mosley 1996; Morduch 1999, 2000); many MDPs have a high percentage of nonpoor clients (Gulli 1998, ix). Even the Grameen Bank, which has one of the best records for serving those in poverty, reports that it is unable to reach the poorest 10 percent of its population (Coyle et al. 1994). Some scholars also question whether the better-off of the poor really need MDPs to succeed (Morduch 2000).

Analysts argue that even when MDPs reach poor clients, programs are usually too small to attain the same scale as banks and credit unions that may serve smaller percentages but serve larger absolute numbers of the poor (Gulli 1998; Buckley 2002). Although it might increase the number of clients served, commercialization might also reduce outreach to the poor or certainly minimize the support services that can be offered at a profit (hence the use of the term *commercial microfinance* instead of *microenterprise development)* (Hulme and Mosley 1996; Morduch 1999). Along such lines, some experts argue that MDPs should aim for sustainability rather than self-sufficiency. Sustainability means that programs are cost-effective in that (1) their operating costs are clearly outweighed by their program impact and (2) their programs can be sustained by smaller amounts of outside funds (Otero and Rhyne 1994; Hulme and Mosley 1996; Gulli 1998).

Even if the majority of MDPs remain nonprofit or government providers, the new privatization ideology of businesslike cost effectiveness is likely to pervade the entire MDP organizational field. Commercialization proponents acknowledge that the movement of a few private firms into the MDP industry will shape the conduct of all—profit, governmental, and nonprofit alike. The line between commercial and nonprofit organizations is further blurred by observations that the largest investors in commercial microfinance concerns are public development agencies and nonprofits (Christen and Drake 2002). Many nonprofits, in turn, are funded by grants from private firms and government (Smith and Lipsky 1993). The hegemony of market standards combined with complex interweaving of links among government, nonprofit and for-profit organizations heighten the ambiguity of responsibilities and accountability for social services (Jurik 2004).

Increasingly, many practitioners and scholars argue that there is a fundamental contradiction between program outreach and sustainability goals (Hulme and Mosley 1996; Morduch 1999, 2000; Vinelli 2002). Intensive social and economic support are important for reaching poor clients, but these services greatly increase program operating costs. Increased costs, in turn, undermine MDP sustainability and self-sufficiency. Sustainability desires may converge with demands for successful program outcomes to pressure staff to screen out higher-risk borrowers. Such "creaming" processes may exclude those who are the most lauded targets for MDP services—women and the poor (Blumberg 1995; Kidder 1998).

Although the MDP focus on women has been highly praised for empowering women economically and socially, critics argue that emphasizing women clients to the exclusion of men can heighten women's burden as providers for the family and discourage men's responsibility. Moreover, directing attention to individual women as entrepreneurs distracts from the structural sources of gender inequality (Poster and Salime 2002).

Some case studies challenge claims that localized programs *automatically* lead to collective empowerment. Funding controls and performance standards set by multinational development organizations often thwart local organizing and other collective empowerment agendas by women.

Local community organizing activities can be inhibited by the demands of international and regional funding sources, and the programs favored by many large funding sources adopt a narrow, more technical and business-oriented approach to microenterprise development (Lang 1997; Poster and Salime 2002).

Centralized controls and bureaucratic regulations may limit program responsiveness to the concrete needs of clients. The resulting rules for program operations can be irrelevant or dysfunctional for clients in some localities (Prugl 1996; Alvarez 1999; McMichael 2000.) For example, some women found that rules for gender-segregated groups heightened men's animosity toward them (Poster and Salime 2002). Another study found that women Grameen Bank participants did not control the loans they received; their husbands or kinsmen took charge of the money and sometimes become violent when their wives or kin were denied loans or refused to hand over the money (Goetz and Gupta 1996).

Some researchers report that peer groups for lenders can be extremely oppressive for borrowers who are unable to repay their loans when they are watched and shunned in the community. In the face of this increased community surveillance and sanction, some borrowers return to village loan sharks in order to make microloan payments (Fernando 1997).

Although there are numerous criticisms, MDPs continue to offer hope of individual and community empowerment in the southern hemisphere. Studies continue to document many examples of the empowerment effects of peer lending and economic assistance for women and men in MDPs. In many programs and communities, individuals struggle to realize the progressive potential of MDPs. Despite many barriers to localized controls, northern development organizations do not completely dominate southern MDP operations. Some international funding agencies are supportive of women's organizing and collective empowerment agendas (Alvarez 1999; Johnson 1999). In addition, some southern hemisphere programs have successfully negotiated the bureaucratic maze of funder demands to locate funders more compatible with their goals. On occasion, they successfully appropriate and transform MDP models to fit their localized needs (see Alvarez 2000; Thayer 2001; Poster and Salime 2002).

CONCLUSION

The history of southern hemisphere MDPs reveals innovations, accomplishments, and dilemmas. Although U.S. programs are portrayed as an outgrowth of successful southern hemisphere MDPs, the relationship was not that simple. Modern MDPs are embedded in a complex context of economic crises and change and of accompanying neoliberal ideologies and policies. Although some MDPs were developed by indigenous leaders of the countries in which they were begun, northern ideologies and organizations significantly influence the form and scope of southern MDPs.

Programs also vary considerably; some have developed holistic and activist agendas (e.g., SEWA), whereas others (e.g., ACCION) have focused more narrowly on self-employment lending. Efforts to move toward commercialization, favored by USAID, the World Bank, and others, are most consistent with neoliberal market-centered ideologies. Although these trends may greatly expand service outputs, they threaten to narrow the services available to the poor, and most certainly to limit program scope so that it excludes collective empowerment-oriented agendas.

Some proponents argue that MDPs actually offer a more humane third way residing between free-market ideologies and the traditional liberal reliance on government (Giddens 1998; Schreiner and Morduch 2002). This third way calls for a greater participation from civic society, including NGOs, as well as localized nonprofit organizations in the provision of human services. Regardless of the preference for neoliberal or third-way ideology, both encourage the privatization of public services and the evaluation of even publicly and NGO-provided services in terms of their consistency with businesslike operations standards.

The context of the new economy provided tremendous opportunities for MDP growth and popularization, but these opportunities also posed dilemmas. Contradictions arose for southern MDPs in the following areas: alleviating versus legitimating neoliberal policies, program outreach versus program sustainability, empowering versus overburdening clients as individuals, encouraging collective empowerment versus increasing community surveillance, and facilitating local control in the face of growing national and international standards. Despite these tensions, reports of southern program successes provided an important niche or point of reference for the diffusion of MDPs into the United States during the 1980s and 1990s.

CHAPTER 2

THE EMERGENCE OF
U.S. MICROENTERPRISE DEVELOPMENT

Harvesting a Living from Seeds of Credit, Anti-poverty
Strategy Called Microenterprise Is Growing in U.S.
—GUGLIOTTA (1993)

With a "Microloan" for a Truck, Family Leaves Welfare
—THOMAS (1997)

Sargent Major's Small Business Birdhouse a Golden Egg,
Microenterprises Are Rural Nebraska's New Lifeblood
—HAMMEL (1999)

Banking on Women, . . . She Pulled Her Family out of
Poverty by Building Business Skills
—DePASS (2000)

The context of economic and cultural strain formed by persistent recessions, unemployment, and racial and gender inequality was a fertile environment for the introduction and diffusion of MDPs into the United States in the 1980s. Reports of failed and costly welfare and economic development programs prompted a disillusionment with government interventions. In contrast, MDPs were sold as a mechanism for alleviating the increasing economic insecurity that came with the new economy without the involvement of big government. They targeted economically disadvantaged or marginalized populations such as women, minorities, the disabled, and immigrants and refugees. MDP practitioners not only trained individuals to operate successful businesses, they also managed programs in a cost-effective businesslike manner.

It is not surprising that NGO professionals and U.S.-sponsored international development agencies found receptive audiences for their news about southern MDP successes. A variety of organizations supported the establishment of MDPs or demonstration projects around the country. The newspaper headlines at the beginning of this chapter provide an overview of the promises and media enthusiasm surrounding microenterprise development in U.S. cities. Pioneering MDP practitioners and NGO supporters even formed a self-proclaimed social movement to further encourage the diffusion and institutionalization of U.S. MDPs. This movement included foundation officers, practitioners from a variety of social service organizations, government officials, and members of a variety of social activist groups, including feminists and anti-hunger, disability, and immigration rights advocates.

Although many U.S. programs were originally patterned after famous southern hemisphere MDPs, these models have been significantly transformed in the U.S. context. U.S. MDPs also have been strongly influenced by a history of welfare and economic development programs; many MDPs were pilot tested as components of such programs. At the same time, however, MDPs have played an important part in the redefinition of social investments and services in the era of the new economy, neoliberalism, and new privatization. This era provided great opportunities for the expansion of MDPs in the United States, but ultimately presented contradictions in program practice.

CONTEXT OF OPPORTUNITIES FOR
U.S. MICROENTERPRISE DEVELOPMENT

The U.S. economic, political and cultural milieu since the 1970s was well suited for the emergence of microenterprise. After a period of economic boom that lasted from the 1940s through the 1960s, an increasing percentage of U.S. workers have experienced declining wages and work opportunities. Although the economic crises were less intense for most U.S. citizens than for those in southern hemisphere nations, economic insecurity was a growing problem in the United States. Decades of recession, corporate mergers, declining unionization, corporate downsizing, deindustrialization, and job exportation generated a growing percentage of permanently unemployed and impoverished Americans. Jobs that were temporary, part time, low paying, and without benefits began to predominate, and real wages stagnated or declined for most workers (Rubin 1996; Smith 2001; Rosen 2002).

These employment trends led to a declining sense of stability and security in the United States (Rubin 1996). Moonlighting and work in the informal sectors increased, and, after years of decline, the percentage of self-employed Americans began to rise again in the late 1970s (Portes and Sassen-Koob 1987; Aronson 1991; Blau 1999). Self-employment has historically been viewed as a means for individuals to accumulate assets and bolster themselves and their families during eras of insecurity (Goss 1991). For women, minorities, and immigrants, it has been described as an avenue for upward mobility—a way around glass ceilings and other discrimination that curtail their advancement as employees. Mothers who are self-employed are expected to have more flexibility in caring for children and earning an income at the same time (Jurik 1998).

Economic crises also encouraged political demands to shrink social programs and privatize government services (Dantico and Jurik 1986). Even agencies that remained government-operated began to outsource and subcontract to private firms (Sclar 2000; Jurik 2004). This trend furthered the loss of good-paying jobs with benefits. These government organizations had historically provided an important source of upward mobility for women and minorities who had been denied them in the private sector (Dantico and Jurik 1986). In rural areas, the demise of government subsidies, grain import quotas, and other federal aid to farmers meant that many family farms were lost. There were not enough jobs to fill the void for displaced rural and urban families (Rubin 1996).

These economic conditions and the leadership of the Ronald Reagan administration furthered discourses about the need for unfettered markets and the failure of big government. Government spending on welfare and other services to the poor was viewed as especially problematic (Piven and Cloward 1978, 1991; Blau 1999). Welfare was vilified for promoting long-term dependency, economic marginalization, and a culture of crime and poverty at the expense of tax payers (Piven 2002). The elimination of spending for safety net programs, decreasing government intervention, and a reliance on free-market policies were prominent discursive themes (Blau 1999; Korten 2001). These economic and political shifts and accompanying neoliberal discourses went by many labels: structural adjustment in southern hemisphere nations (chap. 1), and supply-side economics in the United States (Blau 1999).

Despite these shifts in political ideology and policy, many government programs continued but with new goals and directives informed by neoliberal values. There were continuing demands on government to at least help ease problems associated with the new economy (Quadagno 1999; Giddens 1998). MDPs emerged on the U.S. scene in the 1980s. Some were clones of southern program; others grew out of feminist-inspired women's business-support programs or federal and state antipoverty and economic development efforts.

Lisa Servon (1999a) argues that U.S. MDPs are hybrid organizations that combine elements of social welfare and economic development program traditions. Social welfare programs historically focused on services to individuals, whereas economic development programs fostered economic growth in an area. Social welfare programs adopted an individual-level focus, and economic development programs targeted entire communities. Servon is undoubtedly correct that U.S. MDPs are hybrid organizations and that they are informed by these two traditions but with a renewed commitment to local control and innovation. However, the history of U.S. welfare and economic development policy reveals other moments in which this dichotomy between individual- and community-oriented missions was permeable. Moreover, despite many presentations that suggest that MDPs are a clear break with the past, the historical review presented here identifies significant links between these social economic service traditions and the emergence of U.S. MDPs as a poverty-alleviation strategy.

Welfare Policy and Welfare Reform

Historically, in the realm of social welfare policy and poverty alleviation, the United States has avoided large-scale or structurally oriented solutions (e.g., paid family leave and nationalized health care) (Rose 1995). This stance is part of a classic liberal regime that characterizes U.S. political discourse; this relies on the market as the primary form for the distribution of welfare, honors private property, distrusts state authority, and holds individual rights sacred (Goodin et al. 1999).

A significant challenge to the avoidance of governmental intervention in social welfare began with the Great Depression, and President Franklin Roosevelt's New Deal Agenda. New Deal reforms led to a series of enduring federal programs of social provision (e.g., social security and unemployment compensation). One of these programs was Aid to Dependent Children, later renamed Aid to Families with Dependent Children (AFDC) (Rose 1995).

During the 1960s, social unrest and economic prosperity catalyzed President Lyndon Johnson's Great Society Programs, and a programmatic War on Poverty began. Antipoverty programs included job training, community organization, housing and food provision, economic development, and even job creation in the public sector. Although legislation to address the structural causes of poverty (e.g., mandates for full employment or a national minimum income) was proposed during the 1960s and 1970s, it was never passed. U.S. welfare policy generally focused on individual shortcomings and held faith that the market was the best avenue for social distribution (Hirschmann and Liebert 2001; Goodin et al. 1999).

Notable exceptions to the individual-level focus of U.S. welfare programs arose with the Economic Opportunities Act of 1964 and its funding for Community Action Programs (CAPs). These programs had a mandate of "maximum feasible participation" from area residents and clients (Clark and Hopkins 1969). Some CAP projects took the mandate for collective empowerment seriously and recruited the poor to help organize communities around economic opportunities, welfare rights, and other social issues (Clark and Hopkins 1969, 31; Naples 1998a). The controversy surrounding welfare programs was exacerbated by their association with the Civil Rights Movement and organized demands for equal opportunity, including meaningful economic development (Marris and Reins 1969).

The economic recessions of the 1970s and 1980s and a growing white backlash fragmented public support for the War on Poverty programs. In the late 1970s, a proposed Family Assistance Plan, which would have provided welfare recipients with federal support for child care and guaranteed a basic income to the working poor, was soundly defeated (Rose 1995).

During the 1980s, Presidents Reagan and George Bush made deep cuts to safety net programs. Welfare's increasingly vocal critics argued that these programs were too costly, hurt the economy, and eroded work incentives. Within this discourse, welfare dependence, not poverty or unemployment, became the primary social ill (Amott 1990). Although previously defined as deserving of welfare assistance and more or less exempted from work requirements, mothers were increasingly redefined to be able-bodied workers during the 1980s and 1990s (Sidel 2000). Work, self-sufficiency, and personal responsibility were seen as solutions for poverty (Naples 1997). Welfare programs increasingly included mandatory work requirements and penalties for those who failed to conform to the new regime (Rose 1995).

In 1988, Congress passed the Family Support Act to establish an employment education and training program called Job Opportunities and Basic Skills (JOBS). The purpose of JOBS was to ensure that AFDC recipients obtained training and employment and avoided dependence. This legislation required the participation of recipients with children ages three and over (Rose 1995).

In the 1990s, President Clinton promised to "end welfare as we know it." The Personal Responsibility and Work Opportunity Reconciliation Act of 1996 eliminated AFDC; altered national programs for child care, food stamps, and child support; and decreased or eliminated benefits to the elderly, disabled, working poor, and legal immigrants. It replaced the fifty-year system of federally controlled benefits with state-controlled community-development block grants. The grants (TANF) included more stringent time limits and work requirements than did previous legislation. TANF effectively transferred much of the responsibility for poor women and their children to states. Federal guidelines mandated that states require all able-bodied welfare recipients to work after two years of assistance. The new federal funding formulas provided states with financial incentives to cut their welfare spending levels (Sidel 2000; Piven 2002). Many states vigorously cut welfare rolls and discouraged even eligible participants from claiming benefits (Finder 1998, A1, A12; Rogers-Dillon and Skrenty 1999). Despite promises that cuts would bring economic growth that would "trickle down" to poorer Americans, poverty rates expanded (Dillon 2003) and the number of decent-paying lower-skill jobs in urban poverty centers declined (Blau 1999; Bernstein 2002).

Nevertheless, the media and politicians have characterized welfare reform as a huge success (Pear 2003, A25). Research on this success has been difficult because Congress refuses to require the tracking of individuals who leave welfare rolls (Piven 2002). Preliminary studies suggest that individuals who find jobs do so in low-wage and highly unstable employment sectors (Finder 1998; Eitzen and Zinn 2000; Sandoval and Hirschl 2000; Vartanian and McNamara 2000). Moreover, early reports of success in reducing TANF rolls have been attributed to a creaming process: better-off welfare recipients were those most likely to gain quick employment and better wages. Recipients remaining on the welfare rolls at the end of their five-year TANF eligibility period tended to be the most disadvantaged cases (i.e., less educated or mothers of small children) (Eitzen and Zinn 2000; Albelda 2002).

In 2003, at the request of President George W. Bush, the U.S. House of Representatives voted to renew the 1996 welfare law and impose stricter work requirements on poor people who receive cash assistance from the federal government (Pear 2003). The Senate is expected to pass the measure with some small additional support for child care.

Welfare reform exemplifies Quadagno's (1999, 3) characterization of the "capital investment welfare state" with its focus on market-based and private-investment solutions to social welfare. Welfare reform concentrated on spending for the poor (which made up less than 1 percent of the federal budget) and left more costly universal social programs such as Social Security and Medicare in tact. However, as Quadagno notes, other proposals to alter the quantity and form of support for these social programs are in process. The trend toward the capital-investment welfare state is visible in three ways: "first in efforts to restructure public benefits to coincide with trends in the private sector, second, in efforts to reduce collective responsibility for social welfare needs and increase individual responsibility, and third, in proposals to transform public welfare programs from cash benefits and direct services into incentives for personal savings and investing" (3).

MDPs are compatible with this capital investment policy agenda because they support individual investments in self-employment in lieu of reliance on government safety nets (Howells 2000). Thus, the crisis surrounding U.S. welfare policy provided opportunities for MDPs. At the same time, however, MDPs also drew on the welfare-organization field both as a model for some of their services and as a source of legitimation. They were also influenced by the economic development field.

Roots of Microenterprise Development in Economic Development Policy

Although their popularity has grown in the past two decades, the seeds of capital-investment welfare policies can be seen even in economic development policies such as the urban renewal programs of the 1950s. These programs called for public- and private-sector partnerships and market incentives to solve the social problems of U.S. cities. Urban racial discontent and protests during the 1960s produced programs aimed at revitalizing urban minority communities (Portes 1997).

Community development programs were varied, but shared a common reliance on government grants and tax abatements to attract businesses to distressed areas. The hope was that government investments in business would eventually benefit the poor (Squires 1989). Such programs were criticized for serving as a boon for medium-size and large business interests in ways that actually displaced and further impoverished the poor (Bennett, Herring, and Jenkins 1998). Although some programs included requirements for community participation, the resulting efforts were typically only symbolic (Squires 1989).

A few of President Johnson's War on Poverty programs included assistance for small business. For example, the Economic Opportunity Act of 1964 included the Equal Opportunity Loan program. This program made relatively large, unsecured loans (seldom below $25,000), but offered no business training. Huge default rates led to the program's demise (Rodriguez 1995).

The War on Poverty included the creation of community-based development organizations (CBDOs) charged with combining social and economic programs to coordinate resources so as to raise incomes, create jobs, generate enterprises in poor neighborhoods, and provide direct services to the poor. CBDOs included a range of organizations. Community development corporations (CDCs) were neighborhood- or regionally based economic development organizations focused on housing and physical development of inner-city neighborhoods. Community action agencies (CAAs) worked in partnership with local businesses, charities, and public agencies to provide direct services to the poor (e.g., Head Start and small-business development), coordinate resources and referrals, and develop poverty-reduction strategies (e.g., housing rehabilitation) (Puls 1991).

Bank redlining, the policy of systematically denying loans to individuals in designated poor or minority communities, also prompted federal intervention (Oliver and Shapiro 1995). The Richard Nixon administration sought to assist black-owned businesses through several programs. For example, in 1969, minority enterprise development companies (MESBICs)[1] were designated to alleviate the institutional credit gap that discouraged minority-owned business development. MESBICs were private companies chartered and subsidized by the federal government to invest in and finance long-term loans to minority businesses (Bates 2000).

Community development banks (CDBs) were created in response to complaints about redlining and charges that development projects benefited mostly individuals and businesses located outside the targeted communities. The CDB mission was to invest in business and real estate projects that benefited the community. The banks were regulated by the Federal Reserve and received investments from commercial banks (Puls 1991). The South Shore Bank of Chicago is an example of a famous and successful CDB. It was established in 1973 as a full-service commercial bank offering business and community development loans and services (Taub 1994).

Community Development Block Grant (CDBG) programs and Urban Development Action Grants were initiated in 1974 (Puls 1991). They were charged with developing viable communities by providing decent housing and economic opportunities to low- and moderate-income people. Their focus on grants to cities illustrates the movement to decentralize federal power over economic development and social service programs to local communities.

In 1977, the U.S. Congress passed the Community Reinvestment Act (CRA), also aimed at discouraging bank redlining practices (Oliver and Shapiro 1995). Although the purpose of the CRA was to require that banks reinvest in their communities, this initial measure was ambiguous and ineffective (Santiago, Holyoke, and Levi 1998; Hales 1995).

Lending and training programs for small business appear sporadically throughout the history of local economic development, but, for the most part, economic development programs focused more on attracting larger businesses and hoping for the positive effects of trickle-down economics rather than on training and lending to poor entrepreneurs (Balkin 1989). For example, Bates's (2000) analysis of the MESBIC program revealed that, of the 119 MESBICs initiated, only approximately one-half remain operational. Failed MESBICs were those that undertook larger numbers of small, high-risk, noncollateralized business loans or that provided venture capital loans to inexperienced entrepreneurs (Bates 2000). Bates's evaluation suggests that lending to minority businesses can be a successful but limited strategy: lending to poor, novice, high-risk businesses can only continue if it is highly subsidized. Successful MESBIC's found that to survive they had to scale up their lending, relying on some combination of collateral-secured loans and large-scale venture-capital lending to firms owned by highly experienced and educated entrepreneurs. These historical lessons stand in stark contrast to the modern MDP emphasis on lending to very small businesses, including start-ups. They also illustrate the long interest in government assistance to disadvantaged business owners.

Economic development programs were criticized for focusing on (1) building large institutional-style housing and (2) attracting preexisting businesses owned by wealthy individuals that employ individuals from outside the target community (Rubin 1988; Vidal 1995). Community elites or bureaucrats, not poor residents, were the main participants in program decision making (Levine 1989; Naples 1998b). The failure of trickle-down strategies and continuing high unemployment in both urban and rural areas prompted strong criticisms of government-funded economic-development investments (Squires 1989; Bennett, Herring, and Jenkins 1998). Pushes for increased local control and a declining role of big (that is, federal) government in local areas were increasingly reflected in programs of the 1980s and 1990s.

These criticisms converged with the reported business successes of U.S. immigrant groups and of southern MDPs to stir a new wave of bottom-up development planning (Light and Pham 1998). Bottom-up development was consistent with the popular discursive themes of the time such as antigovernment, privatization, local control, and individual responsibility.

Media coverage and scholarly research describe the business success of immigrant enclave economies around the United States among groups that include the Japanese in California, the Chinese in New York, and the Cubans in Miami (e.g., Portes and Bach 1985; Light and Bonacich 1988; Light and Rosenstein 1995). The success of immigrant businesses and reports of mobility from informal-sector to formalized self-employment activities (e.g., Portes and Sassen-Koob 1987) inspired policymakers to encourage business enterprise in economically neglected and abandoned neighborhoods. Increasingly, self-employment was identified as an effective means of self-help to alleviate problems of poverty, unemployment, and neighborhood decline (M. Johnson 1998a).

Under the Reagan administration, Congress passed legislation (Title VII of the Housing and Community Development Act of 1987) that authorized the creation of Enterprise Zones (Wallace 1999). These zones were intended to offer incentives for businesses to move into an area and provide job training for the residents of the area. The program was not funded.

After declining economic development budgets throughout the 1980s, increasing poverty in inner cities and violent racial protests in Los Angeles during the early 1990s recaptured the attention of federal policymakers, but this time with a more decentralized economic development approach. Under the Clinton administration, the Enterprise Zones were reconstructed as Empowerment Zones that required greater levels of community participation in decision making and business development. Associated legislation for this program passed in 1993. The exact meaning of the Empowerment Zone programs varied across states, but common themes included public- and private-sector partnerships, economic development incentives, and community participation in planning and decision making. The programs relied on existing institutions to attract and create businesses, develop infrastructure, and improve public services in impoverished areas (Servon 1998a; Bennett, Herring, and Jenkins 1998). Funding for local microenterprises was viewed as consistent with Empowerment Zone programming.

The CRA was strengthened in the mid-1990s with legislation that launched President Clinton's Community Development Financial Institution (CDFI) initiative. CDFIs are institutions such as CDBs, bank-owned CDCs, credit unions, and loan funds that receive government-subsidized funding to serve low-income, inner-city communities. CDFIs were to fill the gaps left by mainstream financial services (Oliver and Shapiro 1995). However, Bates (2000) cautions that CDFIs are replicating the same risky pattern of subsidized high-risk lending to the poor that led to the demise of the MESBIC program.

In sum, both social welfare and economic development programs adopted well-meaning goals to extend equal opportunity to the poor, offer needed social services, and help rebuild depressed communities to enhance safety and quality of life. Although some programs incorporated extensive community-participation mandates, despite some notable exceptions (see Rose 1995, 84, 104; Naples 1998a; Puls 1991), most fell short of these goals. Services targets were scaled-up to reach people who were better-off and more likely to demonstrate successful outcomes with the limited available resources. Program control typically fell into the hands of local elites and program staff. Instead of being empowered, poor and low-income women and minorities found themselves the objects of increased surveillance and negative labeling if they failed to succeed according to program criteria (Theodore 1998; Bennett, Herring, and Jenkins 1998; Jurik et al. 2000). Indeed, some experts argue that aid to the poor can only be accomplished with continuous government support to overcome the structural barriers to full participation and economic development (Bates 2000; Piven 2002).

MDPs have entered this same policy terrain and have borrowed much from both the welfare and economic development traditions. However, MDPs promised to break with past problems by emphasizing client self-help, and promoting cost-effective program operations. In any case, the crises surrounding welfare and economic development programs provided political opportunities for emerging U.S. MDPs. Practitioners and other advocates mobilized to spread MDP innovations throughout the United States.

MOBILIZING TO DIFFUSE MICROENTERPRISE DEVELOPMENT PROGRAMS AROUND THE UNITED STATES

The diffusion of MDPs was encouraged by groups of practitioners, NGO professionals, activists, and government policymakers. MDP advocacy drew on program models from southern nations, the United Kingdom, and Europe, as well as the discourses of economic development and welfare reform (Servon 1999a). Significant numbers of microenterprise activists had worked in past war-on-poverty programs (e.g., housing and welfare-to-work programs) (Balkin 1989, 1993). After a number of programs were established, advocates formed a national association of MDP providers, describing their activities as part of a microenterprise movement. MDP movement[2] advocates were predominantly middle-class professionals; they did not generally include the poor entrepreneurs who were to be the movement's beneficiaries. There were four types of MDP advocates: (1) women's movement and other 1960s antipoverty social movement and practitioner organizations, (2) NGO professionals from economic development–oriented foundations and corporations, 3) government agencies, and 4) pioneering microenterprise program practitioners. From these distinct but overlapping groups emerged nationally recognized leaders of the U.S. MDP movement.

Women and Antipoverty Groups

MDPs attracted the interest of a variety of activist groups and social program professionals. During the 1980s, women's organizations sought to promote women-owned businesses through networking, training, and lending programs. With their emphasis on serving women, MDPs provided an attractive alternative for women's activist groups (Prugl 1996). Antipoverty and anti-hunger groups also identified MDPs as a means of addressing their concerns (Rodriguez 1995; Oliver 1983). For example, as noted earlier, ME program founders learned about MDPs through anti-hunger activism. Members of anti-hunger groups traveled to other countries and returned to the United States with films about successful southern MDPs such as SEWA and the Grameen Bank. Serious cuts in social service funding during the Reagan-Bush years also led welfare, CAP, and low-income-housing program staff to move into MDP work (Balkin 1989; conference interviews).

MDP advocates lobbied U.S. policymakers to recognize self-employment as a domestic as well as an international strategy for women to gain self-subsistence and, in the case of the growing numbers of women household heads, support their children (Tinker 1989). The idea that women could operate businesses out of their homes and combine paid work and child care was appealing to feminists, hunger activists, and policymakers (Jurik 1998; Ehlers and Main 1998).

Several pioneering women's self-employment programs were established with the support of private, foundation, and government resources. Some programs focused on women regardless of economic level, whereas others concentrated on poor and low-income women. Some were created with funding from nonprofits such as the Stanley, Mott, Ford, and Ms. foundations, as well as support from corporations and private individuals (Raheim 1997).

One of the first organizations of this kind was the Women's Economic Development Corporation (WEDCO). WEDCO was founded in 1982 by Kathryn Keely of Chrysalis, a women's support and counseling center, and

Arvonne Fraser of the University of Minnesota. Although initially not defined as a microenterprise program, WEDCO was the first U.S. program to offer microloans to low-income women. It received a lot of media attention and served as a model for other U.S. microenterprise programs (McLenighan and Pogge 1991). WEDCO tried to increase the chances for survival and success of women's businesses, especially those begun by low-income or unemployed women. The organization provided training, networking, and financing services. It served as an intermediary for financing through local banks and operated three of its own loan funds for individuals unable to obtain bank financing. Its loans range from $200 to $50,000 (Balkin 1989). In the late 1980s, WEDCO added a welfare demonstration project to help women on AFDC start businesses and gain self-subsistence. WEDCO merged with a nonprofit women's career support center in 1989 to form a single agency called WomenVenture. WomenVenture offers a wide range of economic services to women, including job training in traditionally male trade occupations, and microenterprise development (Kaplan 2003; WomenVenture n.d.).

Foundation and Corporate Support

Foundations and international development organizations provided support for the establishment of southern hemisphere MDPs, dissemination and exchange of information about MDPs, and creation of U.S. MDPs. CDBs, private banks, and other corporations also supported the development and operation of U.S. MDPs.

Private foundations and development organizations were integrally involved in exchanges between southern and northern practitioners. During the early 1980s, the Ford and other foundations and development groups (e.g., the Joyce Foundation and the International Fund for Agricultural Development) provided support for reciprocal advisory services between development and banking practitioners from Bangladesh and North American countries. For example, in 1983, the Ford Foundation asked Mary Houghton, president of Shorebank Corporation, a holding company that owns the South Shore Bank in Chicago, to visit the Grameen Bank and to provide technical assistance and assess the bank's work. Houghton did so and then began to adapt the Grameen approach for use in the United States. Her interactions with Jeffrey Ashe (then with ACCION International) reinforced her belief that the Grameen Bank innovations could work in the United States. Houghton formed the steering committee that established the Women's Self-Employment Project (WSEP) of Chicago in 1986 (Balkin 1989).

Foundations were also important in developing research to track and assess microenterprise development. With foundation funding (i.e., from the Charles Stewart Mott and Ms. foundations), the Aspen Institute, a nonprofit educational and research group, established the Self-Employment Learning Project (SELP) in the early 1990s to evaluate and disseminate information about U.S. MDPs.

In 1993, the Ford and Ms. foundations sponsored a conference of North American and Bangladeshi peer-lending programs to exchange ideas and discuss operational issues. This conference stimulated both information-sharing and the further organization of U.S. MDP practitioners (Coyle et al. 1994). Foundation support was crucial to building a national MDP movement and attracting government support for U.S. microenterprise development.

CDBs such as the South Shore Bank often provided loan monies for U.S. MDPs, but private banking concerns also played a key role in the growth of the MDP movement. Banks obtained CRA credits for providing lending dollars to MDPs, but the MDPs assumed all administrative costs and risks associated with each small-business loan; this arrangement reduced the banks' costs for lending to the poor. Thus, CRA credits provided substantial incentives for banks to support MDPs. Banks also provided a source of expertise about business operations and lending activities for novice MDPs. Other private corporations provided monies for MDPs, especially those that wanted to market to small and home-based businesses and home offices.

Government Financial Support: Demonstration Projects

MDP advocates drew on MDP success stories to encourage government support for tests of microenterprise development in the United States. The federal government offered financial support for experimentation and symbolic support through several legislative proposals that were well publicized in the popular media. Despite popular images of MDPs as grassroots local programs that are largely independent of the government social service programs of the past, this history illustrates that early MDPs had deep connections with both the U. S. government and U.S. welfare and unemployment programs.

Several MDP demonstration programs were funded by federal agencies, often with the joint support of state and local governments. Some programs were appended to government agencies and others were subcontracted to local nonprofit organizations (e.g., WEDCO's AFDC demonstration project). Thus, government was influential not only in shaping southern programs but also in pioneering early U.S. MDPs.

Demonstration Partnership Program Community action agencies in New York and Vermont started self-employment programs for low-income people with funding from the U.S. Department of Health and Human Services in 1986. The project was called the Demonstration Partnership Program of the Office of Community Services. Evaluations of this project suggested that self-employment programs were viable economic and social development strategies. With funding from the U.S. Department of Health and Human Services, some CDCs extended their traditional focus on housing and the physical development of inner-city impoverished neighborhoods by starting small enterprise development programs for low income citizens (Raheim 1997).

Self-Employment Investment Demonstration In 1986, the federally funded Self-Employment Investment Demonstration Program (SEID) was implemented by the nonprofit Corporation for Enterprise Development (CfED).[3] Five states (Iowa, Maryland, Michigan, Minnesota, and Mississippi) participated in the program. Under contract, local program operators provided self-employment training, counseling, technical assistance, and either direct loans or assistance in gaining access to credit from a bank. Participants were self-selected for the program and developed their own business plans. Normal AFDC rules were waived so that participants could earn business income without jeopardizing their AFDC grants for the first year of their business operation.

The evaluation of the SEID program included follow-up interviews with a random sample of 120 participants who started businesses. Although SEID participants were similar to other AFDC respondents in many respects, their level of education was significantly higher than that of the average AFDC recipient. Interviews before and after program participation suggest that the survival rate for clients' businesses exceeded the national average for new businesses of similar size. The SEID results suggest that participant businesses created about one new job for every two SEID businesses, but this figure included part-time and temporary employment. Respondents reported significantly more personal and business assets than they had held at the time of enrollment in SEID. One-half of the respondents terminated their AFDC benefits, and the other half added to their benefits with self-employment income. SEID business income gains were modest; respondents reported a median gross income of $8,000

(Raheim 1997). Net business incomes were much lower; the median net income was $3,000 annually (Schreiner 1999c).[4]

Self-Employment and Enterprise Development Demonstration The first U.S. program to draw on the European models of funding self-employment through unemployment compensation was the Self-Employment and Enterprise Development Demonstration (SEED). Implemented in Washington in 1989 and Massachusetts in 1990, SEED was funded by the U.S. Department of Labor and the Department of Trade and Economic Development. Both states modified their unemployment benefit program to fund microenterprise projects among the unemployed. Those eligible for unemployment insurance could volunteer to participate. Volunteers were randomly assigned to treatment and control groups. In Washington, the treatment group was given business training, and, after completing the training requirements, individuals were given the option of receiving their remaining unemployment insurance benefits in a lump-sum payment to finance their business. The usual job search requirements were waived. In Massachusetts, there was no lump-sum payment, but treatment group participants were eligible for twenty-four weeks of payments with no search requirements. They also received self-employment training and counseling.

The treatment group in Massachusetts fared significantly better than the control group in both earnings and work longevity, but there were no significant differences between treatment and control groups in Washington. The effects for treatment groups in both states also greatly diminished over time (Schreiner 1999a). Despite these mixed findings, project evaluators concluded that self-employment was a viable option for some unemployed individuals and argued that legislative changes in unemployment regulations were needed to support self-employment among the unemployed (Benus, Wood, and Grover 1994).

Rivercities of Iowa/Illinois Self-Employment Program Based on the work of these earlier demonstration projects, Illinois and Iowa hosted a three-year demonstration project as a second test of the impact of self-employment training and lending on the ability of AFDC participants to attain self-sufficiency. The Rivercities of Iowa/Illinois Self-Employment Program (RISE) began in 1990. The program included self-employment training, assistance in obtaining loans, and ongoing technical assistance. Again, participants were encouraged to pursue their own business ideas. The evaluation of RISE included a matched comparison group of AFDC recipients who had not participated in any welfare-to-work program except the state's JOBs program (sixty-one matched pairs). RISE participants were off AFDC longer than the comparison group and also scored higher on self-esteem, self-efficacy, and money-management measures (Raheim and Alter 1998). Although the absence of a randomized control group makes these findings equivocal, they nevertheless bolstered MDP activist enthusiasm (Servon 1998b; Schreiner 1999c).

U.S. Department of Small Business Administration Microloan After numerous U.S. microenterprise programs had begun operations, the U.S. Department of Small Business Administration (SBA) was authorized to begin the Microloan Demonstration Program in 1991. The program was encouraged by criticisms charging the SBA with being unresponsive to the needs of very small businesses. The rhetoric surrounding the passage of this legislation promoted microenterprise and welfare reform as related concepts (Howells 2000). The Microloan Demonstration Program was hailed as an important component of federal efforts to overhaul the welfare system by promoting the self-sufficiency of welfare recipients (Senate Committee on Small Business 1991). The chief advocate for this legislation, Senator Dale Bumpers, expressed his strong desire for a microenterprise program in every state "as a tool for combating poverty, unemployment, and underemployment by offering people the dream of successful business ownership" (Senate Committee on Small Business 1994). Microenterprise programs that participated in this demonstration project offered loans and technical assistance to individuals starting or expanding microenterprises. The loans were provided through an intermediary lender with a maximum of $10,000 and an average size of $2,500 (Riley 1995; Small Business Administration [SBA] 1997).

After the passage of welfare reform legislation, the SBA sought to develop a welfare-to-work strategy focused on assisting small businesses that hired former welfare recipients and assisting former recipients seeking to start their own businesses. Several early microenterprise development programs became sites for welfare-to-work demonstration projects (e.g., WESEP of Chicago and the Institute for Social and Economic Development of Iowa City) (Severens and Kays 1997). However, SBA assistance to low-income businesses has been limited by the agency's failure to establish low-income guidelines and monitor the number of low-income businesses that receive loans (Howells 2000, 171).

Government Financial Support: House Select Committee on Hunger

Cheryl Rodriguez's (1995) research details another important, although technically unsuccessful, source of government support for the microenterprise development movement: the U.S. House Select Committee on Hunger in the late 1980s and early 1990s under the leadership of Congressman Tony Hall. Hall assumed leadership of the committee at a time when calls for welfare reform had become increasingly vocal. He was influenced by President George Bush's political agenda and his own commitment to avoid liberal food-provision programs. Hall successfully shifted the Hunger Committee agenda away from food provision and toward microenterprise development. He argued that food programs were temporary and costly remedies at best. He identified microenterprise development as the best avenue for ending poverty and hunger by promoting self-sufficiency among the U.S. poor (Rodriguez 1995, 103).

In consultation with the leading U.S. MDP providers of the day, the committee staff developed the Freedom from Want Act. Hall introduced the bill in 1991 (HR 3033) (House Select Committee on Hunger 1991; Rodriguez 1995). The bill included provisions for domestic microenterprise development such as granting permission for states to waive federal AFDC requirements for people in state-approved microenterprise programs and including MDPs as eligible training activities under federal JOBS training programs. The bill increased funding opportunities for MDPs under existing federal block grant and job-training programs (i.e., it specified that MDPs were eligible for community development block grants).

The major provisions of the act focused on the needs of the poor to find mechanisms for self-sufficiency. Hearings offered testimony from MDP providers and anecdotal examples of women who had been blocked from starting their own businesses by restrictive federal welfare regulations (House Select Committee on Hunger 1991, Rodriguez 1995). As is the case with the consideration of any legislative agenda, what is *not* included is often just as significant as the provisions covered (Jenness and Broad 1994; Naples 1997). The hearings emphasized the importance of MDPs as an avenue for disseminating individualized self-help strategies. HR 3033 did *not* reference innovative program methodology such as peer lending or the potential of MDPs for collective empowerment (e.g., cooperative buying associations, community-action agendas, and the organizing of informal-sector workers). Rigorous assessments of the reported effectiveness of MDPs were also not a consideration. The proposed legislation included no references to the structural causes of poverty and hunger and no stipulations for improving the services of major lending institutions' to small businesses (House of Representatives 1991; Rodriguez 1995, 114–15).

Although the bill never passed, the hearings on HR 3033 and the associated national publicity provided a well-organized mechanism for promoting microenterprise (House of Representatives 1991; Rodriguez

1995). The media coverage of the hearings extolled the virtues of MDPs. Many food-advocacy groups around the country adopted the call for microenterprise development, featuring speakers from leading MDPs at their conferences and sponsoring trips to visit southern hemisphere MDPS, such as the one attended by ME program founders. Food practitioners and volunteers became active in MDP practice and advocacy (Rodriguez 1995; Poster and Salime 2002). This adoption of a pro-MDP focus by hunger movement activists illustrates a concept developed by social movement scholars called *spill-over*, wherein one social movement or interest group borrows themes and objectives from another movement's practice and advocacy (Meyer and Whittier 1994; Jenness and Grattet 2001). This spill-over was important in the diffusion of MDPs around the United States.

Pioneering U.S. Microenterprise Development Programs

The practitioners of early U.S. MDPs not only pioneered models for U.S. practice, they also provided leadership in advocating supportive legislation and program expansion. MDP practitioners became advocates for microenterprise development. The history of pioneering U.S. programs illustrates links with southern MDPs and with U.S. social service programs and social movements.

Kathryn Keely, founder of WEDCO (described earlier), is widely viewed as a pioneer and leader in the MDP field (conference interviews). She was a founder and early president of a national MDP association. As one of the first (if not the first) U.S. MDPs, WEDCO did not have the links to southern hemisphere programs that characterized other prominent U.S. programs but instead exemplifies some of the early connections of MDPs to feminist support for women in business.

WSEP (mentioned earlier) provides a good example of the relationships between southern and northern MDPs. WSEP was established by Mary Houghton after she attended a Ford Foundation–sponsored exchange between Shore Bank and the Grameen Bank. Through her involvement with Shore Bank, Houghton connected the U.S. poverty-alleviation and economic development traditions. WSEP offers training, technical assistance, and lending to individuals and peer groups. It modeled its peer-lending component after the Grameen Bank and its training component after WEDCO (Balkin 1993). Its individual loans entail collateral requirements and are accompanied by fourteen weeks of business training. The Full-Circle Fund, its peer-lending program, is aimed at women who are African American, low income, and welfare recipients. It requires less training than the individual loan program and allows circle participation to substitute for collateral requirements. Loan amounts range from $100 to $25,000, with an average of around $2,000. With federal subsidies, the program offers transportation and child-care assistance for its clients. It also offers savings programs through local banks (Women's Self-Employment Program n.d.).

Another program initially based on the Grameen model is the Good Faith Fund in Arkansas, which started in 1988. It offers both individual and peer lending: peer loans range from $274 to $7,500; individuals loans are larger, ranging from $5,000 to $122,000. Good Faith provides business training, especially for low-income individuals in manufacturing and health care sectors (Mondal and Tune 1993; Taub 1998; Good Faith Fund n.d.).

Another significant Grameen Bank replication in the U.S. was the Coalition for Women's Economic Development (CWED of Los Angeles). CWED was a peer-lending and business-training program also influenced by SEWA (described in chap. 1). Although CWED ceased operations in the mid-1990s, the program served as a model for several highly successful MDPs that are still in operation today, including the ME case study program (described in chaps. 5 and 6).

In addition to the Grameen Bank and SEWA, other programs from southern nations served as models for U.S. programs. Several U.S. programs modeled themselves after ACCION (e.g., the Women's Economic Self-Sufficiency Team in Albuquerque, New Mexico). In 1991, ACCION International started its own U.S. operations and now has affiliates that offer both peer and individual lending in several states (Himes and Servon 1998; Servon 1999a).

In 1987, after consultations with Jeffrey Ashe (of ACCION and USAID), Frank Ballesteros started the Microbusiness and Housing Development Organization (MICRO), an MDP in southern Arizona. Although partially inspired by the ACCION model, MICRO does not use peer-lending strategies (Edgcomb, Klein, and Clark 1996; Frank Ballesteros, 1995 interview). The program combines individual loans (from $500 to $25,000) with intensive technical assistance and networking support. MICRO targets individuals who are recent immigrants, meet U.S. Housing and Urban Development (HUD) low-income-level guidelines, and have been operating their businesses for at least one year (Severens and Kays 1997; Ballesteros, 1995 interview; MICRO Loan Fund n.d.).

After years of working with USAID and ACCION International, Jeffrey Ashe started Working Capital in 1990 (Working Capital n.d.). Working Capital is an MDP in New England that Ashe modeled after the FINCA program. Working Capital offers peer lending and small amounts of technical assistance to low- and moderate-income individuals who are already operating businesses (Anthony 1997). It serves over fifty economically disadvantaged urban and rural communities. Loans start at $500 and increase in increments of $500 up to a maximum of $5,000 (working capital). Organizations in other parts of the United States have modeled themselves after the Working Capital program (e.g., Working Capital of Delaware) (see Ashe 2000).

The FINCA program also served as a model for other U.S. MDPs. In 1989, Women's Entrepreneurs of Baltimore, Incorporated (WEB), opened in partnership with FINCA. WEB offers individual and peer lending as well as training and ongoing technical assistance to women in Baltimore. Loans range from $100 to $1,000 for individual borrowers and from $500 to $6,000 for peer borrowing. FINCA USA, Incorporated, started in Washington, D.C., in 1994, offers peer lending, technical assistance, and savings, with loan sizes from $100 to $6,000 (FINCA n.d.).

Practitioners from these pioneering programs formed networks and joined with funding agencies to establish information exchanges. They aimed to move U.S. microenterprise development beyond its image as a conceptual model or an experiment borrowed from southern hemisphere nations. To do so, they developed a formal organization to further promote U.S. microenterprise development.

RESOURCE MOBILIZATION AND INSTITUTIONALIZATION OF THE MICROENTERPRISE DEVELOPMENT PROGRAM MOVEMENT

The efforts of MDP advocates led to the emergence of a nationally recognized U.S. MDP field. At several foundation-facilitated exchanges, U.S. practitioners decided that they needed a national association to further domestic and international practitioner exchanges and to advance the case for microenterprise development in a more organized fashion (Association for Enterprise Opportunity [AEO] n.d.). In 1991, leading microenterprise advocates (including Kathryn Keely of WEDCO, Jeffery Ashe of Working Capital, Robert Friedman of the CfED, and Peggy Clark of Aspen Institute's SELP) founded the Association for Enterprise Opportunity (AEO) (Cowgill 1998b). According to its original mission statement, AEO provides its members: "with a forum, information, and a voice to promote enterprise opportunity for people and communities *with limited access to economic resources.* AEO also represents the U.S. microenterprise development agenda in the growing international community" (AEO n.d., emphasis added).

AEO has been instrumental in framing practitioner, funding agency, policymaker, and public views about MDPs and their clients. It facilitated the diffusion and institutionalization of the MDP field through publicity, evaluations, legislative advocacy, and the development of standards for best practice (AEO n.d.).

AEO incorporated as a nonprofit organization to facilitate fund raising and advocacy. During the first four years, leaders ran the organization as volunteers. They mobilized funding from foundations that had been supportive of microenterprise (e.g., the Charles Stewart Mott, Ford, and Ms. Foundations), and worked to establish a collective identity for the organization amid the variety of microenterprise-related activities and programs that it aimed to represent. Early AEO conference plenaries and literature linked microenterprise development with poverty alleviation and economic justice, challenged existing notions of entrepreneurship that excluded very small businesses, and described MDP client abilities and work ethics as analogous to those of large-scale entrepreneurs (Cowgill and Jurik In press). AEO developed a glossary of agreed-on terms that helped to construct and diffuse a new discourse of microenterprise development (AEO 1994).

AEO's framing of microenterprise development drew on rhetoric with wide-ranging appeal, described in the introduction. However, it particularly emphasized discourse popular with welfare-reform and new privatization proponents. AEO highlighted microenterprise as a strategy to achieve self-sufficiency and demonstrate the merits and potential of free enterprise. Stories of clients who had moved from poverty to economic independence through microenterprise evoked popular American Horatio Alger–type images (AEO n.d.). Conference plenaries and presentations frequently contrasted microenterprise development with failed social welfare programs that were costly and promoted dependency. Some leaders extolled the businesslike nature of MDPs and their potential to become self-sustainable; others emphasized the need for continued funding, but argued that MDPs were far more cost-effective than traditional welfare programs (conference field notes).

MDP activists also drew on more liberal concepts to boost their programs. These included promises of poverty alleviation, individual empowerment, revitalization and strengthening of disadvantaged communities, and expansion of opportunities to disadvantaged groups of women, minorities, and the poor. Although some AEO leaders and plenary speakers warned that MDPs alone were not a sufficient solution for poverty (see, for example, Litzenberg 1996), the contrast between microenterprise development and welfare programs was a recurrent theme in the association literature. Efforts to qualify MDP services for welfare clients' participation was a common workshop topic (AEO 1997b; see also Pate 2000; Field for Innovation, Effectiveness, Learning and Dissemination [FIELD] 2002).

The AEO also moved to institutionalize itself as an organization. At its fourth annual conference (in 1995), association president Kathryn Keely announced that an executive director and staff had been hired to manage the AEO. This signified a change in AEO organizational structure toward a more bureaucratic and formalized organization. The next year, the organization increased its membership fees to cover the costs of the annual conference and professional staff. These changes in organizational structure coincided with the continuing increase in the number of microenterprise development programs and with the passage of welfare reform legislation in 1996 (Cowgill 1998b).

Over the next several years, AEO continued this formalization process and expanded its size and influence. By 2001, AEO employed fifteen paid staff members and transformed its board of directors from a working board to a policymaking entity. The organization formalized training materials and established regional training institutes for practitioners. It provided the leadership for establishing a Working Group of funders and advocates to develop the first set of U.S. Microenterprise Standards (AEO n.d.). The expanding influence of AEO can best be seen from a description of its involvement in MDP-related legislation.

Evolving Policy Agenda of the Association for Enterprise Opportunity

Soon after the formation of AEO, members began to advocate for legislative and regulatory changes conducive to microenterprise development programming. Recall that leading MDP practitioners had been consultants in the development of and advocacy for the Freedom from Want Act proposed in 1991 by the House Select Committee on Hunger. Once AEO was established, it quickly identified stable and consistent government funding as essential for the maintenance and expansion of the MDP movement. The group developed an agenda and mobilization strategies to introduce and support MDP-friendly policies (AEO 1997a, 1997b).

The Clinton administration provided a supportive symbolic and legislative climate for the microenterprise movement and AEO activism (W. Clinton 1997; H. Clinton 1999). President Clinton and Hillary Rodham Clinton supported the development of the Good Faith Program in Arkansas, and during his 1992 presidential campaign, candidate Bill Clinton endorsed the concept of microenterprise in a *Rolling Stone* magazine interview (Grieder et al. 1992). Hillary Clinton spoke at an AEO conference and was involved in the Microcredit Summit in 1999.

Initially, AEO lobbied for legislation that *indirectly* supported microenterprise development. Gradually, the organization developed its own legislative agenda that contained explicit provisions for MDP activities (Cowgill 1998a) and, over time, AEO prominence and effectiveness in legislative advocacy increased substantially.

One example of supportive legislation attractive to the AEO was the revision of the CRA. Although microenterprise development was not a primary focus of the CRA, MDPs benefited tremendously from this legislation. Banks were a major source of loan monies for MDPs, and the CRA gave banks an incentive to provide such funds. So, AEO actively advocated for the legislation to strengthen the CRA. A strong CRA was also consistent with the Clinton administration's objectives to create jobs, encourage small businesses, and build partnerships in impoverished communities.

The revision of the CRA in the mid-1990s created a clearer and more effective set of rules that emphasized actual lending to poor communities (Santiago, Holyoke, and Levi 1998). The act created a tripartite system that evaluated banks by the loans made in targeted communities (the lending test), investment in targeted communities (the investment test), and the number of full-service branches in targeted areas (the service test). The revised act also created the CDFIs discussed earlier. Partnering with CDFIs allowed banks to fulfill their CRA obligations without having to directly provide services themselves; CDFIs include community development banks, credit unions *and* microenterprise loan funds. After the passage of the revised CRA, CDFIs grew rapidly from thirty-five in 1985 to hundreds by 1999 (Santiago, Holyoke, and Levi 1998). Also in 1997, the CDFI fund began the annual Presidential Awards for Excellence in Microenterprise for U.S. programs. This award provided important recognition and publicity for the microenterprise movement.

AEO activists supported the Assets for Independence Act that was part of the Community Opportunities, Accountability, Training, and Educational Services Act of 1998. Like the CRA, this act offered indirect support for MDPs. It included demonstration programs to encourage asset accumulation among low-income people through a system that used savings accounts in which amounts committed by participants were matched by government funds. To qualify, individuals had to be TANF recipients or meet other income and net-worth tests. By encouraging asset accumulation strategies among the poor, this program indirectly supported microenterprise development (Oliver and Shapiro 1995; Sherraden 1991).

AEO also supported several pieces of legislation that contained *embedded provisions* for microenterprise development (Cowgill 1998b). For example, AEO influenced the content of both welfare reform and SBA legislation. AEO strongly advocated TANF guidelines that would provide recipients the opportunity to retain benefits while starting a business (Howells 2000). Although provisions varied from state to state, TANF enlarged state discretion to set income and asset limits. The states vary widely in income cut-offs (from $400 to $1,760 per month). Asset limitations also vary. TANF permits states to set aside money to carry out a program to fund individual development accounts (IDAs) (Howells 2000, 104–5), which can be used for microenterprise activities.

AEO and other microenterprise proponents lobbied for provisions within the SBA Reauthorization Act of 1977 that provided additional monies for microloans and for welfare-to-work self-employment projects. Title II of the SBA Reauthorization Act of 1997 created the Microloan Program as a permanent program within the SBA. The reauthorization also provided funds for women's businesses and business centers (Women's Business Ownership Act). Many MDPs became authorized SBA women's business centers. AEO lobbied for the U.S. Department of Labor's Welfare-to-Work Initiative, legislation to allow CDBG funds to be used for MDPS, and for the Self-Employment Assistance Program (SEAP) that allowed states to provide funds from unemployment insurance to unemployed individuals who wanted to start their own businesses (Maroney 1998).

AEO also promoted legislation that was explicitly focused on microenterprise. In 1998, the Program for Investments in Microentrepreneurs Act (PRIME) was introduced in Congress. PRIME aimed to provide $105 million annually to support training and technical assistance for microentrepreneurs. It was significant for MDP training activities that the bill also emphasized the acquisition of business skills as a prerequisite for a successful business. For every dollar of state, local, and private-sector monies invested in programs that participate in PRIME, the federal government would invest $2. AEO was instrumental in developing PRIME. Members of AEO's PRIME subcommittee met with bill sponsors, including Senators Edward Kennedy and John Kerry. The AEO subcommittee also advocated changes that were incorporated in the legislation: international programs would be eligible for PRIME funding, a larger percentage of PRIME funding could be allocated for organizational operations purposes (e.g., staff time), and the bill would not be included in existing CDFI legislation (AEO 1998).

In supporting the PRIME measure, MDP advocates again invoked a discourse that contrasted microenterprise development with the problems of traditional welfare programs. For example, in his opening speech, James Leach, chair of the House Banking and Financial Services Committee, framed microenterprise development as a logical sequence to welfare reform: "Welfare reform legislation passed by this Congress in the last session seeks to move disadvantaged Americans from dependency and poverty to independence and prosperity. This redirection in policy underscores the appropriateness of microenterprise activities" (House Financial Services Committee 1999). Four AEO members testified at the House Banking Committee hearings in support of PRIME. Their testimony emphasized the importance of microenterprise development as a method for poverty alleviation. Peggy Clark, executive director of the nonprofit Aspen Institute, which has been active in national MDP evaluation studies, submitted written testimony that included the following: "We have seen very strong outcomes among the poor entrepreneurs served by microenterprise organizations. These results tell us that microenterprise is an effective poverty reduction strategy that builds the self-reliance of people who are poor" (House Financial Services Committee 1999). Jason Friedman, the vice-president of an MDP in Iowa (the Institute for Social and Economic Development), testified: "PRIME is absolutely critical to the stabilization and evolution of the microenterprise industry. Combined with the SBA program and other federal supports, it will create a unified and coherent infrastructure to stimulate the creation of thousands of microenterprises owned by low income individuals" (House Financial Services Committee 1999).

The PRIME legislation was passed in 2000, but no funds were allocated for the program. When President George W. Bush assumed office, he initially opposed releasing funds for the PRIME program. AEO mobilized its membership to advocate for PRIME funding. In October 2001, $15 million of the originally proposed $105 million were released for this program. The allocation funded grants to approximately eighty MDPs. AEO received two grants from this allocation for research and capacity-building projects (AEO n.d.). AEO continues to lobby for more PRIME funding. In addition, it has lobbied for further MDP-friendly definitions of eligible services and asset restrictions for TANF recipients in the renewal of welfare reform legislation (FIELD 2002).

As the national microenterprise movement matured, the number of MDPs continued to multiply. Research describing and documenting the effectiveness of U.S. MDPs began to appear. This research also provided insights into problems faced by U.S. programs. Practitioner exchanges revealed significant differences between southern and northern hemisphere programs. These differences were reflected in practitioner discourses as well as in actual program design and operations.

GROWTH OF MICROENTERPRISE DEVELOPMENT PROGRAMS
IN THE UNITED STATES

Two large studies have charted the growth of MDPs in the United States. The Charles Stewart Mott Foundation conducted a series of annual surveys ranging from twenty-one to thirty-one programs over a four-year period, 1990 through 1994 (Charles Steward Mott Foundation 1993, 1994). In 1991, with funding from the Ford and Mott foundations, the Aspen Institute (as part of the SELP project) began to conduct a series of research studies, including a biannual survey of U.S. microenterprise providers. Both the Mott and Aspen surveys documented the expansion of U.S. microenterprise development over time.

The Mott findings report an increasing range of program services including individual- and peer-lending methodologies, increasing loan sizes, and training/technical assistance components. The report concludes that efforts to "bolster program sustainability" have led to a shift in client target populations beyond the very poor to a focus on "working poor" and "more moderate income" clients. The practitioners in the Mott surveys were especially concerned about loan delinquencies and defaults, expanding loan volume, and maintaining sustainability while still serving the "most disadvantaged customers" (Charles Stewart Mott Foundation 1994; Klein 1994).

The biannual Aspen Institute survey of MDPs conducted by SELP is the largest study of programs to date. It targets community development agencies, SBA Microloan Demonstration Projects, and other organizations involved in microenterprise development. In later surveys, SELP added AEO membership lists, and AEO encouraged its membership to participate in the study. Program responses have been published in a biannual Directory of U.S. Microenterprise Programs. There have been five surveys; the most recent was published in 2002 (Walker and Blair 2002). However, Aspen researchers estimate that fewer than one-half of existing MDPs respond to their survey (Walker and Blair 2002).

Like the Mott study, Aspen surveys indicate significant growth in the number of MDPs. The 1992 directory profiled 108 programs; the 2002 directory described 427 programs. Of these programs, 72 percent (308) were practitioner agencies (direct-program providers) and 28 percent (119) offered support services to MDPs (e.g., funding or staff training) to practitioners (Clark and Huston 1992). According to the 2002 directory, the 308 practitioner programs served over 99,000 individuals in fiscal year 2000, an average of approximately 361 individuals per program. At the end of fiscal year 2000, responding lending programs had disbursed over $213 million since their inception (Walker and Blair 2002). The 2002

Aspen directory reports that 65 percent of their U.S. MDP respondents were established between 1991 and 1999 (Walker and Blair 2002, xv).

It is interesting to note that despite the strong emphasis on lending in most MDP literature, 36 percent of U.S. programs surveyed offered *only* training or technical assistance services. The vast majority of MDP clients (90 percent) received training or other program services, and only 10 percent of the clients received loans (Walker and Blair 2002). Despite practitioner and advocate emphasis on credit, these findings suggest that MDPs are far more training than lending oriented (Microcredit Summit 1997). Training is more consistent with a U.S. social welfare–social service orientation than it is with an economic development or southern hemisphere microcredit orientation.

Moreover, given the emphasis on peer lending in the literature (e.g., Wahid 1993c; Brill 1999), it is also surprising that the vast majority of U.S. MDP lenders offered individual rather than peer loans. Only 11 percent of all surveyed U.S. MDPs (and 18 percent of programs that offered loans) provided peer-lending services. Individual lending is more consistent with traditional U.S. banking and economic development practices than with southern hemisphere MDP models (M. Johnson 1998b).

A significant percentage of MDPs serve women (62 percent of programs report that at least half of their clients are women) and low-income people (70 percent of MDPs said that over half of their clients were low income) (Walker and Blair 2002). Past directories have noted the percentage of programs that serve AFDC participants (e.g., 48 percent of programs in 1999). Earlier surveys also broke out the average percentage of poverty-level clients served; approximately 30 percent of those served on the average across programs were identified as poverty-level-income individuals (Severens and Kays 1997). This figure is lower than some other estimates of low- and poverty-level income MDP clients (e.g., Edgcomb et al. 1996). Interestingly, information on welfare and poverty level clients is no longer included in the Aspen directory surveys (Walker and Blair 2002). Nevertheless, the percentages of women, minority and low-income clients suggest that MDPs have persisted in serving significant numbers of disadvantaged business clients and have not been scaled-up to the extent that characterized U.S. economic development programs in the 1950s though 1980s.

U.S. TRANSFORMATION OF MICROENTERPRISE DEVELOPMENT

The Aspen surveys were suggestive of common issues and significant differences between U.S. and model southern hemisphere programs such as the Grameen Bank. These issues were elaborated in practitioner exchanges and early U.S. MDP evaluations. Two reports about the first five years of U.S. pioneering MDP operations provide considerable insight into the transformation of southern hemisphere models to fit the U.S. context.

First are findings drawn from a five-year study of seven of the oldest U.S. MDPs. The study, conducted by the SELP group, began in 1991 and concluded in 1996. This SELP study sample comprised both individual- and peer-lending MDPs (see Edgcomb, Klein, and Clark 1996; Clark et al. 1999). According to SELP, the program sample "shared a focus on poverty alleviation, an emphasis on client responsibility instead of charity, and an incremental approach to training and lending" (Edgcomb, Klein, and Clark 1996, 1–5). These programs reach large numbers of women (73 percent of clients), minority (60 percent of clients), and poor (43 percent of clients with incomes below poverty level). MDPs reported a variety of strategies to serve clients. Some focus more on offering credit and keeping training costs to a minimum (referred to as credit-led programs); other programs emphasize training and require the completion of a course prior to borrowing (referred to as training-led programs). The longitudinal study concludes that the MDP clients experience significant business successes, asset growth, and improved household incomes. The researchers argue that these findings apply to clients who are poor entrepreneurs (Clark and Kays 1995).

A second group of findings come from the reports of thirty providers from Bangladeshi, U.S., and Canadian programs who attended a 1993 peer-lending conference. Several practitioners from programs in the SELP study were also participants at this practitioner exchange conference. The conference presentations and recommendations were published in Going Forward (Coyle et al. 1994).[5]

In addition to SELP and Going Forward projects (Coyle et al. 1994; Edgcomb, Klein, and Clark 1996), there are other ethnographic and evaluation studies of U.S. MDPs (e.g., Balkin 1993; Mondal and Tune 1993; Rodriguez 1995; Taub 1998; M. Johnson 1998a, 1998b; Servon 1999a, 1999b). This emergent body of research suggests differences between U.S. MDPs and their Bangladeshi model. The most recent studies outline some key problems faced by U.S. MDPs (Bhatt 2002; Schreiner and Morduch 2002; Hung 2002; Vinelli 2002). Together, this emerging body of research suggests five ways in which U.S. practitioners have transformed southern models of microenterprise development.

First, U.S. programs emphasize up-front business training more heavily than do southern hemisphere MDPs. U.S. practitioners argue that the increased complexity of operating a business in the United States makes more training essential (Edgcomb, Klein, and Clark 1996; Taub 1998; Servon 1999a).

Second, U.S. practitioners report more problems with peer lending models. They suggest that the great geographical distances separating clients, increased anonymity, and the highly individualistic U.S. culture make peer-lending programs time consuming and expensive to operate. This has led some U.S. programs to increase staff supervision of peer lending or to discontinue it altogether. Some U.S. programs that began with peer lending alone have added individual loans to reduce costs and offer a fuller range of services to clients (Mondal and Tune 1993; Coyle et al. 1994; Taub 1998; Servon 1999a; Bhatt 2002; Bhatt, Painter, and Tang 2002).

These first two factors lead to a third reported difference for U.S. programs—higher operating costs. The provision of additional training and supervision of peer lending makes U.S. programs more costly and challenges sustainability goals. Thus, it is not surprising that obtaining consistent sources of funding for program operations has emerged as a major concern for U.S. programs (Edgcomb, Klein, and Clark 1996; Bhatt 2002; Bhatt, Painter and Tang 2002; Vinelli 2002).

A fourth difference centers on the percentage of poor clients served. At the Going Forward conference, Bangladeshi organizations reported that they did not reach the poorest 10 percent of their population. However, northern programs reported even greater difficulties in reaching the poor. Practitioners argue that this difficulty stems from the fact that "in the North American context, self-employment is one of the most challenging ways to work one's way out of poverty" (Coyle et al. 1994, 6). Practitioners reported that serving the poorest North American clients meant increased costs for business training and other social services such as child care and transportation. In addition, business lending to the poor was typically associated with higher lending costs due to an increased number of defaults. These tendencies heighten the dilemma of program sustainability (Edgcomb, Klein, and Clark 1996; Bhatt, Painter, and Tang 2002).

In response to these concerns, some experts (Balkin 1989; Mondal and Tune 1993; Charles Stewart Mott Foundation 1994; Clark and Kays 1995; Anthony 1996; Edgcomb, Klein, and Clark 1996; Taub 1998) recommend a reframing of U.S. microenterprise development as a strategy for the working poor and moderate-income people, especially those who are more highly educated; have prior business backgrounds, special skills, and support networks; and are highly motivated to run their own businesses.

Given the broad range of skills necessary to run a small business in this country, it is no surprise that most of the people the microenterprise-loan programs serve have a personal safety net: some education, a support net-work of family and friends, and experience in their line of business. The ma-jority of participants do not fit the underclass stereotype that attracts the lion's share of the attention in the media and in Washington. It's time for policymakers and funding sources to recognize the niche microenterprise-loan programs fill and set their sights elsewhere for solutions to the problem of urban poverty. (Bates and Servon 1996, 27)

One Going Forward conference participant suggested that this dilemma be resolved by reframing U.S. program target groups in a "more inclusive" manner by focusing on "those who suffer a 'poverty of access' to credit and other business services. Agonizing over these categorizations tends to obscure an important strength of peer lending: it has significant impact on the culture of poverty (often characterized by low self-esteem, a perceived lack of control over one's life and circumstances, and little hope for the fu-ture), and that is by no means the exclusive domain of the poorest" (Coyle et al. 1994, 7). In this reframing statement, the target population of MDPs is transformed from those who are materially poor to those who are cul-turally poor. The culture-of-poverty concept is thereby extended to include those with low self-esteem or those who do not have access to credit.

Similarly, AEO changed its 2001 mission statement to broaden the tar-get population for microenterprise development and de-center economi-cally marginalized individuals as the major target for MDPs. This revision deleted older language that defined the organization as being committed to "expanding enterprise opportunity for people and communities with *limited access to economic resources.*" In contrast, the new mission state-ment reads, "AEO supports the development of strong and effective U.S. microenterprise programs to assist *under served entrepreneurs* in starting, stabilizing, and expanding businesses" (Association for Enterprise Oppor-tunity n.d., emphasis added).

Not all advocates agree that services to poverty-level clients should be deemphasized. Some researchers and advocates continue to argue that mi-croenterprise development is a key method for poverty alleviation even among the poorest of the poor, including welfare recipients and others below the poverty line (Raheim and Bolden 1995; Raheim 1997; see also discussion in Brokaw 1996). SELP evaluators have been among those ad-vocating microenterprise as a poverty-alleviation tool, even for those with incomes below the poverty line. Their follow-up interviews with program clients bolster their claims. These findings suggest that 62 percent of clients who started the program below the poverty line significantly in-creased their incomes during the five-year study period. Twenty-three

percent of poor clients interviewed increased their family incomes to figures *above* the poverty line (Clark et al. 1999). However, these findings
are equivocal because the study suffered from the research design flaws
common to southern MDP evaluations, especially the lack of an adequate
comparison group of non-MDP clients (see chap. 1).[6]

A fifth program difference is that U.S. MDPs rely on a narrower, "less
integrated approach" than southern MDPs. As the conference presentations suggested:

> A comparison of the Bangladeshi and North American programs illustrates
> how mission affects program design and implementation. BRAC and
> Proshika [Bangladeshi programs] seek a structural alleviation of poverty
> through empowerment of the poor. Their mission to address the systemic
> nature of poverty has important program implications. The many facets of
> poverty require interventions in multiple sectors including education,
> health, the status of women, environmental protection and employment. . . .
> While the North American programs share similar values and would largely
> concur with the Bangladeshi colleagues on the need for structural change,
> their strategy focuses more narrowly on the economic development com-
> ponent of poverty alleviation. They are in the business of facilitating entre-
> preneurship and self-employment. . . . [A]s the agents of technology
> transferral, they have been driven more by interest in the peer lending model
> itself—the need to test it, adapt it, make it work and demonstrate its viabil-
> ity as a poverty alleviation strategy—than by an overarching mission.
> (Coyle et al. 1994, 4–5)

This suggests a strong divergence in northern and southern MDP approaches. The northern programs are focused on the scientific-like trans-
feral of peer lending as a technology for encouraging self-employment.
The programmatic focus shifts from poverty alleviation and collective empowerment strategies to the narrower goal of self-employment advocacy.
This narrowing is consistent with the individualized focus favored by U.S.
welfare programs of the past. As noted earlier in this chapter, broad structural foci that include community organizing agendas have historically attracted the ire of U.S. lawmakers and funding sources (Marris and Reins
1969). The statement also suggests that the effect of self-employment on
poverty alleviation has been assumed rather than carefully tested. This approach is consistent with assumptions made in the proposed Freedom
from Want legislation described earlier (House of Representatives 1991).

Although most MDP research to date has centered southern programs,
the Aspen Institute established a research and development fund in 1998.

The Microenterprise Fund for Innovation, Effectiveness, Learning and Dissemination (FIELD) is "dedicated to the expansion and sustainability of microenterprise development efforts, particularly those aimed at poor Americans" (FIELD n.d.). The organization provides research and development grants and produces a variety of reports to promote U.S. MDPs. These include a four-volume report that describes the best practices" in the field (FIELD n.d.). Research continues to highlight the dilemmas identified in earlier research, but also tends to take for granted a more narrow, individualized approach that centers on self-employment training and lending as technology (e.g., Bhatt 2002; Buckley 2002). These studies continue to lack adequate comparison groups and direct, long-term measures of program success (e.g., Alisultanov, Klein, and Zandniapour 2002).

CONCLUSION

U.S. MDPs are both something old and something new. This chapter has mapped the connections of U.S. MDPs with southern programs, with U.S. welfare and economic development traditions, with government and nongovernment funding sources, and with a number of social activist groups. A variety of social movements and interest groups spilled-over to support microenterprise development—feminists advocating women in business, antipoverty and anti-hunger groups, and community development organizations, to name a few. This spill-over was no doubt both a cause and an effect of the widespread appeal of microenterprise development in the United States.

U.S. MDPs are also integrally connected to the opportunities, problems, and discourses of the new economy. MDP advocates presented an ostensibly nongovernmental self-help program that aimed to integrate marginalized individuals into the market economy through self-employment training and lending. These programs were consistent with neoliberalism, and they furthered welfare reform and new privatization agendas through their success statistics and stories about poor women and men whose lives had been changed by MDP services. Their reports suggested that programs could operate in a cost-effective and businesslike manner and still lift significant numbers of poor and low-income people out of poverty without costly government welfare and social service programs. Given the U.S. disillusionment with government welfare services, MDPs offered an attractive alternative and hope for a poverty alleviation method that could actually thrive in the new economy.

Despite their heavily promoted image as government outsiders, U.S. MDPs were significantly promoted and influenced by government funding and services in the areas of economic development, welfare, and unemployment and job development. Many early MDPs were actually experimental components of welfare and unemployment programs. As we see in the next chapter, some are still components of government-funded economic development programs.

There were reported divergences between U.S. and southern MDPs. Early comparisons suggest that, compared to their southern hemisphere precursors, U.S. MDPs had greater difficulties with peer-lending models, and were more narrowly focused on self-employment training and lending to individuals than on collective empowerment programming. Of course, these apparent tendencies can also be associated with the individualism that is evident throughout U.S. culture and social policy (Heclo 1986). U.S. programs also found it difficult and costly to help the poor become entrepreneurs without significant expenditures for training and support services.

Thus, U.S. MDPs experienced not only myriad successes but also contradictory demands in program practice. A more complete understanding of the successes and dilemmas of U.S. microenterprise development requires a more in-depth analysis of MDP practice, including the emergence and transformation of particular programs over time and of practitioner strategies for coping with contradictions, which begins in the next chapter. This in-depth analysis also maps the ways in which program practice is linked to the institutions and contexts beyond each local MDP. This analysis further explicates the interrelationships among context, contradictions, and practice in the embedded process of microenterprise development.

■
□ ■
□ ■
□ □ ■

CHAPTER 3

CHARACTERISTICS OF U.S. MICROENTERPRISE PROGRAMS

COAUTHORED WITH JULIE COWGILL

> [E]veryone says Bangladesh [the Grameen Bank] is the model,
> the one to imitate. But a lot of practitioners are saying that
> it does not translate into the [U.S.] culture.
> —MDP PRACTITIONER

> The peer group process was very cumbersome for clients,
> when you know, they really wanted to be on their own, spending
> their energy on marketing their business. . . . We found it very
> difficult to find people who were willing to join groups.
> —MDP PRACTITIONER

For a more in-depth look at U.S. microenterprise development across a variety of programs, we interviewed practitioners from fifty programs across the nation. This chapter considers their accomplishments, problems, and strategies. The two quotations that begin this chapter are drawn from these data. Like the discussions in the preceding chapter, they suggest both the importance and limitations of the Grameen and other southern hemisphere models in U.S. program practice. Consistent with an IE approach, our interviews yielded insights into practitioner work experiences and the connections among programs, as well as glimpses of the ways in which extra-local organizational processes informed local program practice. We considered points of convergence and divergence in practitioners' discussions of program goals, client populations, services, and changes over time.[1]

We relied on a combination of random and purposive sampling techniques to identify practitioners working in a variety of programs that reflected the range of U.S. MDPs. However, as suggested by IE researchers, we were less concerned with gaining a perfectly representative sample than with obtaining a grasp of the variety of MDP experiences and the institutional processes that shaped practitioner experiences (DeVault and McCoy 2002).[2]

Practitioners described both enthusiastic support for and rapid growth in their microenterprise development work. They credited southern hemisphere programs as important points of reference, but, as suggested in the statements that begin this chapter, they also emphasized the need to modify and to some extent tailor them to U.S. practice. Practitioners attributed such changes to the individualism so characteristic of the culture and to the complexity of doing business in the United States.

Despite program commonalities, there was also considerable variation across MDPs. Practitioners identified a range of respected MDP traditions or niches that they could reference in justifying their programs. The newness and variation of the MDP movement provided practitioners with opportunities for agency and for innovations as they mixed and adapted models and methods over time. The programs in this sample most often assisted the businesses of low-income individuals, especially women and minorities. Some programs targeted immigrant, refugee, disabled, displaced, and underemployed workers. Most practitioners described new, small-scale sales- and personal-service-oriented, owner-operated concerns including enterprises in child care, baking, furniture assembly, word processing, and computer or office equipment repair. Such businesses were generally labor intensive. Some MDPs also assisted larger and more established businesses that needed loans as large as $35,000. The hope was that these larger businesses would provide jobs for disadvantaged individuals.

Our analysis of practitioner interviews elaborates connections between extra-local organizational demands and local MDP practice. Despite the popularity of MDPs as a method for assisting some of the population groups most negatively affected by economic restructuring, demands from external funding sources promoted contradictions in practice. In response, practitioners developed innovations and also shifted their goals, target populations, and lending models in ways that drifted from important MDP claims to serve the poor, provide an alternative to welfare, and empower borrowers through peer-lending groups.

PROGRAM TYPOLOGIES

The interviews provided an overview of the variety among U.S. MDPs. Table 3.1 provides a summary of the organization structure, location, and other characteristics of the fifty programs. A few served statewide or

TABLE 3.1

MDP program characteristics

Characteristic	Number	Percentage
Region of the United States		
Northwest	19	38
Southwest	7	14
Midwest	12	24
Northwest	5	10
Southeast	7	14
Area served		
Urban	15	30
Rural	14	28
Both urban and rural	21	42
Organizational structure		
Independent organizations	24	48
Microenterprise network	6	12
State/quasi-state organization	4	8
Subsidiary of existing organization	16	32
Number of lending programs		
One program	32	64
Multiple programs	18	36
Age of program		
1–4 years	17	34
5–9 years	27	12
More than 9 years	6	54
Mean age	14 years	
Median age	9 years	

multistate regions; most targeted smaller areas. Programs ranged from less than one to twenty-five years of operation, but most were less than ten years old, reflecting the nascency of U.S. microenterprise development. Less than one-half of the sample (48 percent) were independent organizations; the majority were part of larger organizations or networks. Sixty-four percent of the sample reported some type of significant expansion since inception. Two programs reported that they were not in an expansion mode at the time and were aiming to "consolidate and improve" their services.

Researchers and practitioners have categorized MDPs using several criteria. We initially focused on distinguishing peer-lending programs such as the one in our case study from MDPs that offered only individual loans. Practitioners (e.g., Coyle et al. 1994; Clark and Kays 1995) also emphasize that there is a distinction between programs focused more on lending and those focused more heavily on training. For example, programs are defined as credit-led or minimalist when they offer lending services with little or no business training. Training-oriented programs typically offer business courses and require them as precursors or accompaniments to borrowing.

Margaret Johnson (1998a) and Lisa Servon (1999a) offer typologies that reflect the differential and convergent roots of MDPs in Grameen peer-lending and U.S. social service and economic development traditions. Economic development–type programs target specific geographical areas or places with the primary aim of developing or attracting businesses to provide jobs for residents. In contrast, Grameen peer-lending and social service models are blended into more entrepreneur-centered programs, which aim to develop and empower entrepreneurs, especially poor women, through business training, loans, and other services. Johnson (1998a) argues that an orientation toward either place or entrepreneurial development shapes other aspects of the program, such as the type of lending, terms of lending, and amount and type of training. For example, economic/place development programs typically offer only individual loans with more banklike terms and do not offer business training and social services. In contrast, entrepreneurial-centered programs typically rely on Grameen-style peer lending, avoid collateral requirements, and offer business training and social support services. Johnson (1998a) also identifies a third, hybrid organizational type that combines peer- and individual-lending methodologies.

Our findings support some of Johnson and Servon's generalizations. Correlational analyses suggest that, on average, place-based programs (n = 17) offered less training, made larger loans, and worked with larger businesses and more moderate-income clients than other programs. They served significantly fewer women and poverty level clients than other programs. They also tended to be older programs and a part of state agencies (differences significant $p < .05$). An example of a place-based program is detailed in the appendix to this chapter.

Sixteen of the fifty MDPs offered peer lending. Nine of these offered *only* peer loans, and seven fell into Johnson's hybrid category offering peer *and* individual loans.[3] Compared with place-based MDPs, the sixteen peer programs served higher percentages of women, welfare, and poverty-level clients on average. They were typically newer than the place-based programs, and were less likely to receive state funding. Their funding was more likely to come from private businesses ($p < .05$). The appendix to this chapter provides a more detailed example of a peer program.

Approximately one-third of our sample consisted of hybrids, but in a form different from that discussed by Johnson.[4] Like MDPs in the economic/place development tradition, they offered only individual loans, but, like programs in the social service tradition, they typically offered extensive training and social supports. They tended to be newer than other place and peer programs. These individualized programs drew more on the U.S. job training and welfare service traditions than did the Grameen-like peer-lending or place/economic-development-oriented types of MDPs. Table 3.2 provides a list of the fifty programs with their research pseudonym, region served, and lending type. On average, individualized programs offered the most training of the three program types and served significantly more women and poverty-level clients than did place-based programs ($p < .05$).[5] The appendix to this chapter provides an example of an individualized-type program from our study. Table 3.3 summarizes client demographics across the various types of MDPs.

Despite the limitations of typologies, we found it necessary to refer to program types because MDP practitioners frequently invoked them to categorize their programs. These categories provided important reference points for MDP practitioners as they planned and justified their program practice. One practitioner from an individualized program that targeted women said, "One thing that's real important is to make a distinction between those programs that view themselves as credit led and those who view themselves as training led. We are a training led program. . . . We're focused on human development . . . that's the key part of what we're doing. People feel good about themselves, but a lot more important, they get some skills, too. . . . I think it's worth the investing in, but . . . that is why it is important to make the distinction and not be lumped together with credit led programs when we are being considered for funding" (#38). Such interview comments provided insights into the ways that national discourses about the MDP organizational field (i.e., in AEO and media coverage) informed staff perspectives and practice.

The existence of multiple reputable program models and practices in the MDP literature and conference discourse provided new and experienced practitioners alike multiple and varied organizational niches within which to locate their programs. A practitioner from a recently established peer program that targeted low- and moderate-income people said, "We modeled ourselves after [an established] peer model. Its core philosophy is our, kind of mantra. We paid for it because we wanted an established, respected model" (#44).

IE researchers (e.g., DeVault and McCoy 2002) have warned against reifying typologies and ignoring the practices that produce them, and our research reinforces this concern. Interviews indicated the fluidity, cross-fertilization, and dynamic blending of organizational forms among MDPs.[6] A practitioner in an individualized program that targeted

TABLE 3.2

Fifty-program sample overview

Program Pseudonym (ID)	Region	Program Type	Lending Type
Women's Enterprise, Inc. (1)	Southwest	Individualized	Individual
Economic Opportunities, Inc. (2)	Southwest	Individualized	Individual
Women in Microenterprise (3)	Southwest	Peer	Peer/Individual
Winning Enterprises for Women (4)	Northwest	Place-based	Individual
Women Entrepreneurs Development (5)	Southeast	Peer	Peer
Rural Business Program (6)	Midwest	Peer	Peer
Southern Entrepreneur Group (7)	Southeast	Peer	Peer/Individual
Business Development Fund (8)	Midwest	Individualized	Individual
New Entrepreneurs Fund (9)	Midwest	Place-based	Individual
Women's Business Development (10)	Northeast	Peer	Peer/Individual
State Business Program (11)	Northeast	Place-based	Individual
Microenterprise Fund (12)	Southeast	Peer	Peer
Step Lending Program (13)	Midwest	Peer	Peer
Midwest Self-Employment Program (14)	Midwest	Individualized	Individual
Southwestern Enterprise, Inc. (15)	Southwest	Individualized	Individual
Northern Entrepreneurs, Inc. (16)	Northeast	Individualized	Individual
Northern Economic Initiatives (17)	Northeast	Place-based	Individual
State Disability Services (18)	Northeast	Place-based	Individual
Community Business Services (19)	Southeast	Place-based	Individual
Business Development Program (20)	Northwest	Place-based	Individual
Working Community Development (21)	Northeast	Place-based	Individual
Workers' Business Support (22)	Southeast	Individualized	Individual
Midwestern Women in Business (23)	Midwest	Individualized	Individual
City Business Development Services (24)	Southwest	Place-based	Individual
Small Enterprises, Inc. (25)	Northeast	Place-based	Individual
Vocational Rehabilitation Services (26)	Northeast	Individualized	Individual
Southwest Community Lending (27)	Southwest	Place-based	Individual
Self-Employment Enterprises, Inc. (28)	Northwest	Peer	Peer/Individual
Individual Business Development (29)	Northwest	Place-based	Individual
State Business Programs (30)	Northeast	Place-based	Individual
Enterprise Loan Program (31)	Midwest	Individualized	Individual
Women, Inc. (32)	Midwest	Individualized	Individual
First Nations (33)	Midwest	Peer	Peer/Individual
Northern Nations Fund (34)	Northeast	Peer	Peer
Northeast City Fund (35)	Northeast	Individualized	Individual
Western Self-Employment Project (36)	Northeast	Individualized	Individual
Women-Owned Enterprises, Inc. (37)	Midwest	Individualized	Individual
Women Entrepreneurs Support (38)	Midwest	Individualized	Individual
The Business Network (39)	Southeast	Peer	Peer
Microenterprise CDC (40)	Northeast	Place-based	Individual
State Community Loan Fund (41)	Southeast	Place-based	Individual
Women Entrepreneurs Program (42)	Midwest	Peer	Peer/Individual
Women's Business Loan Fund (43)	Northwest	Individualized	Individual
Entrepreneur Networking, Inc. (44)	Northeast	Peer	Peer
People in Enterprise (45)	Northeast	Peer	Peer
Western States Self-Employment (46)	Southwest	Individualized	Individual
Northeastern Urban Entrepreneurs (47)	Northeast	Place-based	Individual
Northern Enterprise Networks (48)	Northwest	Peer	Peer
Community Development Program (49)	Northeast	Place-based	Individual
First Lenders' Program (50)	Southeast	Peer	Peer/Individual

TABLE 3.3

Mean percentages of demographics served by program types[a]

Population Served	Place (%)	Peer (%)	Individualized (%)	Minimalist (%)	Training (%)	Total (%)
Women (n = 38)	43[b]	72	74[c]	52[c]	73	66
Welfare (n = 32)	16	21	23	14	23	20
Poverty level (n = 28)	22[c]	26	42[b]	22[c]	35	31
Low income (n = 38)	38	37	40	38	38	38
Moderate income (n = 32)	33[d]	31	16[c]	33[d]	23	27
Minority (n = 27)	27[d]	59[d]	26	25	53	45
Start-ups (n = 44)	12[d]	28[d]	26	19[d]	35[d]	22

[a]Because many programs did not keep records on certain client demographics, there is a large percentage of missing data. This makes it difficult to draw any firm conclusions about the demographics of clients served from this table. (Missing data on demographics ranged from 24 to 54 percent; see numbers of cases in each demographic category for the exact number of cases available.)

[b]The t-test for differences of means between the program type (coded 1) and the other two program type(s) (coded 0) was significant at p < .001 for a one-tail test. Comparisons are made (a) among place, peer, and individualized or (b) between minimalist versus more training-oriented programs.

[c]The t-test for differences of means between the program type (coded 1) and the other program type(s) (coded 0) was significant at p < .05 for a one-tail test. Comparisons are made (a) among place, peer, and individualized or (b) between minimalist versus more training-oriented programs.

[d]The t-test for difference of means between the program type (coded 1) and the other program type(s) (coded 0) was significant at p < .10 for a one-tail test. Comparisons are made (a) among place, peer, and individualized or (b) between minimalist versus more training-oriented programs.

displaced factory workers exemplifies this blending and changing of MDPs over time: "We are an economic development program and locate ourselves within that tradition. Those are the conferences I attend. Those industry standards have been our model. We recently have also begun thinking of ourselves as microlenders. That has involved some reorientation, and now I come to AEO conferences [i.e., microenterprise development practitioner conferences]" (#22). This program originally planned to assist large worker-owned businesses, but shifted focus because there was not enough demand for such projects. We found other examples of blending—many peer programs had incorporated individual lending, and some had dropped peer lending altogether.

We also found that differentiating training- from credit-led program types was far more complicated than it appears in the MDP literature (e.g., Edgcomb, Klein, and Clark 1996). Although many practitioners were quick to identify their program as conforming to one side of this dichotomy, their descriptions of program practice suggested more of a continuum of credit and training emphases. Some training oriented-programs offered little or no training courses themselves, but relied on training through partnering with other community agencies. Some self-proclaimed credit-led programs offered extensive technical assistance to their borrowers. Only two MDPs in the entire sample offered no training or technical assistance, and even these programs had lists of technical assistance services for routine client referral.

Finally, although service to women is emphasized by Servon (1998b) and Margaret Johnson (1998a), this program dimension is not sufficiently captured by the typologies described so far. Six programs in our sample viewed themselves as women-centered organizations and tailored their services to women. A practitioner in one of these, an individualized program targeting low- and moderate-income women said, "We focus specifically on issues about women's entrepreneurship . . . issues that a woman might have . . . when trying to start-up a business, especially for the first time. . . . We try to rewrite a lot of the scripts for them that have been built up over a lifetime, so that they can come out of the program saying, "Yes, I can do this. I am smart; I am wise . . . and I can be in business" (#1).

Other programs emphasized service to women, but to a lesser extent; thirteen had the word *women* in their title and served at least 75 percent women. Although some of these had initially designed their programs with the needs of women in mind, most did not differentiate the services they offered to women and men clients.

Thus, although practitioners invoked typology talk, it was difficult to neatly classify programs into discrete categories. Practitioners were equally adept at mixing and matching components from different program types. One respondent, who directed a peer program targeting low- to moderate-income individuals, said, "We are flexible and creative. We have been doing our peer lending . . . we have found that people don't want to meet in little groups. So, they like to meet once a month as a full group, and then we have borrowers' groups for the people who actually borrow money. . . . So we've got our own hybrid, but it seems to be working for us" (#13). Almost uniformly, practitioners described some form of experimentation or model blending in the course of their program's development.

Practitioners also indicated an interest in promoting the improvement and often expansion of the services provided by their program. They wanted these services to perform a social good. The nature of that good was defined in varying ways, including the support of economic development and employment opportunities in disadvantaged or depressed communities, offering training or credit opportunities for poor and otherwise marginalized entrepreneurs, and empowering poor and marginalized groups. Practitioners believed that there were many opportunities and much support in their communities for microenterprise development activities. But interviews were suggestive of the ways in which everyday program practice and the pursuit of objectives were informed by the extra-local demands and popular discourses surrounding economic development and social welfare issues.

LENDING, TRAINING, FUNDING, AND PROGRAM DILEMMAS

Although most IE analyses focus on qualitative data, in her analysis of Canadian mental health statistics, Smith (1975) explains how a critical examination of statistical information reveals the ways in which organizational work is done. In this section, we examine the lending statistics from the MDPs in our study. These statistics suggest a disjuncture between MDP practice and discourse about the importance of microcredit for the poor.

Despite the strong identification with business credit in the MDP movement (Microcredit Summit 1997) and practitioner discourse, the ratio of borrowing to nonborrowing clients for the programs in our sample suggests that this characterization is problematic. Overall, the programs in our sample served an average of twenty-two nonborrowers for every borrower served. On the average, self-identified minimalist programs had much lower nonborrower-to-borrower ratios than did training-identified programs (see table 3.4). However, there was also considerable variation

TABLE 3.4

Means and ratios for nonborrowers/borrowers by program types[a]

	Place	Peer	Individualized	Minimalist	Training	Total
Borrowers	42	29	35	62	28	35
Nonborrowers	285	256	399	251	345	316
Ratio of nonborrowers to borrowers	11	18	33[b]	7[b]	28	22

[a]*The numbers of borrowers and nonborrowers in this table are the averages computed for each program type. The ratio was computed for each individual program; these ratios were then averaged for each program type. The figures in the Total column are the means computed for the total sample of 50 programs.*
[b]*The t-test for differences of means between individualized (coded 1) and place- and peer-type programs (coded 0) were significantly different, as were the differences of means between self-defined minimalist (coded 1) versus training-oriented programs (coded 0). Significant at the p < .04 level.*

across programs even within credit- and training-oriented categories. This ratio is consistent with the survey findings reported in chapter 2. They underline the extent to which microcredit takes a back seat to training services in U.S. MDPs. This tendency presents problems for MDP practitioners because training and other services are costly.

Table 3.5 contains information about the amount and variety of MDP funding sources. Program operations budgets ranged from $18,000 to

TABLE 3.5

Source and amount of operations funds[a]

Funding Sources	Number	Percentage
Federal government	25	50
State government	20	40
Local government	16	32
Foundations	30	60
Banks	20	40
Individual donations	9	18
Churches	5	10
Businesses	9	18
Fees/consulting	10	20
Operations funds		
$200,000 or less	18	36
$200,001–400,000	17	34
$400,001 and above	15	30
Mean operations budget	$309,298	
Median operations budget	$257,000	

[a]*Due to multiple funding sources, percentage totals exceed 100.*

over $1 million. The average operations budget was approximately $300,000, and the median was slightly less at $257,000. Funding for programs came from a variety of sources, but foundations, government, and banks were the most frequently named funding sources and provided the largest percentage of dollars for the sample programs.

Funding was the lifeline of MDPs, and the maintenance of funding support represented a key mechanism whereby the extra-local social and economic milieu influenced the inner-workings of these programs. It was the problem most frequently noted by practitioners. Funding-related problems were equally prominent across MDP types. Funding concerns included the need for more operations monies, an overall instability of funding sources, worries about support for training or lending programs, and meeting the requirements of funding agents in order to retain existing funding.

Several MDPs received foundation or government grants to begin their programs, but eventually had to search for more long-term funding sources. A practitioner for a place-based program that targeted unemployed low-income women and minorities in a rural area said, "The first thing [in program development and operations] is making sure that you have enough funds. . . . [T]he agency that I work for, [has] put out approximately $30,000 a year for my salary, plus money for my part time secretary salary, space, rent and telephones, and you know, they're not going to continue to do that forever. So you've really, really got to be careful about your funding" (#20).

Respondents expressed concern about declining foundation support for existing MDPs and the increasing competition for scarce monies. A practitioner of an individualized MDP targeting refugees said, "As we continue to open more and more of these programs, there's actually becoming less and less money that's going to be distributed among more and more programs" (#26).

Even MDPs that did not name funding as their most significant challenge spoke in interviews about fund-raising efforts and strategies. Funding concerns rippled through every aspect of program operations, including the definitions and framing of program goals, target and service populations, the amount and type of training offered, and the administration of peer- and individual-lending programs.

Funding opportunities and expectations produced several contradictory demands for MDP practitioners. First, MDP field maturation and increasing competition for funding were associated with demands for standardization (i.e., emerging best practices) and quantitative outcome measures of program success (e.g., Klein 2002a; 2002b; Nelson 2002; Von Pischke

2002b). Some practitioners were supportive of this move, but others suggested that such accountability demands stifled program innovation, evaluation, long term planning, and service quality enhancement. Second, demands for cost effectiveness and success indicators pressured practitioners to increase their loan volume and reduce training and client support costs. But without sufficient training and support services, practitioners were afraid to make loans to more disadvantaged clients. Thus, demands for sustainability and cost effectiveness limited efforts to extend credit to poor entrepreneurs (also see Morduch 1999; Bhatt, Painter, and Tang 2002). Third, pressures to increase loan volume but maintain low rates of default pressured practitioners to increase the predictability and efficiency of the lending process. Such concerns led some practitioners to abandon or reduce the autonomy of borrowers' circles in peer-lending programs. The desires for stability were an incentive for undermining such circle empowerment goals. Practitioners developed strategies to meet these challenges and strike a balance among competing and contradictory demands.

SHIFTING GOALS, FRAMES, AND PROGRAM EVALUATION

Funding requirements shaped (and reshaped) the goals and orientation of MDPs, both in presentations to the public and within the organizations themselves. A practitioner at a place-based program said, "Primarily, our goals are set with the assistance of our funding sources" (#41). Another practitioner from a peer program said, "Over the years, and as we have learned about the program, we've had some policy changes. But a lot of these changes are passed down to us from funders" (#12). When asked about the goals for her program, a third practitioner said, "They are almost a given since we are grant-based" (#26).

From Social Work to Business Standards

Practitioners' descriptions of the ways in which they had changed both the presentation and practice of their programs over time were reflective of new privatization discourse. Programs reported that they were becoming more businesslike. Some, especially place-based programs, had been striving for a businesslike identity from their inception. Others, especially peer and individualized programs, initially defined themselves as vehicles for poverty alleviation, but were trying to move to a business frame of reference. Practitioners sought to convey this business image to funders and clients. A business frame entailed communicating to clients that loans had to be repaid and communicating to funders that programs were professionally run, efficient, and cost effective. Businesslike programs conformed to proper accounting practices and showed demonstrable outcomes of their effectiveness. They also professionalized their boards of directors by including more representatives of banking and other corporations over time, a common tendency among maturing nonprofit organizations, especially in this time when business models are increasingly the standards for best organizational practice (see Smith and Lipsky 1993; Johnston 2000; Freedman 2002).

The following statement is from a practitioner in a program that changed its initial orientation to adopt a business model; the individualized program had formerly been a peer-lending demonstration program targeting women on welfare. She said, "We have been more flexible than we should have been, and maybe a little more "social workey" instead of business-like. We've changed. . . . You have to communicate to your clients that these are loans not grants" (#14). Once this program's federally funded demonstration project ended, it changed goals, eliminated peer lending, and scaled up its target population to include more low- and moderate-income rather than poverty-level-income clients.

Some practitioners sought to increase their businesslike images to funders by emulating banks. Nine programs described themselves as becoming more banklike in their operations, modeling banking practices in lending and developing quantitative measures of their cost effectiveness. These strategies were most applicable to larger-volume MDP lenders. A practitioner at a place-based program that targeted women and minorities in a rural region said, "We are becoming more bank-like. We want them [clients] to get used to what is it like out there to run a business. . . . We make better loans and have fewer losses now and . . . are more respected in the community out there, we have better ties with the community and more potential funding sources as a result" (#9).

Another practitioner at an individualized program that worked with a bank to administer most of its loans stressed the need for more integration of banklike efficiency standards: "I'm sure you've seen the numbers from the organizations around the country, in terms of loan funds that can't realize $300,000. And it takes $400,000 to administer that loan fund over a year, . . . that's ludicrous. . . . The business expertise does not exist in the nonprofit sector. . . . What I would like to see happening is staff trained as bankers as well as community development workers. . . . My advice is that we [MDPs] get with the bank and model ourselves more after them" (#38).

This business model was compatible with MDP field and funder efforts to promote increased standardization and accountability for MDPs (see

Bhatt 2002). Noted outcome measures of interest to funders included service utilization, high loan repayment rates, and increasing clients' business successes (e.g., number of employees, increased business profits, and increases in household incomes). Most practitioners viewed program cost effectiveness as closely associated with program sustainability. Programs were pressured to show that they could cover significant parts (if not all) of their operations with profits from lending, fees for services, and the sale of program curriculum, accounting documents, or software. Cost effectiveness meant serving as many clients and producing as many business successes as possible at the lowest cost. Three practitioners thought that their programs could reach self-sufficiency, that is, completely cover all their operational costs with profits from lending and other services. A practitioner at a peer program focused primarily on lending rather than training described this strategy: "[W]e are constantly . . . working on moving this whole thing to the next level, you know, building scale, becoming sustainable, creating an impact. You know, we never stop looking at how can we do this, how can we jump on to the next level, and do it better. How can we get more people involved, how can we . . . meet our own expenses" (#44).

However, the majority of practitioners simply aimed to produce successful outcomes at lower costs than other types of job-training, development, and lending programs. For example, a practitioner at a peer MDP targeting low-income women and minorities emphasized cost effectiveness in lieu of self-sufficiency: "I don't think anyone [in the United States] has been able to figure out how to attain the kind of sustainability or self-sufficiency scale that they have in the developing world. . . . People in the United States are struggling with how we can make this an effective and efficient tool to provide credit" (#39). Along these lines of outcome-oriented cost effectiveness, another practitioner said, "We evaluate our effectiveness through our job creation . . . and our cost is maybe $2,200 per job. So we think that's a pretty good number" (#30).

Practitioners were generally positive about accountability demands. A practitioner at a peer program agreed that outcome accountability was essential to clearly establish the impact of MDPs: "I think that a factor that should be taken into account is the size of the programs, when they started, and how many people they've reached. . . . [T]he only way that you're going to know the impact that we're making is by looking at how many people we have been able to benefit . . . and at what cost" (#44).

Practitioners attributed the demand for businesslike operations to the maturation and growth of the MDP movement, the increased competition for funding, and funders' desires for standard business practices. The demand was noted across organizational types and thus indicated the degree to which business models of operations were an increasingly common expectation for MDP practice.[7] Yet, given most programs' mission to serve disadvantaged clients, the market-efficiency model was a challenge.

The Trade-Offs of Market Efficiency

A few practitioners ($n = 5$) were skeptical about what they described as the uncritical application of private-sector efficiency standards to the MDP field. One respondent argued that market-oriented outcome measures pressured MDPs to "sacrifice program quality by demanding quick and easy success measures" (#43). Practitioners also suggested that the "production" of successful outcomes discouraged the inclusion of some educationally and economically disadvantaged clients and encouraged practitioners to ignore less easily measured, longer-run outcomes. According to a practitioner at an individualized program that targeted refugees: "And it's coming from a desire to do something good, but we all get caught up in numbers. . . . You get so caught up in that, [and] you get very confused as to who your target market is . . . what your goals are . . . who you're going to serve, and how to really give them a quality education. It should be working with people, . . . people who really need the help, . . . and not just to fulfill a number" (#26).

Funding demands also shaped routine program operations such as record-keeping. When they received grants for particular programs, MDPs sometimes had to revamp their record-keeping systems to conform to the requirements of government sponsors (e.g., the SBA). If resources permitted, they hired additional staff to handle the requirements associated with the grant. When resources were insufficient, these duties fell to existing staff.

Practitioners were also concerned about the effects of cost-efficiency demands on program planning and evaluation. Several argued that efforts spent to meet funding demands diverted staff energy from needed evaluation and improvements in program quality.[8] One practitioner explained:

> My experience is that you find a lot of nonprofits that are . . . competing with each other, and they get caught up in that aspect instead of the aspect that really drove them [to develop the program]. . . . [I]t's spending 50 percent of your day competing for funds, and that is a lot of wasted time . . . when you could be doing good . . . or learning how to improve what you are doing . . . or coming up with new ideas. . . . We do the reports and keep records depending on what our grants require. Our evaluation is internal.

We need more information on how our program works, and we don't do enough evaluation, but we have a very small staff. (#22)

This businesslike model for MDPs accords with new privatization ideologies that call for the adoption of idealized standards of market efficiency and cost effectiveness in the provision of public services (Quadagno 1999; Morduch 2000; Jurik 2004). It may also represent, however, a displacement or drift from the initial promises of MDP-movement advocates.

Extra-local pressures appeared in internal organizational practices in myriad ways. For example, it was difficult to distinguish practitioners' own views about how the program should be run from their perceptions of funder desires and client needs. These orientations literally blurred into practitioners' theory of office, that is, their general approach toward doing their job (Jurik and Gregware 1992).

ADJUSTING AND SCREENING TARGET/SERVICE POPULATIONS

Although most MDPs aimed to serve low income or otherwise marginalized populations, the actual target and service populations were strongly influenced by the availability and requirements of funding sources. Funding pressures encouraged staff to carefully consider the cost effectiveness of training and lending services to severely disadvantaged clients.

Multiple Targets

MDPs with multiple services ($n = 18$) often had different targets for each program component. These variations were often a result of donor requirements for each component. As an individualized program practitioner put it: "We have one program which basically targets immigrants and refugees. We have another program . . . [with] a really high Cambodian population. . . . And then we have a program that works with the federal government [to serve] low income and welfare recipients" (#26).

Four MDPs in our sample were funded as part of federal welfare-to-work demonstration projects. Several place-based programs had been established by state governments as economic development programs. Some programs in the northeast targeted displaced factory workers, whereas rural programs offered support of microenterprises to supplement dwindling farm-worker incomes. Three place-based programs included special services for displaced homemakers that drew on available government funding in this area. Five MDPs (including place and peer types) focused their programs on refugees in response to the availability of government funding targeted for these groups (also see Howells 2000). Funding concerns and program experiences led to shifts in MDP target populations over time.

Shifting and Screening Target Populations

One of the most frequently occurring changes reported by our respondents was a shift in target population. Ten programs reported such changes. The rationales for this shift included funding availability, community needs, desires for program expansion, and concerns about default rates associated with a particular target group.

Three programs reduced their recruitment of welfare clients when their federal demonstration grant ended. Also, some programs shifted or planned to shift their female target population focus to include men. One-half of the programs that served all women (three of six) reported that they were planning to expand to include men. Two additional programs in the sample had already removed the word *women* from their titles to indicate their inclusion of men clients. One program added services for displaced homemakers, and another added programming for youth in response to new funding availability.

Service population data (see table 3.3) suggest that most of the fifty programs served significant percentages of women, minority, and low-income clients. However, almost uniformly, practitioners stressed the importance of screening MDP clients. Although some screening was designed to increase the delivery of services to targeted disadvantaged clients, programs primarily screened, or creamed, to select more capable clients (Edgcomb, Klein, and Clark 1996; Cowgill and Jurik In press). The loan manager at a large place-based program that targeted African American and women entrepreneurs described the rationale for this process: "[B]y *creaming* them [clients] a little bit . . . now we're not dealing with the people who say "Yeah, I'm *thinking* about a business." . . . We provide loans to people who *already* exhibit strong entrepreneurial characteristics, and that's a key distinction" (#21).

An example of one of the most more rigorous screening processes was described by a practitioner from a program that offered both peer and individual lending: "We have a very intense screening process to even get *into* the program. [People] have to turn in an application, take a math test, submit a writing sample, do a group activity, [take] an individual interview, and [complete] a personality interview. . . . We usually have seventy-five to eighty people apply to the program and then we select thirty of them" (#10). Over time, practitioners developed their own assessment categories or typifications to identify clients who were most likely to succeed in their programs. Screening occurred formally and informally at different stages across programs: before admission, during training, during technical assistance, and before lending (see also Balkin 1993; Servon 1999a).

Profiling the Right Clients

MDP practitioners developed typifications of the "right client" for their program.[9] The clarity and feasibility of a business concept, indicators of past business experience, and particular business-related skills were important cues for practitioners as they decided which clients to serve and how best to allocate clients among service modalities. One practitioner said, "They have to have a viable idea and the experience to know how to run the business" (#10). Another practitioner said, "We carefully assess their business plan and decide whether the idea is feasible, that is, practical for them to accomplish. If it is, we help them prepare it to get a loan" (#22). On the one hand, it was essential for practitioners to make informed and experienced judgments about lending; on the other hand, the resulting typifications can introduce stereotypes that disadvantage the very clients that MDPs claim to target.

Practitioners expressed desires to maintain a neutral businesslike orientation toward clients, a stance that avoided the sorts of moralizing judgments associated with traditional welfare programs. Despite such intentions, profiles of the "right client" often entailed implied or explicit moral assessments of clients' characters. An individualized program practitioner said, "We have certain qualities that we look for in participants. . . . They have to have a good business idea, and they have to seem to us to be motivated and hard working individuals" (#2).

Motivation was the most frequently referenced attribute of a good client. In practitioners' descriptions of methods for assessing client motivation, absence from program events, tardiness, and the absence of emotional displays of energy and enthusiasm were the defining features of clients who "lacked the motivation to succeed" in the program. A practitioner from a peer program targeting anyone who "is or wants to be self-employed" emphasized the connection between motivation and clarity of business concept: "I think our program is designed to be very reliant on people coming in and being very motivated or becoming more motivated as they learn business skills and get support from their peers. I also don't think that this model, as it's presently being run, works very well for people who don't have a clear idea about wanting to go into business. They have to be motivated" (#45).

Some practitioners used the term *serious* to distinguish the more committed from the less committed clients. The practitioner working in the program for displaced factory workers said, "It [the MDP] is really tailored to people who are much more serious, and more driven, and a little more developed. . . . We find the people who are most successful come to us already having garnered those key skills and motivation, and the drive to empower themselves. It's what they bring to the table. . . . Our role is, You know what business you want to do, you're serious about it, you've done the research and some basic work around it. Good. We can provide you with a loan" (#22).

Seriousness was associated with a more developed and researched business idea. Client loyalty to the MDP was also an important cue for practitioners. A peer-program practitioner described her most successful groups: "[G]roup one is the most active and they're out there doing their business, and they are more apt to come to meetings, the trainings, and there's a good relationship between them and the program" (#34).

Realism was another important attribute of the "right client." The business idea needed to be clear and practical given the client's resources and past work experiences. A practitioner with a peer MDP emphasized realism: "We are looking for women in [our state] who are unemployed and who want to start a business because they really love what they're doing. . . . In the [loan] interview, we just try to find out how interested they are and how realistic they are about it" (#5). This practitioner associated realism with the client's level of commitment. Several practitioners noted that clients' resources affected their ability to present themselves as good clients—motivated, serious, and committed to a business. Prompt and regular meeting attendance and well-researched business ideas required financial and educational capacities that often eluded many poor and low-income clients.

Concerns about Poverty Level and Welfare Clients

Practitioners were generally positive about program clients and attributed client disadvantages to structural forces such as unemployment, divorce-related poverty, and lack of economic or educational opportunities. Some questioned the effectiveness of microenterprise development for the highly disadvantaged (e.g., individuals living at the poverty level, individuals with very little education, and welfare recipients). In some cases, practitioners noted problematic characteristics associated with the poor. Two practitioners, one in a place-based and the other in an individualized program said, "There's the issue of bringing someone off of a long term dependency on the system and have them learn to become independent. This is where we've had the biggest problem with the training for our population" (#18) and "Working with individuals who are receiving AFDC, you . . . wonder especially with those that have been on for a very long time, what are some of the barriers to them finding either self-employment or employment . . . people have to assume responsibility and they have to step up to the plate" (#14).

Another practitioner from a place-based program that targeted African American and women clients justified his program's decision not to target poverty-level clients:

> A lot of programs . . . are trying to be full-scale service providers and it's very costly, very time intensive, and they don't always have a lot to show for it because often times people aren't really starting their businesses and getting them running. . . . The program is so involved with those people and their businesses that if you remove the program, the business falls. . . . We have to think about what we do best, and . . . what we *don't do* best is providing full-fledged counseling, literacy, and credit counseling. . . . My conclusion so far with microenterprise development is that I don't think loan programs are the most suitable method for helping the poor. As opposed to other things like job training and placement. I just don't think it [microenterprise development] is very feasible for the poor. (#21)

Practitioners associated services to poverty-level and welfare clients with increased rates of business failures and loan defaults. In part, they feared that such increases would hamper fund-raising efforts. A staff member at an individualized program that had terminated its peer and welfare component said, "You have to select your loan clients carefully . . . if you try to work with severely disadvantaged groups . . . you're going to be out there begging for money all the time, and there is a cost when somebody has to pick up the tab" (#14). A peer-program practitioner argued that employed clients fared better in her program: "They're not mediocre; they all have jobs. They don't rely on a fixed income of any kind like welfare or that type of thing. Most of them have an eight-to-five job. Here it seems like those type of people are the ones that are really making the program work" (#34). These MDP screening processes reflect common practices in welfare and social service programs. Whenever program staff must allocate scarce resources, they develop methods and categories for determining which clients merit organizational services (Lipsky 1980; Miller 1989; Holstein and Miller 1996).

When it came to lending, practitioners' concern about identifying the "right client" were at their peak. A practitioner of a place-based MDP described her program's image of good and bad clients and its need to feel "comfortable" with its borrowers:

> We'll be doing our side looking at their credit, calling their references, kind of testing the viability of their business plans and doing our due diligence. . . . We've really gained a lot of information on how to assess the repayment potential of a particular client . . . there's just some clues there. If people have a lot of late payments, that's a clue. If people have collections, we don't do a loan to them. . . . Sometimes people say this is done and this is done, why can't I get the loan? [I tell them] well, the short answer is we're just getting to know you and until we feel really *comfortable* with who you are, that you're going to stick around. You know, some people just have red flags as far as lending, maybe they haven't lived somewhere for very long. Maybe they don't seem to have any ties to the local community. So then we want to be satisfied, you know that they're going to be here long enough to repay the loan. (#4)

Her program had evolved from an individualized, training-oriented program to a place-based, credit-led MDP that, in the practitioner's terms, "operated more like a bank." As it had grown, the program became more concerned about scaling up clients to reach sustainability.

Screening efforts were complicated for MDPs whose central mission entailed serving poor and very-low-income clients, especially when their funding was linked to this commitment. Some programs resolved this dilemma through stratified screening strategies whereby they provided some basic services to all clients and then carefully screened clients for advanced or riskier services such as lending (also see Servon 1999a).

STRATIFIED SERVICE STRATEGIES

Some MDPs attempted to balance service to highly disadvantaged clients with concerns about loan losses and overhead by developing stratified service systems. They offered unique types of training and lending methods for different types of clients. A practitioner at an individualized program describes how training and lending varied among different types of clients: "We have several training programs . . . one that meets once a week for fourteen weeks and takes them through all aspects of their business development. . . . We have another especially for public aid [welfare] recipients, and it meets twice a week instead of once. We have a program that bridges the gap between business start-up and those that are expanding. . . . Our welfare clients do a lot more training and many wind up not borrowing at all" (#14).

Training was an important screening mechanism to determine client advancement to lending stages. As exemplified by the nonborrower-to-borrower ratio discussed earlier, most MDP clients never receive loans. This stratification process is enhanced when training is a prerequisite to borrowing. Twenty-six percent of programs ($n = 13$) required the completion of training prior to borrowing. A practitioner from a place-based program said, "We developed the training program for essentially screening applicants. Once the applicant has gotten through that initial step [training], then we look for a business plan. . . . And once the business plan is approved . . . then the loan is cut"(#18). And a peer-program practitioner with a strong welfare-to-work component said, "We do a lot more training with our poverty level and welfare clients. . . . Once they go through the business training, many of them learn that they are not cut out for self-employment. We lose a lot that way, but it's important that they found out before they borrow" (#42).

Most service stratification occurred between the training and lending stages of programs. Even programs that did not require training courses often limited some clients to business counseling and technical assistance alone, when clients could not assemble an acceptable business plan or had insufficient collateral to secure the loan.

For peer-lending MDPs, the addition of individual-lending services was a strategy for boosting the number and size of loan offerings. Individual loans were expected to generate revenue for the program by making larger, collateral-secured loans devoid of some of the administrative costs associated with peer lending. The recipients of individual loans were typically more experienced entrepreneurs with greater access to resources than those associated with peer borrowing. A practitioner described the stratification in her program between peer and individual loans: "For our individual loans, they have to be in business for at least a year and with these people . . . we really collateralize these loans. They have to have financial statements, they have to have tax returns, they have to show their business is succeeding . . . and . . . they don't have to go through our training program. . . . We are hoping the individual loans will generate some profits for our program to cover our training and peer lending services" (#7).

In this program, low-income clients were served by smaller peer loans; individual loans typically went to more-moderate-income clients. Stepped lending (the process of offering successive loans of increasing amounts to successful borrowers) was also an often-cited method for stratifying client-service delivery between more and less disadvantaged clients (Clark and Kays 1995).

Prior research (Servon 1999a; Servon and Bates 1998) suggests that service stratification typically means that more highly disadvantaged clients participate in business-training programs and receive small loans, whereas larger loans and more specialized technical assistance programs serve a clientele that is better-off in terms of education, business experience, and income level. In our sample, practitioner perceptions were consistent with these generalizations. We would have liked to compare program statistics for client demographics across service categories, but we were unable to do so because so few programs kept these data. For example, one practitioner said, "We keep track of the data that our funders require. There are other things we should keep track of, but we just do not have the time" (#12). Record-keeping practices were thus strongly shaped by extra-local funder demands.

BALANCING TRAINING AND TECHNICAL ASSISTANCE WITH COST EFFECTIVENESS

Most programs (64 percent; $n = 32$) made business training available to clients, but training varied in terms of structure, location, and timing. Table 3.6 summarizes the number and types of programs that offer training and technical assistance (e.g., business counseling).

Because funding sources were typically more interested in providing money for loans than for operations, MDPs had strong incentives to keep training costs to a minimum. A practitioner at a credit-led, place-based program said that a primary goal was to build a lending program without building a whole new bureaucracy: "We have total assets of . . . around $400,000, and operating costs of around $65,000. . . . I look at most loan programs, and they have a loan pool of about $100,000, and operating costs of about $400,000. . . . Then you have to go after grant money to pay for your $400,000 staff" (#24). Practitioners struggled to find ways of offering needed training and technical support to clients at the lowest possible cost.

TABLE 3.6
Training and technical assistance offered, by program type[a]

	Place, $n = 17$		Peer, $n = 16$		Individualized, $n = 17$		Total, $n = 50$	
	Number	Percentage	Number	Percentage	Number	Percentage	Number	Percentage
Business training offered								
Yes	5	29	12	75	15	88[c]	32	64
No	12	71	4	25	2	12	18	36
Length of training[b]								
Under 10 weeks	4	24	9	56	9	53	22	44
10 weeks or more	1	6	3	19	6	35	10	20
Mean number of weeks	2 weeks		5 weeks		7 weeks[c]		4 weeks	
Technical assistance offered								
Yes, on demand	13	76	13	81	15	88	41	82
Yes, required	3	18	2	13	2	12	7	14
No	1	6	1	6		–0–	2	4

[a]Percentages are based on the total number of programs of each type.
[b]Includes workshop format
[c]The t-test for differences of means between this program type (coded 1) and other programs (coded 0) was significant at p < .05 for a one-tail test.

Minimalist Strategies

Some practitioners argued that minimal-training programs were the best strategy for maximizing impact and minimizing costs. Four programs emphasized credit to such an extent that they offered neither business training nor technical assistance. Several respondents disparaged training-intensive models. One practitioner at a state-run program that targeted clients with disabilities said, "The reason for the large operations budgets of most programs is the high level of technical assistance they're involved in. But what a lot of them don't measure is what are the returns on that technical assistance dollar, versus returns to capitalization [lending]" (#18). This illustrates that even state-run MDPs had to be concerned about the bottom line.

Some programs valued training but tried to tap into services offered by other providers. A practitioner at a large place-based program that targeted women and African American entrepreneurs without regard to income explained, "We found that there are technical assistance providers that provide both ongoing one-to-one TA and up-front training classes . . . so we don't feel the need to duplicate that" (#21). Yet many practitioners believed that too few training and support services were problematic. Training and technical assistance served multiple purposes that included developing clients' entrepreneurial abilities, providing business skills, creating or improving business plans, and preparing clients for the borrowing process.

Technical Assistance Instead of Training Courses

Some practitioners relied on technical assistance (TA) as an alternative to the costs of more generalized business training. Although less expensive than formal business courses, TA was still costly. Even some self-espoused credit-led programs offered technical assistance to borrowers, and in some of these programs technical assistance was extensive. A practitioner at a credit-led peer program explained her circle training process: "[The circles] go through a group development process where they put together a set of by-laws, elect officers, [and] they go through a budgeting workshop where they learn to understand cash in and cash out and how to calculate this for their own businesses. They go through a loan review practice where they learn how to evaluate loans" (#44).

Most practitioners feared that without TA support, their clients would fail, and loan delinquencies would be prohibitive. This was a great concern in programs that targeted start-up businesses and highly disadvantaged clients. A practitioner in a individualized program that targeted welfare clients said, "Staff have to do lots of ongoing technical assistance, and we need a lot of money to be able to support that effort" (#32).

Practitioners experimented with different methods to increase the efficiency of TA offerings. Three programs moved to workshop formats in an effort to decrease the costs of one-on-one technical assistance. The sole staff member of a credit-oriented, place-based program explained, "I would say though, that . . . about 60 percent of my counseling or teaching is done one-on-one. . . . If I have a lot of people at one time . . I take an afternoon . . . and we work together as a group. I'll do a session on . . . cash flow and . . . I might do billing sheets and income statements" (#20).

Some practitioners (20 percent) emphasized the need for additional training and/or TA in their programs. One practitioner at a credit-led, place-based program lamented the lack of time to assist applicants: "What I think is the weakest with our program is . . . we [should] concentrate a little bit more on quality than quantity, . . . have more time to spend with each potential applicant and . . . more time with each borrower. . . . I think they really need more attention paid to them" (#9). Most practitioners emphasized the need to provide more than business basics, especially for disadvantaged entrepreneurs.

Beyond Business Training

Some programs (20 percent, $n = 10$) offered extended services to their highest-risk borrowers. These services went beyond the basics of business training and technical assistance to include workshops on topics such as "cleaning up a poor credit history," self-esteem, fear of success, or other personal issues. The types and the average number of these programs for MDPs are listed in tables 3.7a and 3.7b. Programs with the highest percentages of poverty-level, welfare-to-work, women, or disabled clients were most likely to offer such courses.

Ehlers and Main (1998) criticize MDP training for neglecting the structural barriers such as gender and racial/ethnic discrimination that confront disadvantaged microentrepreneurs. As described in chapter 2, Coyle et al. (1994) distinguish the approach of North American MDPs from the broader structural change missions adopted by many southern hemisphere programs. The missions of southern programs' typically go beyond offering business credit and training to include community organizing and political action. The North American focus, according to conference presentations, is directed more toward the "transfer of technology" and

TABLE 3.7a

Additional services provided, by program type[a]

	Place, n = 17		Peer, n = 16		Individualized, n = 17		Total, n = 50	
	Number	Percentage	Number	Percentage	Number	Percentage	Number	Percentage
Transportation	1	6	3	19	3	18	7	14
Child care	1	6	4	25	5	29	10	20
Client advocacy	5	29	5	31	4	24	14	28
Citizenship	0	0	0	0	1	6	1	2
Literacy	0	0	0	0	1	6	1	2
Counseling	0	0	3	19	4	24	7	14
Community organizing	0	0	2	13	0	0	2	4
Life assessment	1	6	3	19	1	6	5	10
Legal interpretation	1	6	2	13	5	29	8	16
Housing services	4	24	3	19	2	12	9	18
Nutrition/fitness	0	0	2	13	1	6	3	6
Savings	0	0	7	44	2	12	9	18
Social services (e.g., household budgeting)	0	0	1	6	2	12	3	6

[a]Percentages are based on the total number of programs for each type. Respondents sometimes listed more than one service, and many respondents listed none at all. Thus, percentages do not total 100.

TABLE 3.7b
Mean number of additional services offered, by program type[a]

	Place	Peer	Individualized	Minimalist	Training	Total
Mean	0.16[b]	2.56	2.29	1.11	2.28	1.86

[a]The numbers of social service programs (from table 3.7a) that all programs offered were added together to compute a social service index. Scores on the index range from 0 to 7 with a median of 1 and a mean of 1.86.
[b]The mean additional social service index score for place-based programs (coded 1) was significantly lower than the mean for the other two MDP types (coded 0), p < .001.

"facilitating self-employment" than toward collective or community empowerment (Coyle et al. 1994, 4).

Our research supports this generalization. We found that only a minority of programs (16 percent, $n = 8$) included community organization or community empowerment goals among their major program objectives, and only two organizations worked directly on political empowerment issues. According to a practitioner at a peer program that targeted low-and moderate-income clients: "We've been able to make a lot of connections between our program and different Latino groups, or with groups working on welfare, countering some of the more vicious parts of welfare reform, and we've joined an organization which [is comprised of] about six organizations in the community who have sponsored debates of the local state representatives and city council elections. . . . So we have members [clients] become politically active in bringing the issue of micro-business development to politicians" (#45).

An even smaller percentage of programs reported that they addressed societal-level or structural barriers to women, minority-owned, or very small businesses in their training or technical assistance programs. Twelve percent ($n = 6$) of the sample programs (three peer and three individualized MDPs) addressed structural barriers. Most of these programs were geared toward women and focused on issues of sexism confronting women in business. Three programs that targeted women welfare recipients examined the convergence of gender and economic disadvantages. They reflected the goals of the women's movement—developing alternative, gender-sensitive services for women. A practitioner from a program that targeted women on welfare reported:

Our training is a healthy combination that covers personal and societal barriers. Women who are motivated and aspire to become self-employed face a number of regulatory battles and obstacles to developing a business, everything from taxes to licensing, certification to zoning laws and the like. There are a number of barriers that prohibit women from developing their dreams into a reality. . . . There are a number of personal and social issues that prohibit women from becoming self-employed, whether it be a lack of education, a lack of the skill or talent they might need to develop that business, either in their personal household, or maybe the community in which they live, lack of transportation, lack of housing. . . . We deal with those in the training. (#42)

Although most practitioners agreed that more comprehensive training was vital for reaching highly disadvantaged client populations that might lack basic business and life skills, few U.S. MDPs offered such training. Those that did sought to justify it to funders by redefining their program success in qualitative human development terms rather than in quantitative output measures. A practitioner in an individualized program that targeted moderate income clients exemplifies this approach: "One of the ways that we increasingly look at the success of our program is not through the number of loans that we make. We look at it in terms of how we assisted the client. Because I think at the heart of the issue, we're coming to the conclusion that it's not credit that improves people's lives, it's education" (#36). However, the majority of programs shied away from comprehensive service models. They feared that their program would not be sufficiently cost effective in the eyes of funders and their larger community. The most common strategy for extending services while maintaining cost effectiveness was to connect with other organizations in the community.

PARTNERSHIPS

Fewer than one-half of our MDPs (48 percent) were independent organizations. The majority (52 percent) were part of larger organizations or networks, but, regardless of their level of independence, all had significant links with the community through partnerships with other private, government, and nonprofit organizations. Partnering was a common strategy used by programs in an attempt to offer the most training and lending services for the least money. A practitioner in an individualized program that targeted low-income women and minorities said, "A big part of what we do here . . . is work in partnerships with different organizations. . . . But not, you know, trying to go in and do it on our own, no, but work with these other agencies, banks, programs, and organizations. You know, kind of in tandem, and really have an impact, and leverage the funds that we have" (#23).

Lisa Servon (1999a) notes that partnership networks are a central aspect of MDP operations, and our data agree. The operations manager for an MDP that targeted women entrepreneurs with more established businesses described the wide array of partnerships that her organization developed: "We have a very strong alliance with a lot of different groups. For instance . . . we work closely with the Small Business Center . . . SCORE. . . . We also get and give referrals and do joint programs with the [local] minority and women's incubator. . . . We have excellent rapport with the area banks. . . . We have a good strategic alliance with organizations that work with low to moderate income people. . . . Those are just some of the alliances that we have out there" (#37).

The most common partnerships were with local banks (54 percent), small business development centers (52 percent), social service agencies (42 percent), and community development groups (40 percent). Partnerships helped extend MDP lending and training services without expanding program infrastructure. With regard to lending, a practitioner at a small individualized program said, "Our loan program is now done in a bank, which to me, is much more efficient in cutting loans, than [loans done] by the nonprofit directly" (#38). Thirty-eight percent of programs ($n = 19$) were able to make loans directly to clients, and the rest loaned through intermediary organizations (e.g., CDCs or banks).

Some MDPs offered their training and technical assistance through community partners. Programs that served highly disadvantaged clients made additional support services available through community partners. A practitioner at a peer program that targeted welfare clients said, "We understand that what we do as a microenterprise development agency is very limited in scope, and in order to develop and start a business, there are a number of things that . . . happen in a woman's life . . . everything from issues that include domestic violence, health, education, training skills. And there are a number of different things that we don't do as an agency so we're not a panacea for the women that we work with. So, we have to do a number of referrals to outside agencies, organizations, and social service groups" (#42).

Twenty percent of programs ($n = 10$) reported that they linked clients with child-care support and 14 percent ($n = 7$) networked clients with transportation subsidies. Twenty percent of programs ($n = 10$) developed partnerships with child care providers and 24 percent (n = 12) obtained funding for transportation assistance to aid clients in their business pursuits.

Drawbacks of Partner Services and Supervised Partnership Strategies

Ultimately, practitioners across program types were concerned about the long-term sustainability of their programs, and partnering was one way to expand but keep program costs down. Yet close partnerships to enhance important client services required extensive monitoring. As a result, they were time consuming for staff and complicated their efforts to provide consistent services for clients. One practitioner at an individualized program said, "I partner with an agency here that offers business counseling. I find that the counselors, who are all volunteers, are of really mixed quality and relevance for my clients' businesses. I have to try and watch who my clients get. Again, I am the only staff member for technical assistance, and I need to be able to use them, but it takes time to make sure my clients get good counselors" (#22).

A few MDPs developed extensive guidelines for selecting and monitoring their partners' service quality. Practitioners sought to improve partner services through a strategy we call *supervised partnerships*—the MDPs played a large role in designing the services that partners provided. For example, one program designed a business course curriculum that was offered at a community college. The MDP had a lot of input into the choice of the teachers for the courses. Another MDP helped design the training and guidelines for counselors from a partnering agency that provided technical assistance for its clients.

Thus, although partnership strategies were key to MDP cost effectiveness, they were not without problems of quality and relevance. They also made MDPs appear more cost effective than they perhaps really were. One practitioner described what he saw as the hidden costs of minimalist programs' reliance on partnerships, "I don't think they're self-sufficient. Their costs are just born by other local organizations" (#36). Although supervised partnerships improved quality and relevance, their maintenance required significant allocations of staff and other program resources (see also Ashe 2000).

LENDING STRATEGIES

Balancing Numbers

Although lending processes varied somewhat according to program type, they seemed to vary most along the lines of lending methodology (i.e., peer versus individual methods). Table 3.8 provides information about the number and amount of loans (including the mean and median loan

TABLE 3.8

Means and medians for total loans, by program type[a]

	Place	Peer	Individualized	Total
Number of loans				
Mean	21	27	35	23
Median	13	26	15	11
Number of individual loans				
Mean	21	21	35	25
Median	13	15	15	14
Number of peer loans				
Mean	N/A	19	N/A	N/A
Median	N/A	15	N/A	N/A
Amounts of individual loans				
Mean	$16,782[b]	$15,203	$ 6,533[c]	$12,404
Median	$12,476	$ 2,925	$ 5,749	$ 7,750
Amounts of peer loans				
Mean	N/A	$ 1,262	N/A	N/A
Median	N/A	$ 1,014	N/A	N/A
Minimum loan				
Mean	$ 2,754[c]	$ 298[b]	$ 520	$ 1,262
Median	$ 1,000	$ 300	$ 200	$ 500
Maximum loan				
Mean	$61,294[b]	$26,187	$17,036	$36,598
Median	$25,000	$ 8,000	$10,000	$10,000

[a]N/A, not applicable.
[b]The t-test for difference of means between the program type (coded 1) and the other two program types combined (coded 0) was significant at p < .05.
[c]The t-test for differences of means between the program type (coded 1) and the other two program types combined (coded 0) was significant at p < .01.

amounts) offered by each program type for the fiscal year preceding our interviews. Table 3.9 provides an overview of lending policies.

The funding sources were influential in determining lending requirements. Variations in collateral requirements across loans within the same MDP were quite common. Such policies were a reflection of the type (individual versus peer, first versus repeat loans) and amount of the loan, but they also reflected variations in demands across funding sources. A loan officer for a place-based program said, "For the microloans that we do internally, we have a lot more flexibility in the collateral area. . . . Because it's our money, and there's nothing hard and fast like we want a $1.25 for every dollar we loan. . . . The SBA loans . . . are a different story. There you're dealing with the banks and we have seven banks that are in the program with us. Every bank is different . . . and some are more lenient" (#29).

TABLE 3.9
Lending policies, by program type[a]

	Place, n = 17		Peer, n = 16		Individualized, n = 17		Total, n = 50	
	Number	Percentage	Number	Percentage	Number	Percentage	Number	Percentage
Overall policies[b]								
Practices character-based lending	9	53	12	75[c]	12	71[c]	33	66
Requires collateral always	8	47	6	38	7	41	21	42
Requires collateral at times	6	35	1	6	6	35	13	26
Conducts credit checks	12	71	1	6	10	59[c]	23	46
Allows co-signers	2	12	0	0	1	6	3	6
Staff or committee approval for all loans	17	100	6	38[c]	17	100	40	80
Step lending	1	6[c]	10	63	4	24	15	30
Direct lending	7	41	6	38	1	6	19	38
Interest rates								
Current market rate	1	6	1	6	4	24	6	12
Over current market rate	6	35	6	38	5	29	17	34
Below current market rate	4	24	3	19	4	24	11	22
Subsidizes interest rates	3	18	1	6	4	24	8	16
Not reported	3	18	5	31	0	0	8	16

[a]Percentages are based on the total number of programs for each type.
[b]These overall policies are not mutually exclusive categories, so percentages do not total 100.
[c]T-tests for differences of means between this program type (coded 1) and the other program types combined (coded 0) were significant at the p < .05 level or better for a one-tailed test.

Although some funding sources encouraged MDPs to emulate banking practices, most MDPs remained nontraditional lenders. Thirty-six percent offered multiple types of loan services including varying loan types (e.g., peer and individual loans), loan amounts, and lending criteria. Fewer than one-half required collateral for loans, although some took collateral when available. Sixty-six percent practiced some form of character-based lending on at least some of their loans. Even some of the programs that tried to emulate traditional bank-lending procedures still offered some character-based loans. One practitioner at a rural, place-based MDP said, "So much of our lending is based on character, probably character makes up about 80 percent of the decisions. So, we rely real heavily on the history of the person—their financial history, their work history—just kind of general character issues, because in most cases, we aren't adequately secured by any means" (#9). Pressures to be conservative in lending practices were limited by the MDP mission to reach borrowers who would be denied loans by traditional banks. The effort to balance careful lending with reaching a large population of borrowers was a constant struggle for practitioners.

Boosting Loan Numbers

Chief among outcome measures requested by funders were the number of loans issued, the rate of loan default and delinquency, and the impact of loans on client businesses. Thirty percent of respondents ($n = 15$) named lending as one of their organization's primary problems. Lending concerns included the need to make more loans, competition with other programs and banks for good borrowing clients, and fluctuations in loan repayment rates.

MDPs, especially those whose primary function was lending, had to be certain that they were making sufficient numbers of loans to justify their existence. A place-based practitioner described the significance of this for his funding: "[W]e're evaluated according to our contract [which says] we have to have so much money out each year. Like at the end of this year's contract, I am to have 80 percent of my funds out there, and if not, I'm in noncompliance with the contract" (#20).

Building up loan volume was a strategy used by some programs to enhance the prospect of sustainability for the organization. A practitioner at an individualized, credit-led MDP said, "We try to get the dollars out on the street, especially some of our larger loans. [That is] the way that we can subsidize our other services, like TA" (#22). However, several other practitioners described difficulties in obtaining sufficient clients for lending. A practitioner in a two-year-old peer program said, "[G]o slow on trying to build up your loan fund pool, because what we are finding is that the demand for the loans is not as big as what we had thought it was going to be" (#13).

Two practitioners attributed their difficulty in finding sufficient numbers of borrowers to "the increasing competition for better-risk clients" who still met the income or demographic criteria for the program's target population. A loan officer at a seven-year-old place-based program blamed SBA-subsidized programs for increasing competition from banks:

> Even though we're participants in the SBA Microloan program, we think the SBA blew it by starting the LowDoc program as well, because even though they say it's not a competitive program, it does compete with us. And so, if you have to go through us and make a business plan and show how the business makes sense, or you can go to the bank, and fill out a two-page application, and the government's going to guarantee 90 percent of that loan, which one is going to be easier? The answer is going to be the bank. So mostly, the people we end up getting are the people who are definitely not bankable at all. (#17)

Thus, competition with banks and other lending sources for clients led to fears that MDPs would be left with the highest-risk clients.

Practitioners also cautioned that too much lending growth increased defaults if it caused staff to lose touch with clients or become too lax in approving loans. A practitioner with a seven-year-old peer program said, "We had a great amount of success early on when we could spend a lot of time with each group, but . . . as we started making more loans . . . well, now we each have to have work with fifteen to twenty groups. We got to the point that I didn't know everybody's name even, you know, and our sources were diluted, there's no doubt about it, and we started to see the default rate go up . . . [but] if we're going to stay in business we need to have a lot of clients" (#12).

Although they differed on the acceptable repayment rate, all were interested in showing stability in loan repayments. A practitioner in a five-year old individualized MDP said, "It makes it so much easier to plan and manage . . . and you know what to tell your funders . . . if you have a reasonably stable rate of repayment, whether it be 98 percent or 88 percent" (#2). Uniformly, practitioners stressed the importance of showing good loan repayment rates to potential funders.

Assisting the Right Borrower

As described in a previous section, practitioners regard screening for the "right client" to be most crucial at the lending stage. Still, no matter how right the borrower, it was still essential for MDP staff to maintain considerable contact with the borrower. Contact meant ongoing communication and technical assistance. A practitioner at a peer program with one of the most comprehensive service offerings in our sample said, "Let's say they are late on their payments and we try to work with them to figure out why. . . . Then they stay away, like we are trouble and we [are] after their money. . . . [R]eally, we are just trying to help them and try to figure out what's going on. . . . Of course, we would like our money back also, but at the same time we need to help them. We need to help them run their business and maintain good records and keep them going" (#33).

A practitioner at a place-based program agreed, "We found through experience that our post-loan technical assistance is absolutely critical, especially in the first year of the loan, and if you don't have resources to do it, you're just going to be spending your time collecting" (#40).

Communication and technical assistance were crucial components for promoting business success and minimizing defaults. Unfortunately, such services increased program operating costs and necessitated more funding.

Step Lending

Step lending was used as a strategy for controlling risk in 30 percent of the programs. This strategy was more popular among peer and individualized MDPs than among the place-based programs in our sample (χ^2, $p < .001$). Step lending is an extension of the screening and service stratification strategies described earlier. Of the fifteen programs that used stepped lending, 62 percent ($n = 10$) were peer, 24 percent ($n = 4$) were individual, and only six percent (n = 1) were place-based programs. The loan manager at the place-based program most articulately explained the process, "Staged [step] loans . . . help people build up a track record slowly and steadily and [with] the first step, the loan is $1,000 and we have not required collateral. At the higher stages, we might [require collateral]. . . . We're requiring that people show us that they've been in business for at least six months. But, six months is still very much a start-up by conventional standards" (#21). Step lending helped to manage the risk associated with high-risk borrowers. Peer lending was another mechanism for managing risk.

Strategies for Administering Peer Lending

Despite the reported advantages of peer-lending methods for encouraging client support and loan repayment, this model could be stressful and expensive. Although reports suggest that it allows programs to reach the poor with small loans and involve clients in the administration and repayment costs, it also introduced instability and uncertainty into program management (see Ashe 2000). The "additional administrative costs" associated with circles led two programs to discontinue peer lending during the year preceding our interviews. At the time of our interviews, a third MDP had just decided to eliminate its peer-lending program. Problems with peer lending included tensions within circles, poor circle attendance, and members' liability for one another's loan repayments. Some practitioners said that clients were just not interested in circle participation. A practitioner evaluated her programs' experiences with borrowers' circles of poor and low-income clients:

> They've been positive and somewhere in between. The peer group lending model has been exciting. . . . What it allows us to do is to bring women together for support and for loans. So that's the exciting part of it. It is a challenge, because when you bring groups of women together and they are totally dependent on each other's characteristics and behaviors to operate effectively, it becomes difficult sometimes to get people to want to work together over the long period. . . . [C]ircles have life cycles like anybody else, . . . so we have strong circles that start out, they'd go through a rocky period, [and during] that rocky period we have to really work to maintain that circle and keep it together, and then they recover . . . where they are doing well. And then you have members of a circle that become very successful. They may not want to continue to be part of the circle, because maybe they don't have time to meet . . . so all the circles have life cycles. (#42)

Although some abandoned peer lending altogether, other MDPs kept borrowers' circles in modified forms (also see Taub 1998). These practitioners developed mechanisms for controlling and stabilizing the circle process. For one MDP, circles became an option rather than a requirement: "When we first got started, we modeled [peer lending] after the Grameen Bank, but we've made a lot of changes. [A]fter they go through our seven-week program, they [now] have the option of joining a group or staying an individual member" (#7). Another MDP modified its requirements so that circle members were not held accountable for one another's loans. Two MDPs modified their circles' size to deal with erratic attendance.

Some MDPs avoided direct staff intervention, but increased efforts to socialize borrowers and encourage them to monitor one another more carefully. A respondent described why her program added a tracking mechanism for circle members: "You have people who can't make the [circle] meetings all of the time. So we developed this thing called a membership information chart which has every member's name on it, if they have a business, if they're attending. . . . they have to have at least 70 percent attendance to borrow money. And this chart will let the members know if one of their members has fallen behind on attendance, payments, etc. (#7)

Some programs sought to shape circles through written procedures. One practitioner at a program for low- to moderate-income clients described her program's guidelines: "[Clients] have to attend nine weeks of meetings . . . [and] they have to write a loan application, read through all the guidelines and expectations, and agree to become members. . . . At the very end, they do a loan review and then apply for a loan" (#13).

Other programs increased direct staff intervention. One program increased staff direction of the circles: "[A] circle banking director goes to all the meetings. . . . She doesn't necessarily run the meeting, she's just there to help with whatever questions they have, and if they had an idea, she can kind of help them through it" (#33). Several programs formalized staff control by screening clients for circles and approving circle decisions. Sixty-nine percent ($n = 11$) of peer programs stipulated that staff assign clients to circles. Thirty-eight percent ($n = 6$) required circle approval of loans, and 19 percent ($n = 3$) added requirements that staff must approve business plans before clients were allowed to join circles. One practitioner emphasized "the symbolic importance of staff veto power over circle decisions" (#39), even though she acknowledged that this power was rarely used. At the time of our interviews, four other programs were considering implementing staff-approval policies for circle lending decisions. The practitioner detailed this change in her program: "Our facilitator has final say on the loans. He hasn't rejected any, but he does evaluate them. . . . Adding his review was designed to give people reasons to take the [loan review] process more seriously" (#39).

Although client autonomy and input into the lending process has been praised as an innovative and effective avenue of client empowerment in peer-lending programs (e.g., Anthony 1997; Servon 1999a), many U.S. practitioners argue that it is not the most effective model in highly individualized U.S. urban or decentralized rural communities (Coyle et al. 1994). Only two peer-lending programs in our study maintained a high degree of circle autonomy. Both targeted low- to more-moderate-income rather than poverty level clients: "I think we are one of the few programs where they

[circles] make all of the decisions. We have no screening process, they decide. . . . They not only do business with each other and help each other,
but they become involved in other community activities" (#44).

And as noted earlier, only two programs directly attempted to link circles to political activism or empowerment. A practitioner at one of these
said, "We're really involved in a lot of community . . . and political activities. . . . We have members become politically active" (#45).

Thus, in an effort to promote repayment stability and reduce administrative costs of failed circles, most peer-lending programs increased controls over circle decision-making processes. Such increased stability might
be of great benefit to program clients as they pursue their businesses in a
more predictable and uniformly helpful circle situation. For example, it
might remove the pressures associated with the loan default of a circle colleague. But, although typical of maturing organizations (McCarthy and
Zald 1973; DiMaggio and Powell 1983), this centralization and bureaucratization of authority undermines the gains and collective empowerment
so often associated with more autonomous MDP borrowers' circles (e.g.,
Auwal and Singhal 1992; Anthony 1997).

CONCLUSION

Using the IE approach, we have mapped a series of links between the local
practices of fifty MDPs and extra-local institutional conditions. Our
analysis reveals a complex of relations in which the work of MDPs was
embedded. It explores both common and divergent dimensions of the field
and the ways in which local MDP practices were organized by and in re-
lation to other programs and institutions. These MDPs were attempting to
respond to issues of poverty and economic stagnation characteristic of the
new economy. Most programs helped small-scale enterprises; some also
assisted larger businesses that might create jobs in economically depressed
areas. The fifty programs traced their roots to a combination of southern
hemisphere microenterprise development, welfare, and economic development programs. Indeed, some began as components of economic development programs and CDBs. Many were independent nonprofits, but even
some of those began as federally funded welfare-to-work demonstration
projects. The plurality of influences facilitated the development of diverse
MDP models and gave practitioners room to mix models and experiment
with innovations.

Practitioners often described a tension that arose as they tried to help
marginalized groups succeed in the new economy and still operate

sustainable, cost-effective programs. Assisting disadvantaged clients entailed more extensive training and assistance than that associated with lower-risk borrowers. These services were costly and most funding sources were more interested in providing monies for lending than for operational expenses and programming.

Practitioners in the fifty programs employed a variety of strategies to respond to this tension. They stratified services and partnered with other providers to reduce the costs and risks of lending to the poor. Some attenuated the autonomy of peer-lending groups, and some developed profiles to select only the best of high-risk clients. In either case, despite the publicity surrounding lending, most MDP clients never received loans. Some practitioners decided that MDPs were not appropriate for the poor, and scaled-up their clients with a redefined mission of assisting the credit deprived rather than the poor. Most practitioners aimed for a businesslike image that distanced their programs from what they saw as a social work mentality.

Even as they drifted from the common goals that initially had characterized the MDP movement, most programs were still different from traditional banks. And most continued to assist businesses owned by or employing members of disadvantaged groups. Although some practitioners embraced a market model, a few tried to challenge it by defining their program's success in qualitative human development rather than quantitative business output terms. In either case, this extra-local new privatization trend was part of the terrain that practitioners had to negotiate.

This chapter has presented a sample of fifty U.S. MDPs. Chapters 4 and 5 trace the emergence, implementation, and institutionalization of one MDP, the ME program, over time. This case study elaborates the interactions among staff, clients, and extra-local funding sources that give further life to MDP practice.

APPENDIX

Example of a Place-Based Program

The Community Development Program (CDP, #49) is an example of a place-based economic development program from our sample. Founded in 1994, it was set up as a limited liability corporation and funded by state grants, foundation support, and investments from private banks. CDP targeted fifty-three investment communities in its state. These were areas that the state deemed economically disadvantaged, and some of those communities contained enterprise zones. CDP made individual loans ranging from $5,000 to $500,000. The applicants for the program must have been rejected by a bank or able to obtain only a portion of their funding from a traditional lender. In order to receive a loan from CDP, clients' business plans were assessed for their potential to create jobs in the target community. CDP offered technical assistance to borrowers in the form of management support services to enhance business capacity. It did not require business training or collateral to qualify for lending. A lending committee evaluated each loan application, ran a credit check on the applicant, and reviewed the business plan to judge its feasibility and likely impact on community job creation.

Example of a Peer Program

The Southern Entrepreneur Group (SEG, #7) is an example of a peer-lending MDP from our sample. SEG served a rural area in the southern United States. It offered both peer and individual lending and had a special program for welfare clients. Its goals included promoting client networking and self-sufficiency and providing alternatives to welfare and business training. Target clientele included women, minorities, and dislocated workers. Participants who entered the peer-lending component of SEG were required to complete a seven-week training program prior to borrowing. The program also offered a twelve-week training program designed for clients who were on welfare. Graduates of both training sessions were eligible to join borrower circles of five to eight people. Peer-lending amounts fell between $150 to $5,000, and lending decisions were made by circle members. Individual loans were larger than peer loans on average and did not require training as a prerequisite. These loans were approved by committee. SEG operations were funded by local private foundations. Loan funds were provided by an economic development bank and the SBA. SEG loaned primarily to ongoing businesses; only 18 percent of their loans were made to start-ups. At the time of our study, SEG had twenty-four groups and had disbursed 137 loans (sixty individual and seventy-seven peer loans) that totaled over $600,000.

Example of an Individualized Program

The Midwestern Self-Employment Program (MSE, #14) is an example of an individualized MDP from our sample. Located in a large midwestern urban area, this program was initiated in 1990 as part of a federal demonstration program designed to help AFDC clients transition off welfare and into self-employment (see chap. 2). The primary goals of MSE included poverty alleviation, providing access to credit, and promoting self-suffi-ciency. The program's literature described its commitment to developing entrepreneurs: "Entrepreneurship and business development is a viable strategy for addressing the alleviation of poverty, and creating a climate of self-sufficiency, ownership, and asset accumulation." MSE provided the most intensive training programs in our sample—an eleven-week class that met for five hours per day, three days per week. MSE also provided business and personal support services (e.g., counseling and transporta-tion to classes). The program was primarily funded by city and state sources, but MSE also partnered with banks, state agencies, a local uni-versity, and foundations. Loans were made directly by MSE and ranged from $500 to $10,000. All loans were approved by a lending committee. At the time of the interview, in its fifth year of operation, MSE had grad-uated 325 of the 455 people who entered its training courses and had ex-tended twenty-three loans totaling over $54,000.

□
□ ■
□ □ ■

CHAPTER 4

FORMING A MICROENTERPRISE PROGRAM:
CASE STUDY PART I

COAUTHORED WITH JULIE COWGILL

> We want to help women get off welfare and keep
> off welfare. Having their own businesses can allow them
> to feed themselves and their families. . . . A lot of immigrant
> women in our city already have small businesses and
> a small loan can help them grow those businesses.
> —ME PROGRAM FOUNDER

> Our borrowers' circles will give women the
> opportunity to come together and help each other. That is
> what I like so much about the Grameen model. The borrowers
> make the decisions; they work together. This is a small
> step toward community building.
> —ME PROGRAM FOUNDER

These statements summarize the guiding vision that was part of Micro-
Enterprise, Incorporated (ME), a peer-lending MDP in a large western
U.S. metropolitan area that we call Southville.[1] The images contained in
these statements and the image of women at home making tamales to sell
(noted earlier) were frequent sources of inspiration throughout the early
ME planning sessions. Within the first year of operations, however, a different, more complicated reality emerged. It was a source of concern to
many working in this MDP as staff or volunteers that some of the very
people they most wanted to assist were not being well served by the program. The life circumstances of clients made it difficult for ME's narrowly
focused program and limited resources to foster successful businesses
among its disadvantaged clients. The gradual recognition of the gap between ME services and client needs led to a reassessment of the initial program objectives.

Consistent with an IE approach, our research began with the disjuncture between needs and services.[2] Through observations, interviews, and program records, we examined the experiences of volunteers, staff, and clients.[3] We compared ME program experiences with the issues identified in the national sample of 50 MDPs described in chapter 3 and traced the connections among national conditions, regional context, and the establishment of this local program. This ethnography reveals the ways in which microenterprise development must be coordinated with the demands of clients' lives and other social organizations and conditions. It also maps the ways in which changing social, economic, and political contexts provided both opportunities *and* contradictions for practitioners and clients. Thus, extra-local arrangements informed internal program dynamics and, hence, program practice.

This chapter describes the planning and formalization of the ME program. The first part details the context and planning; the second part describes the implementation of the ME program including start-up, training and lending, and conflicts between staff and clients during the first year of operation.

CONTEXT AND PLANNING

ME was founded in 1993 by a small group of women who had had lengthy histories as volunteers and activists in state and local civic affairs. As noted in the introduction, several of the founders had been involved in campaigns to fight world hunger and heard about microenterprise development at a 1992 hunger conference. The director of a west coast microenterprise program made a presentation at that conference. She argued that hunger could only be stopped when individuals were given the means by which to support themselves, and she identified microenterprise training and credit as a means for women to "lift themselves out of poverty." This speech was a part of the publicity campaign surrounding the Freedom from Want Act (see chap. 2).

After the conference, several Southville women activists formed a task force that eventually established the ME program. Some task force members visited the Grameen Bank and SEWA programs described in chapter 1. Task-force membership included a blend of professional and volunteer community activists from local social service agencies, local businesses, and universities, in addition to some grassroots community activists. This wide representation facilitated information gathering and support from a variety of community agencies and groups. Gradually, a steering committee was formed to spearhead the formation of a new MDP. This committee consisted of mostly white, upper-middle-class women; some were employed professionals and others worked as community volunteers. There were few women of color in the group, and only one committee member had life experiences that in any way resembled those of the program's initial target group (she had started out poor and operated a fledgling microenterprise). But the committee did have many direct and indirect connections to elite local and state business leaders and political officials; these proved invaluable in the mobilization of the political and business sectors to fund program start-up and later expansion.

Planners envisioned a program to assist poor and low-income women to develop microenterprises. Images of poor, immigrant women running small, often informal businesses to feed their families were invoked throughout the planning process. These discussions exemplified the ways in which the ideal ME client was gendered, class-specific, and racialized. Yet most committee members had little direct experience working with poor populations. One member said, "I have never actually *known* any poor people, but I have spoken with a lot of people who have worked with the poor" (Kate). Consequently, discussions often took on an idealized and overly optimistic view of how basic business training and very small loans might "change the lives of poor women." Planners hoped that the program would exert a lasting effect through borrowers' circles that encouraged clients to form networks and help one another. These early planning discussions frequently referenced stories from SEWA, the Grameen Bank, and other southern hemisphere programs.

Needs Assessment for an MDP

The steering committee formed a subcommittee to conduct a multiphase needs assessment to inform the program design. The first part of the study entailed an examination of the local economic context to see whether conditions suggested the need for an MDP. As noted in the introduction, national concerns about underemployment, welfare reform, and women's increasing involvement in the paid labor force were salient to many in the Southville area. Despite a reported boom economy, the state in which Southville was located suffered from an overrepresentation of low-wage employment opportunities. Its average income levels fell below national averages, and its per capita income was 86 percent of the national average. The average rate of income was also growing more slowly than the national average, and Southville reported a relatively high cost of living when compared with other large U.S. metropolitan areas. Eleven percent of the state's families lived below the poverty level, and 32 percent of those families were female-headed. Sixty percent of those who used public assistance were women. Moreover, the area's large tourism and service industries relied on a steady flow of immigration from Mexico and other Central American countries. Women of color accounted for 46 percent of the total unemployment rate for the state.

In the absence of large-scale high-paying employment opportunities in core business sectors, self-employment was a frequent method for easing the economic insecurity experienced by many Southville citizens. Subcontracting was a common form of self-employment that was popular with employers who desired the flexibility that was so integral to the new economy. The Southville region was often rated by national business magazines as an area highly supportive of self-employment ventures, especially home-based business. The state legislature was a conservative Republican stronghold that was pro-business, anti-union, and generally opposed to welfare programs. Given this context, it was not surprising that the proposal for a Southville MDP attracted the enthusiasm of business, government, social service, and volunteer groups.

The second part of the needs-assessment study entailed the compilation of a list and description of all existing small-business training and lending services in Southville. This analysis revealed that there was little small-business training in the area. Furthermore, basic training in business start-up and business loans below $10,000 were virtually nonexistent.

Third, a small sample of U.S. MDP providers and local social service agencies was contacted for information about their programs. Five of the ten MDP practitioners responded to the study. These practitioners described their clients as predominantly women with children, especially women of color living on low incomes at or near the poverty line. They recommended that any new lending program develop a clear target population and associate with well-known agencies to boost client trust. Practitioners warned that (1) working with start-up businesses would reduce program success rates, and (2) tensions would arise in managing borrower's circles with mixed-gender and mixed-race membership.[4]

Fourth, a systematic sample of 25 local social service providers for the poor suggested that there was an unmet need for microenterprise training and lending in the Southville area.[5] In their recommendations, respondents frequently referenced the economic climate of Southville. They suggested that the MDP target Southville County poor and low-income people, especially women and minorities, for training and lending amounts of approximately $5,000. Respondents perceived that low-income women who were aspiring entrepreneurs were underserved by existing small-business lending and training programs. They believed that most clients for a microenterprise program would be women located in service, craft, and food enterprises and, to a much lesser extent, in nontraditional construction and plumbing enterprises. One respondent who worked with a training program for women in traditionally male blue-collar occupations warned: "You need to network with some of the programs for women in plumbing and construction. Those are the kinds of businesses that can make a living for women. The kinds of businesses in your traditionally female industries, you know, cake baking, childcare, crafts, do not make enough money to keep a woman's family going" (Eva).

Respondents recommended that the program provide basic business skills and facilitate networking and mentoring groups. More than one-half of the respondents recommended that the training be offered in both English and Spanish, be sensitive to cultural differences, and foster the personal growth of clients. Three respondents suggested that planners identify how the program can work effectively with informal businesses run by immigrants. A respondent from an immigrant advocacy organization said: "You're going to need to decide if you will work with undocumented immigrants or just the informal businesses of citizens. A lot of poor people operate businesses on the side and 'under the table.' They don't report their earnings. If they went 'legit,' they would have little money left over from the business after taxes, and their business is too sporadic anyway. So, you have to decide if you are going to serve this group. . . . There is a need for you to serve them . . . but you need to decide how you are going to approach that, justify it to your funders and so forth" (David).

Some respondents urged that microenterprise program planners adopt a holistic approach to aiding poor entrepreneurs. The approach and programming that they suggested were similar to some of the more comprehensive southern MDPs. Three respondents argued that the microenterprise program should develop collective marketing and advocacy strategies for clients. In order to accomplish this aim, they suggested partnering with other community groups. A respondent from an organization that served the American Indian community stressed the importance of sensitivity to cultural differences among potential clients and to the personal and spiritual growth dimensions as well as the profit margin aspects of the enterprises: "A lot of our people here feel uncomfortable with marketing their crafts. They see their craftwork as a way to preserve their culture, their heritage. But if a microenterprise program could be sensitive to their concerns and help develop some collective marketing strategies that helped to, yes, *sell* the crafts, and *also to educate* the buyers about the culture associated with the crafts, well, that would help earn an income for Indian peoples, but not go against their culture by forcing them to do individualized marketing" (Agnes).

As another example of a holistic perspective, four respondents argued that training and technical assistance could only be effective if the program also provided links to child care and transportation for low-income clients. As one put it: "Any program of this kind, if it really wants to serve a low income clientele has to confront the issues of childcare, especially for a *women's* business training program. Transportation is also a major barrier. The program should network with other agencies to provide such assistance. Otherwise, many poor clients will not be able to complete the program you propose" (Mae).

Designing the Microenterprise, Incorporated, Program

With the results of the needs-assessment study in hand, the steering committee members contacted local businesses and requested donations to begin the program. The funds raised were sufficient to hire a part-time staff member who developed additional funding proposals to start the program. In 1993, the program incorporated as a nonprofit tax-exempt organization. The board members viewed nonprofit status to be an essential strategy for gaining legitimacy within the community and for garnering contributions from businesses and foundations.

A board of directors was formed and began the tasks of designing the program and seeking additional funding to begin operations. Board members networked with local businesses and social service practitioners and attended the national AEO meetings to interact with other MDP providers. The program founders sought to have the board represent their community in terms of demographic characteristics and areas of interest or expertise. The board included workers from social service agencies, employees of local banks, officers from large local businesses, university faculty, and former clients of social service programs assisting low-income women. The first board was approximately 80 percent white and 70 percent women. However, the composition of the board changed frequently as some members left due to changing career demands and new members were added. Board members were also added from businesses that made significant donations to the program; several corporations required board representation when making large donations.

Initial discussions by the steering committee and later by the new board of directors took the advice of MDP practitioners and local community service providers seriously. The group identified poor and very-low-income inner-city women, especially women of color, as their target population. They also planned to include immigrants and former welfare recipients. Board leaders explored the possibilities of obtaining waivers so that, for a specified business start-up time period, women on welfare would be permitted to accumulate small levels of business assets without losing their benefits. One board member described the rationale for targeting women: "We decided to target women because they are the ones who are overburdened by child care and housework responsibilities. These responsibilities make it hard for them to work in jobs outside the home. They need to be able to work out of their homes and on flexible schedules" (Lisa).

Early in the planning process, the board decided that the MDP would use a peer-lending model similar to that of the Grameen Bank and the U.S. program featured at the hunger conference (as discussed earlier). A small contingent of planners and board members envisioned the adoption of the Grameen-style peer-lending model as an avenue for encouraging collective support and community organization among poor women. Two board members emphasized the image of borrowers' circles as a means for building networks and cooperative relationships among poor women in business. A steering committee leader and future board member spoke about prospects for borrowers' circles to form networks for marketing their products (e.g., group buying networks) or for further involvement in civic affairs: "I believe that this program should build solidarity among poor women running small businesses. . . . They may decide to form collective markets or to organize their communities . . . somehow to work together to improve their lives. The borrowers' circles are the key to doing that" (Lisa). The board members hoped that such involvements would lead to networking with other child-care and transportation support service providers to assist women-owned businesses.

Early Alterations in the Program Plan

Throughout the planning process, several board members solicited corporate and community donations and helped the paid staff member to prepare proposals soliciting government and foundation funding. They also sought feedback from other MDPs through AEO. They hired a consultant from an existing microenterprise program—the MDP director who had spoken at the 1992 hunger conference. Conversations with the consultant as well as with numerous prospective donors gave rise to several proposed alterations in the program plan.

First, advisors encouraged planners to narrow the program focus to make it more manageable and to increase the targeted income level for client eligibility. Program funders and, later, the majority of board members argued that it was important to avoid a holistic approach at first and to narrowly limit the program to business training and lending. One board member said: "It would be nice if we could offer all these services, childcare and transportation, but we can't. They will take up too many resources. We simply have to focus our energies in a manageable direction" (Teri). Discussions with other MDP practitioners further reinforced the idea that programs more narrowly focused on self-employment were easier to operate and raise funds for, especially in the early program stages (also see Freedman 2000). This advice was consistent with the U.S. practitioners' emphasis at the Going Forward conference described in chapter 2 (Coyle et al. 1994).

Second, potential donors strongly suggested that the word *women* be deleted from the proposed program name. Initially, the program's name included the words *women* and *network*. Drawing on the discourse of reverse discrimination that became popular in the 1980s, donors argued that having the word *women* in the name implied that the program would discriminate against men. After several donors made such comments, the board held a contentious debate, and gave the program a gender-neutral name.

During the debate, all board members favored including men clients in the program, but a sizable minority (30–40 percent) wanted to keep the word *women* in the program name. "Those supporting the name change argued that the new name was more descriptive of what the program did and that it was more inclusive of men. A board member said, "We can still make it clear in our program description that we are *especially* targeting women, but at least the new name does not suggest we actually want to *exclude* men. And, to secure funding, we need to make the name change" (Kate).

Another board member argued for the name change by asserting that the name was not so important. She believed that the very structure of the program would discourage middle-class men from participating: "There is this fear that white, middle class men will take over the program. That is not going to happen. The white, middle class men will *naturally* exclude themselves, because men don't want to ask for help, and they will not agree to be in the borrowers' circles. They will get money for their businesses in other ways" (Abby). This member described how borrowers' circles would be seen by men as less appealing because they have other alternatives for credit and do not feel the same need for support from fellow clients that women do.

Several board members argued that it was important to preserve the original name so that women would be encouraged to apply to the program. This group feared that, given the disadvantages women face in most business-lending programs, many women might be lost without overt targeting. A board member who worked as a social service provider that targeted women in the area said: "We need a program name that tells women that they are welcome, that they will be comfortable" (Sara).

Some board members also opposed the change because they did not want to drop the word *network* from the program name. They were concerned that the acronym of the new name contradicted the cooperative elements of the program. One board member who had a strong background in grassroots activism suggested, "If we change the name as proposed, our new acronym suggests a highly individualistic approach. It undermines the tone of cooperation that our program is going to require. It implies that clients are just in it for themselves" (Tina). The board ultimately voted to change the name, but agreed that the new acronym would not be used in the program literature. This caveat was quickly disregarded in practice, however. For example, the first program newsletter featured the disputed acronym in its title.

A third proposed change was to alter the program's target population. Funders and consultants warned of the difficulties associated with a focus on very poor women, especially current and former AFDC recipients. The board discussed the issue and agreed that the initial focus should be directed more toward the "working poor" who met HUD low-income guidelines shown in table 4.1. These criteria were significantly higher than the U.S. poverty level income designations shown in table 4.2.

Despite the adoption of the higher HUD income guidelines, the ME board leadership reasserted its desire to maintain a dedicated pool of

TABLE 4.1

HUD low-income figures for 1995 for ME's county

Family size	Gross Annual Household Income (dollars)
1	23,300
2	26,600
3	29,950
4	33,300
5	35,950
6	38,600

Source: *U.S. Department of Housing and Urban Development, http://www.huduser.org/datasets/il/fmrold/fy95s8.doc.*

TABLE 4.2
Federal poverty level figures for 1995

Family size	Gross Annual Household Income (dollars)
1	7,763
2	9,933
3	12,158
4	15,569
5	18,408
6	20,804

Source: *U.S. Bureau of the Census, Current Population Survey,*
http://www.census.gov/hhes/poverty/threshld/thresh95.html.

funds for serving very poor women and recent welfare recipients. One board member continued to work diligently (although without success) to obtain state waiver provisions that would increase the allowed assets for welfare recipients starting their own businesses.

Securing Operations Funds

Early in 1994, ME applied for a CDBG from the city of Southville. The grant proposal requested $100,000 to provide the funds to hire an executive director and a program manager and to begin the training program. The proposal was submitted under the economic development category of the CDBG program. The CDBG officials disqualified microenterprise development for that category and shifted ME's proposal to the social service category. This second category had a cap of $50,000 per grant and included over 50 other applications, whereas the economic development category had no cap and received far fewer proposals. Pursuant to this reclassification, ME's proposal was denied. As a result, the officers from ME's board of directors mobilized community supporters and met with CDBG officials to appeal the decision and request reconsideration under the economic development category. They obtained advice on their appeal from MDP practitioners in other areas of the country who had experienced similar barriers with CDBG funding. Several board members also attended the city hearing on ME's appeal. The appeal was successful, and in 1994 ME obtained CDBG economic development funding to start its operations.[6] This grant also served to define the geographical target area for the grant—a section of Southville with a heavy concentration of poverty-level and low-income households and a high concentration of African American and Latino/a residents.

Securing the grant meant that ME had sufficient funding to hire two full-time staff members: an executive director and a program manager. The executive director had extensive managerial experience working in programs for poor women, particularly in the realm of welfare-to-work programs. The program manager was a recent college graduate with a family background in nonprofit work and a study focus on Latin American economic development issues. She also was fluent in Spanish. Both staff members were white, college-educated women from middle-class backgrounds.

Once operation monies had been obtained from the CDBG, a line of credit was secured from a local CDB for making loans to clients. The bank was uncomfortable with the peer-lending model proposed by the ME program, so it demanded that 100 percent of the loans be guaranteed. Again, ME board members drew on contacts with local elites and successfully lobbied the state to guarantee the loans for the early program stages.

Late in 1994, ME staff and board members held client-recruitment orientations in the targeted area. Throughout these early stages, board members were active in all aspects of the program's development and implementation—client recruitment, training, publicity. Members mobilized contacts within the community to gain the necessary resources and guarantees for each new phase of program implementation. Even before the program opened, several members arranged publicity in local newspapers and on radio and television stations. Similar to experiences in other MDPs (described in chap. 3), the day-to-day involvement of ME board members and other community volunteers diminished with program maturity and the hiring of additional staff.[7]

Both the national and local contexts were inextricably linked to the formation of the ME program—economic recession and high unemployment, the conservative antiwelfare national and local milieu, the spillover of the hunger movement campaign to MDPs, connections to local agencies, links to government and business elites for funding support, and MDP field consultations. The start-up of the ME program elaborates these links by describing how the ME leaders altered their goals in response to community and funder expectations.

PROGRAM IMPLEMENTATION

In many ways, the ME program was planned as a traditional formal organization. Yet the nascency and inventiveness of the MDP field, a source of its attraction for funders, provided ME founders with the room for innovation in the program. The initial ME program was a kind of organizational hybrid that included a traditional hierarchical and bureaucratic management and training structure but also participatory peer lending and women's advocacy components.

ME staff and board negotiated a contract with a Small Business Development Center (SBDC) at a local community college to develop training materials and teach the client-training sessions. Board members decided that ME would be a training-led program. In other words, both new and experienced entrepreneurs would be required to complete a course of training prior to receiving a loan from the program. ME staff worked with the teachers at the SBDC to develop a training package relevant for ME's targeted clientele. The planned training consisted of a four-week Starting Your Business Workshop for clients who were starting a new business. After graduation from the beginning course, start-up clients would join with clients who had been in business for six months or more and take a ten-week Business Plan Workshop.

Upon graduation from the second workshop, clients would be eligible to form borrowers' circles of five people each. The circles would be formed by clients during the last days of their training session. They would elect officers, write by-laws, and review one another's business plans and loan applications. Pending the approval of others in their circle, members would receive their first loans. If a member defaulted, the other members of that circle would not be allowed to borrow for a six-month period.

By the end of 1994, the ME staff and board members were enrolling the first class of clients. ME held public orientations and visited church and grassroots community leaders in the target area to get the word out. Although the board postponed offering classes in Spanish until sufficient funds were raised, the chair of the ME board of directors developed a Spanish version of the client recruitment script and spoke on several Southville Spanish-language radio stations to publicize the program to Southville Latino/as. These efforts were successful in recruiting clients for the program.

Training Sessions

ME's training workshops began in early 1995. Forty-one clients joined the first ME training class, the four-week Starting Your Business Workshop. The fee for this course was $15. It covered basic business skills and focused on helping individuals evaluate their suitability for self-employment and exploring the feasibility of their business ideas. Individuals who missed more than one class or who were late on more than one occasion were prohibited from borrowing in later program stages.

When the four-week workshop ended, the ten-week Business Plan Workshop began. More than 80 percent of the first four-week class joined the ten-week class. The first ten-week class included 33 graduates of the first workshop and seven other clients who had been in business for at least six months, for a total enrollment of 40 students. Individuals who missed more than two classes of this course or who were late on more than two occasions were prohibited from borrowing in later program stages. The fee for this workshop was $45.

Class members were eligible for additional one-on-one counseling from SBDC business counselors. The four-week-class members were eligible for two hours of individual counseling and the ten-week-class members were eligible for six hours of counseling. Consultations were geared toward helping the clients complete a business plan by the end of the ten-week workshop.

Those attending training sessions reflected ME's original target population—poor and low-income women and minorities. The demographic characteristics of the first ME training sessions are described in table 4.3. These data suggest that the typical ME client in this first cohort was a woman of color who had a high school education or less, had a household income that met the HUD low-income standards (see table 4.1), and had not yet started a business. The median household income was approximately $13,000 for the four-week class, and $16,000 for the ten-week class. About one-third had gross household incomes at the poverty level for their family size, and 12 percent ($n = 5$) of the four-week and eight percent ($n = 3$) of the ten-week class received one or some combination of the following public assistance, food stamps, or AFDC at the time of their entry into the program. Five percent ($n = 2$) received state disability. Roughly 40 percent of this class consisted of single parents. A survey of clients from both the four- and ten-week classes in the first cohort revealed that 87 percent were the heads of their households and 68 percent were employed at the time of training. Approximately 35 percent of the first cohort of clients had had at least some college. Although women made up the majority of the first training cohort, males made up a significant portion, 40 percent, of the group. This composition was consistent with the changes made in ME design to be more welcoming to male clients.

Table 4.4 provides information from the survey about the type of businesses planned by this first client group. In line with other studies of MDP clients (e.g., Charles Stewart Mott Foundation 1990; Ehlers and Main 1998; Servon and Bates 1998; Clark et al. 1999), most ME businesses

TABLE 4.3

Demographics for four- and ten-week training classes, 1995[a]

Characteristic	Four-week, $n = 41$		Ten-week, $n = 40$	
	Number	Percentage	Number	Percentage
Sex				
Male	16	39	16	40
Female	25	61	24	60
Race/ethnicity				
African-American	19	46	22	55
White	5	12	4	10
Native American	3	7	2	5
Hispanic/Latino/a	12	29	10	25
Mixed race	2	5	2	5
Highest educational attainment				
High school or less	17	41	15	38
Vocational training	9	22	11	28
Some college or AA degree	7	17	6	15
Bachelor's degree or above	8	20	8	20
Personal income year before				
$7,500 or less	8	20	8	20
$7,600–12,500	13	32	13	33
$12,600–23,000	14	34	15	38
$24,000 or more	3	7	3	8
Missing	3	7	1	3
Median personal income	$11,500		$12,000	
Average personal income	$12,516		$13,344	
Household income year before				
$10,000 or less	10	24	8	20
$10,100–15,000	10	24	10	25
$15,100–21,000	11	27	9	23
$21,100–35,000	7	17	9	23
$35,100 or more	2	5	2	5
Missing	1	2	2	5
Median household income	$13,200		$15,600	
Average household income	$17,328		$18,888	
Already in business?				
Yes	6	15	16	40
No	35	85	24	60
Single parent?				
Yes	15	37	17	43
No	26	63	23	58
Number of children living with client				
0	20	49	17	43
1–2	14	34	18	45
3 or more	7	17	5	13
Poverty, low income, and moderate income				
Meets federal poverty-level standards	14	34	10	25
Meets HUD low-income standards	23	56	25	63
Moderate income and above	3	7	3	8
Missing	1	2	2	5

[a]Due to rounding error, some percentages do not total 100.

TABLE 4.4

Type of businesses planned by the first client cohort
(four- and ten-week students combined survey, n = 38)

Business Type	Number	Percentage
Sales	9	24
Child care/assisted living	4	11
Travel/hospitality	4	11
Computer-focused (programming, desktop publishing)	4	11
Personal services (hair, housecleaning, shopping)	4	11
Other services	4	11
Sewing clothes and sales	3	8
Other small-scale production/manufacturing	3	8
Combination of several activities	3	8
	38	103[a]
Home-based business	24	63
Wanting to move outside the home	11	29

[a]*Due to rounding error percentage total exceeds 100.*

were small, labor-intensive ventures. The largest percentage fell in the sales category, followed by child care/assisted living, travel, computer, personal, and other service ventures.

Some individual examples from ME's first client training cohort illustrate the nature of these planned businesses. Carole was a Latina who had worked as a waitress, cook, and manager of small restaurants. After her former employer went out of business, she decided to open her own restaurant in Southville. Carmen worked in a factory and wanted to expand her own business making and selling children's clothing. Joey, an African American man, had always worked in food services and wanted to open a mobile vending business. Data from ME's first cohort also support claims that MDPs have special appeal to individuals in home-based businesses. Most (63 percent) planned to operate their businesses either within or based from their homes. For example, Betty, an African American woman who worked in child care, wanted to expand her own home-based child-care facility. She hoped to combine this paid enterprise with caring for her own small children. The members of the classes had experienced a variety of problems common among poor and low income individuals in the new economy: unemployment, underemployment, disability and other health issues, family-care conflicts, transportation difficulties, and legal problems. Observations of and interviews with the students revealed many commonalities among the participants, but there were also interesting variations in interactions, benefits, and evaluations of ME training across gender, race, ethnicity, and class groups. For example, an

African American woman who had worked at a variety of low-income service jobs and as a salesperson for Tupperware-type companies said, "Well, I find that the jobs here in [this state] take your self-esteem away from you in terms of pay as well as policy. As a counselor of mine once said: 'I'm 56 years old, and after a while you get tired of working for people that are stupider than yourself.' Well, that is how *I* feel" (Marge).

The classes were well attended and positively evaluated despite some rough spots in early curriculum design and administration by the SBDC that offered them. Despite positive evaluations by the first cohort of clients, there were dilemmas surrounding training and lending. Such difficulties are common when any program begins operation (see also Jurik et al. 2000), and the implementation process invariably involves changes in design and objectives (Sabatier 1986; Wittrock and de Leon 1986). But in addition to this, the passage of the first client cohort through the ME program also suggested a significant gap between the ME program design for successful businesses and the life circumstances of disadvantaged clients.

Despite these problems, clients developed a variety of strategies for accommodating conflicting program demands for self-reliance and competitiveness, on the one hand, and peer cooperation and support, on the other. Clients also challenged perceived program problems, unexpected changes in operations, and some staff interventions in circle matters. ME staff members were generally responsive to criticisms, endeavoring to clarify and improve program services as quickly as possible. But the staff members were simultaneously being pressured by the program lending source to more carefully scrutinize and oversee the circle approval process. Although the staff members resisted some of the bank's demands, they also feared the eventual withdrawal of future lending support and gradually developed strategies for exerting more control. The contradictions surrounding their experiences led to strategies that informed the operations of the maturing ME program. We examined the initial staff and client experiences in each program phase: training, borrowers' circles, lending, and repayment stages.

Client Evaluations of Training Quantitative course evaluations of ME's first training cohort were overwhelmingly positive.[8] More than 90 percent of the students in both the first four- and ten-week classes described training as satisfactory overall. Ninety percent of those surveyed in both classes described their interactions with instructors and counselors as positive. Clients described training as beneficial in several ways. It helped them gain business skills, evaluate their business concept, increase their confidence, and develop supportive relationships with other prospective entrepreneurs and counselors at the SBDC.

In interviews, class members were very positive about training, but more willing than in the quantitative evaluations to include criticisms or areas in need of improvement for the training sessions. A typical positive comment by students was that courses in the first four-week sessions gave them reality checks for business ideas. Five class members either abandoned or altered their original business ideas. Even clients with business experience said that the ten-week workshop helped them enhance their skills and learn how to operate businesses more effectively. According to one member, the course helped her determine the "weak points that brought me down before" (Setera). Another participant reported that, prior to the training, she would indiscriminately withdraw money from her business. She explained how the classes improved her management skills and commitment to the business: "Now I know why my business has not been successful. Now, I won't draw a salary. I'll just put all the money back into the business" (Jane). Class members were especially positive about the individual counseling sessions. One commented, "They helped me with all of the legal and technical addresses and information that I would need. . . . That could have been overwhelming in a big city such as this. . . . They helped me with the rules and regulations that I needed too" (Marge).

There were gender differences in student perceptions of training needs and instructors. Women class members almost uniformly singled out one woman counselor as especially supportive and helpful in building their confidence. "She helped me feel good about myself. My self-esteem went way up . . . if you don't feel good about yourself, you're not going to succeed" (Carmen). Men students were less positive about this counselor. They described her supportiveness as "unnecessary and time consuming" because they believed that they already possessed the kind of confidence that she could provide. They expressed a desire for more critical feedback on their businesses and less time devoted to confidence building.

Most class members were positive about the relationships they formed with other students in the workshops. Bonding was both shaped by and reflected in classroom seating arrangements. Those sitting in close proximity during classes tended to interact more, and later, to select each other for their borrowers' circles. A respondent described the camaraderie that she experienced and related how she picked other members of her circle: "I paired off with Carole right away and with [looked at Maria, another class member] because they could help my business and I could help theirs" (Carmen). As ME planning consultants had warned, client networks tended to reflect (consciously or unconsciously) the racial and gender tensions in the larger community. Observations revealed that African American and Latino/as associated most with others of the same race or ethnic group. For example, Carole, Maria, and Carmen were Latinas and shared similar views about the meaning of business professionalism.

Some clients were unable to forge strong bonds. White clients appeared to have more difficulty than racial minority clients in forming close links with classmates. Slightly less than one-third of all clients and the majority of white respondents reported on the surveys that they "did not have time" to interact and form bonds with classmates.

Problems with Training Sessions Staff, instructors, and clients identified several issues with both the quality and completeness of training-course materials. The quality of teaching and counseling was uneven across instructors. There were also class- and gender-related issues that hampered student attendance, grasp of class information, and satisfaction with class content. A better understanding of these problems can be gained by considering their connection to issues of class, gender, and race relations—issues that went beyond the ME organization. Microenterprise development was embedded in this larger social context, which sometimes gave rise to conflicting obligations and tensions.

In part, the problems with instructor commitment stemmed from significant federal budget cuts to SBDCs just before classes began. The cuts strained resources and burdened instructors and counselors with additional and unexpected responsibilities that were unrelated to ME's workshops. The supervisor of the instructors was overloaded with other responsibilities, and did not exercise the quality control over course content and delivery that had been initially promised. Some instructors were distracted and ill-prepared. One counselor missed several appointments with ME class members and was generally described by clients as "lacking commitment" during counseling sessions. A student suggested, "The counselors should be as committed as the client . . . and they should listen to what the client wants and help them get there. My counselor did not keep her appointments and I would wait for 20 or 30 minutes or she would cancel" (Naomi).

Instructors adopted a traditional orientation to business training that was ostensibly "neutral" and not focused on the gender, race, and class dynamics in business life (see Ehlers and Main 1998). Instructors and staff viewed it as a sign of respect to treat microenterprises as they would any other business venture—treating even small entrepreneurs as they might treat larger entrepreneurs. As a result, the courses were insufficiently tailored to the needs of very small businesses; some sessions focused on issues that related primarily to large businesses. Clients described such sessions as "irrelevant and boring."

At other times, despite their efforts to be race- and class-"neutral," trainers exhibited clear race- and class-laden assumptions that clients found offensive. One evening, a counselor was discussing a woman's business idea. The idea was to sell art that was produced in her neighborhood, a low-income community with a large concentration of African Americans. The counselor suggested that items the woman planned to sell would be more accurately described as "crafts." The client responded, "It is art. Art is more than just what white people sell up in Northland (richer area of town known for its art galleries) for hundreds and thousands of dollars" (Carole).

Unconscious racial bias was evident in the array of predominantly white and upper-middle-class speakers who were invited to ME workshops. Class members reported dissatisfaction with the guest speakers. They said that the topics were not well coordinated with the course subject matter and that speakers' social class and business size did not reflect the realities that characterized ME client business and life experiences. One client criticized a speaker who was a wealthy woman starting a business with financing from her ex-spouse: "She talked about how she and a friend went out and put flyers on a car in their *mink coats* when her business was starting out. How can I relate to that? At my level, I could take the coat, hock it, and that's my start-up capital" (Ben).

The speakers focused on individual achievement, financial success, and bootstrap capitalism—starting with little or no capital and building million-dollar businesses. In response to client requests for a speaker who was a person of color, instructors brought in a Latino man who described how he had started out poor, but become fabulously successful in a short time. A recurrent theme was that if an individual was "committed enough" and "willing to work very hard," he or she could have business success. ME staff and clients repeatedly requested speakers who would explain how to make businesses work, speakers who would impart skills. Yet the SBDC training staff continued to provide motivational speakers who imparted the ideology of the merits of self-help. Implicit in this storyline was that failing entrepreneurs lacked the necessary level of commitment.

Training staff also selected speakers whose businesses were at a level far beyond those of ME clients. One class member described the problem as follows: "The speakers need to identify with the group at large . . . we need speakers who have been in business three to five years, who could talk about the true nuts and bolts. I felt the people in business for 15 years or more didn't understand as well and have forgotten what it's like to start-up, to be a single woman starting a business with no savings" (Naomi).

It was especially significant, given the racial, ethnic, class, and gender composition of the students, that barriers of racism and sexism in business were never addressed by instructors or guest speakers. Neither the structural conditions that disadvantage small-scale entrepreneurs in the U.S. economy nor strategies for coping with structural challenges were included in ME training courses. For example, although instructors identified subcontracting and government procurement as a viable option for ME businesses, no discussion prepared clients for the competitive disadvantages faced by small firms or for the potential racial and gender discrimination that they might face in this bidding process.[9] As noted earlier, most ME clients were developing small, labor-intensive, home-based businesses. Considerable research suggests that such ventures lead to self-exploitation as the entrepreneurs and family members work long hours to survive (see Jurik 1998). For women, this schedule creates stress and conflict with other family responsibilities (see Christensen 1988). Previous research, including the national study in chapter 3, finds that most U.S. microenterprise training programs ignore structural barriers to client businesses and the difficulties of operating small businesses in the corporate-dominated global economy. Such discussions are typically viewed by both instructional and MDP staff as beyond the purview of business training (Ehlers and Main 1998). This view was shared by the SBDC instructors and by most ME staff and board members.

Some clients experienced difficulties comprehending the course material. Such problems were indicative of the challenge involved in offering self-employment training to disadvantaged individuals. The greatest problems of this sort were experienced by older women with lower levels of formal education. Some of these women suggested that the length of time for classes be expanded for those who felt "rusty in the education world." They were often hesitant to ask questions during classes because they felt that they were "behind" the progress of other students. ME resources were simply too limited to offer multiple training sessions for students with varying capabilities.

Another problem was the attrition rate for clients with limited resources. Clients who did not have access to dependable transportation were more often late or absent from class. One client (Marge) said that the area's poor public transportation forced her to spend several hours on buses, transferring several times, to attend meetings. For some, chronic health problems contributed to attrition or a slow rate of progress. One woman described how her health impacted her attendance despite her firm commitment to her business: "There were a few times that I came to that class and it was all I could do to sit there. A couple of times I wanted to sit there and scream because I was in so much pain. But . . . I didn't want to be dropped from class" (Setera).

Some women had problems locating dependable child care. One mother asked to bring her child to class one evening, but ME rules did not permit this. Although such problems might plague any group of students, poor and low-income clients are especially vulnerable to life problems that interfere with their work and/or training activities. During training sessions clients were advised to start small, perhaps to begin operations out of their homes. Discouraged by this advice, a homeless woman said, "How can I start a home-based business when I don't even have a home?" (Marcia). Low-income individuals targeted for MDP training often have inadequate resources to manage the problems of illness, housing, child care, and transportation in their lives. A client described Marcia's plight: "She lived in a shelter and was told by vocational rehab that she had to get a job. When she got a job, it was at night. . . . [S]he worked two weeks and got sick and has been sick ever since. . . . She uses a walker and I go over and check on her. She's known for two years that she's had breast cancer and couldn't have it treated since she had no money" (Jane). The experiences of ME clients reinforce other research regarding the inadequacy of basic business training without additional support and safety-net services for poor women (Ehlers and Main 1998).

Despite these problems, ME's training was generally well received by the clients in the first cohort. But, as the shift from training to lending approached, problems among clients and between clients and staff intensified. Such problems were, in part, a function of ME organizational dynamics, but these dynamics were informed by the larger social context and relations beyond ME.

Making the Transition from Training to Lending: The Circles

In the concluding weeks of the Business Plan Workshop, tensions developed over the upcoming lending process. Clients claimed that the staff had provided contradictory information about the transition from training to borrowers' circles. In some cases, clients actively resisted what they perceived as ambiguities and inconsistencies in program rules.

First, clients protested ME's rule that borrowers' circles must comprise individuals from the same gender group.[10] During the ten-week workshop, one man challenged ME's gender segregation rule as "sexist." He argued that men and women would be dealing with one another in business, and should be interacting in the peer lending circles as well. Other men agreed: "I didn't like the sexist rule that they had about only men or women in a circle. To be honest, Ben wasn't the only one who was offended" (Jim). Although some women supported same-gender circles, others agreed with the men. "I would listen to what people would say and where they were in their businesses. That was more important than the gender of the person. I could understand that gender problems could arise, but didn't consider that to be a problem" (Sonia).

A second source of tension surrounded the process of circle admission. Clients had not been informed that staff approval was necessary for admission to borrowers' circles; ME's rulebook specified that the completion of training and a business plan were the requirements for entry into the lending stage. Clients discovered that staff were *informally* screening businesses for their feasibility prior to permitting clients to join circles. In response, staff argued that the "rejected" clients had not fully completed their business plans or that their businesses had financing needs beyond ME's scope. Clients countered that ME staff and the SBDC trainers had promised to work with them to scale down or change businesses before the end of the ten-week session. One woman expressed her frustration that the staff had waited until the end of the course to inform her cohort that some businesses were not acceptable for lending: "Tell the people up front. Don't wait until eight weeks into the program and tell them this business is not acceptable. Tell them so they have time to adjust and think of something else" (Marge).

Throughout the transition period, ME staff met with clients, listened to grievances, and tried to resolve disputes in a satisfactory manner. In the case of the same-gender circles rule, the staff changed the rule to permit mixed-gender groups. In the conflict over circle screening, the staff relented in some cases and helped clients revise their business plan. In a few cases, staff stood firm, arguing that the businesses were not appropriate for the ME program (e.g., those involving pyramid schemes or selling Tupperware). The staff members promised clients that they would revise the rules to clarify that business plans would be screened for feasibility prior to circle admission. They also promised they would communicate problems earlier in future classes so that clients could modify their business plans in time to enter circles. Although clients were still angered by the unexpected screening, they described the staff as "responsive and flexible" in dealing with complaints. Despite the fairly successful resolution of problems through the ten-week class, greater tensions were yet to come. The lending process was fraught with conflicts between the staff and clients and among the clients themselves.

Lending Phase

This phase of the ME program began with the formation of four peer lending circles and ended with the distribution of the first loans. Immediately after the completion of the Business Plan Workshop, the ME staff held two meetings to assist with circle formation and introduce the clients to the newly hired circle facilitator. The facilitator's job was to attend weekly circle meetings, guide the circles to certification for lending, assist with the loan application and review process, and mediate any disputes among members. One-half the graduates of the first ten-week class joined borrowers' circles.

Prior to the loan application, circles were required to complete several tasks as part of their certification for lending. These activities included electing officers, developing by-laws, sharing life stories, naming their circle, and opening a group savings account. ME required that members elect three officers: a president to conduct circle meetings, a secretary to record minutes, and a treasurer, who along with a ME staff member controlled the mandatory loan loss reserve fund.

After certification, the circles reviewed one another's business plans, loan applications, and repayment capabilities. The circles determined the loan amounts and the order in which loans would be made to members. ME's distribution sequence called for two people in each circle to receive the first loans. After each had made two bi-weekly payments, two additional members of the circle could receive loans. The final member of the circle would receive a loan after the second group of borrowers had each made two payments. Each circle member was eligible for first loans of up to $1,500 with up to eighteen months to repay. The interest rate on the loans was set at 2 percent above the market rate. Each borrower was required to contribute 5 percent of his or her loan to the loan loss reserve fund, or circle savings account. During the repayment phase, circle members would have the discretion to use this account to cover a missing payment or to leave a loan in default. If these funds were insufficient to cover a loss, circle members would be ineligible for new loans for six months.

Client Evaluations of Circle Experiences Observations of circle meetings revealed both the strengths and weaknesses of the peer-lending framework. Clients gained much from circle participation, but there were also tensions and struggles among clients and between clients and staff. Some circle problems were clearly due to ME's early stage of development, others were associated with the personality of the circle facilitator, and still others were the outcome of personality conflicts among members. In addition, there were less individualized and transitory problems. Social science research describes the highly individualistic nature of U.S. culture (see Merry 1982; Quadagno 1999) and the resulting difficulty in adapting collectively oriented peer-lending models for use in the United States (see Balkin 1989; Taub 1998). Many clients react unfavorably to group participation requirements (Coyle et al. 1994; see chaps. 2 and 3). The peer-lending model entails fundamental contradictions: it simultaneously calls for the virtues of entrepreneurial individualism and competitiveness, on the one hand, and for group cohesiveness on the other. Borrowers' circles were expected to play the often contradictory functions of support groups, evaluators, and collection agents.

Despite this, most clients in the first ME cohort described collegial relationships with other circle members. A woman with a history of self-employment perceived that her circles members shared her commitment to "business professionalism." She said, "We have good chemistry and there is interest in everyone's plans. The circle tries to get together for coffee after the meeting and I hope we get a chance to watch everyone become successful. It would be a thrill" (Sonia). Circle members offered support for one another's businesses. In one circle, a member needed some mailing labels on short notice. Other circle members helped her meet the deadline. Another group spent part of a circle meeting helping a member devise a solution to an employee problem. Members shared marketing and bookkeeping advice and sometimes traded services.

The most positive evaluations came from clients who felt that they had had considerable choice in selecting compatible circle members. One member who was part of a circle that instantly bonded during training classes said, "It was easy for my circle. . . . I really clicked with the others . . . at the outset, we knew what we wanted and were committed. . . . It would be harder if four people were from [different classes]. . . . I would have felt like an outsider" (Naomi).

Members were less likely to view circles positively when they felt that they had had little choice in the selection of other circle members. One client believed that he had not been properly informed about ME's borrowers' circle process before joining a group. He explained, "There was no choosing. On the day that the circles were being formed, I came in about 45 minutes late and most of the circles were formed. I was the odd man out. I wound up being in that group, but I would not have chosen those particular individuals . . . knowing what was being expected of the groups" (Rashad).

Relationships within circles also reflected gender, race, ethnicity, and class tensions in the larger society. To some clients, it was important to find other people who could relate to their racial, ethnic, or class background. The three Latina members mentioned earlier, who had forged a bond during training, also selected one another as circle members. Their connection was rooted in a common cultural background and a shared definition of business professionalism. Two African American women in the circle also formed a connection with one another. In another circle, four African American women developed bonds with one another. In this circle, shared cultural background converged with a desire to resist what members perceived as excessive organizational control. The women in this circle, all from working poor backgrounds, eschewed the middle-class standards of professionalism adopted by the circle of Latinas just mentioned. One commented, "In the end, we feel that we really were fortunate because we got people that we felt comfortable with and that damn near walked the same streets, had the same desires, same goals and had integrity. . . . I suppose that [others in the workshops] thought they were better than us, outclassed us, different things of that nature" (Marge). In contrast, strong cross-racial bonds between Latina and African American clients were elusive.

Gender relations also infused circle relationships and structure. As noted, the staff withdrew the circle gender-segregation rule at the clients' request. It was not surprising, given predominant societal views about gender and group leadership functions (see Williams 1995), that in the circle elections that followed the men were elected president in three out of the four mixed-gender circles and the women performed the secretarial duties in all four circles. One woman refused to serve as the circle secretary when the male president assigned her the role: "I just don't like being a secretary. Ben said, 'Not even for the sake of the group?' I said, 'Hey, wait a minute, we got to change that, don't make me the fall guy' " (Naomi). The group accepted her decision but quickly elected another woman to serve as circle secretary.

Tensions among Circle Members The circles faced a variety of other problems including personality conflicts and more fundamental tensions between the individualized and competitive demands of business culture and the cooperative demands of circle participation. Some clients resented having to participate in and trust the people in the circles to obtain loans. One client said: "I kind of didn't want to be in a circle with anybody. If you don't know these people, how are you going to trust them? How do you know they're going to do this? How do they know you're going to do it, too?" (Jane). Some individuals were afraid to discuss their business plans with circle members. They feared that others might steal their ideas. These findings parallel reports of practitioners in our national sample of peer programs and reflect the increasing individualization of the responsibility for one's well-being in the new economy (Rubin 1996; Quadagno 1999).

Personality conflicts and communication gaps caused problems within circles. Some circles had problematic relationships or poor communication from the start. But relationships in most circles improved as they progressed toward lending stages. One strategy was to meet separately and develop relationships beyond the circles. Some circles pulled together to resist organizational policies or because of a problematic circle facilitator. One member said, "We never really got to learn each other until . . . one Saturday, and we started to communicate. It's getting better; we call each other and chit-chat" (Setera).

Difficulties in building collective relationships were framed by the simultaneous demands for critical assessment and supportive functions. Circle supportive functions often conflicted with more instrumental business concerns in the peer review of loan applications. The ME staff emphasized that members must constructively critique one another's business plans. In an effort to maintain their group's sense of collective identity, the clients of all four circles generally shied away from offering extensive criticism of fellow circle members' plans. A few circle members argued that a more rigorous review was in order. "It helps to understand the whole lending process and helps you as a business person to make sound business decisions. It's easy to say they are a friend and give them money, but you need to know people on a business level" (Jane). Other members disagreed and felt they knew one another's businesses better than a banker. Some members were particularly critical of the pressures to adopt business jargon in the discussion of their enterprises. This objection was especially characteristic of members who came from poverty-level backgrounds. One individual said, "To us, management is hung up on big words and presentation . . . now to you, if you're hung up on big words that may not sound kosher, but to like-thinking people it's acceptable because we're communicating. We understand what we're saying to one another" (Marge).

In response to concerns about sharing full business plans, ME staff agreed to permit the members to present brief summaries of their plans for circle evaluation. Of course, this provision made the critical assessment of each loan application more difficult. Moreover, the ME staff had told members that once admitted to the circle stage they were virtually guaranteed a loan, thereby making the loan review process seem even more perfunctory.

Member reviews of fellow circle members' loan applications were overwhelmingly supportive and offered little critical feedback. They routinely approved the maximum size loan with little regard for the amount justified by the business plan. The clients emphasized maintaining circle interpersonal relationships during the lending decision process. One member said, "Basically our main objective is to be there and support each other . . . whenever the opportunity arises" (Alan). Another said, "I think we are looking at a lifetime thing. . . . I see that [circle] as a family" (Carmen).

Most members acknowledged that they used financial need as the chief criterion to determine the order of the lending (i.e., which members received the first two loans). Lending decisions were still difficult when the first two lending spots were competitive or when there was a disagreement over who had the greatest need. Sometimes, these dynamics were associated with gender, racial, or ethnic differences. For example, in one circle, two Latina members argued that a third Latina member should receive her loan first. The three had been very close since the formation of the circle. The members made arguments in favor of their position based on the woman's need and proven success of her business. An African American woman in the circle disagreed and argued that her own needs were just as great. The exchange left the Latina member feeling uncomfortable, even though she ultimately received the first loan: "I felt like there was this little war there. . . . It was even like a racist thing, us Mexicans against them. But anyway, it's all settled. It did make me uncomfortable though. . . . I like for us all to agree. Those things come up, we all don't think the same" (Carmen).

Many groups developed strategies for mediating or resolving such interpersonal conflicts. When the lending order became highly contentious, two circles discussed a lottery system to decide the order of loan dissemination. Some circles also had members who clearly sacrificed their immediate interests for others in their group: "There was concern about who would get the first loan of the three who were ready. I liked the idea of picking a number, it seemed fair. We had already looked at everything and no one seemed to have a greater need than anyone else. But, Jim said . . . [that] others had a more immediate need so he backed out, and it takes a unique individual to do that" (Naomi).

Circle members typically avoided criticism of one another's business plans to protect the fragile bonds that were forming within the circles.

There was considerable tension in starting a business and in negotiating the requirements of the ME program, and there were still other life stressors facing ME clients. To a significant degree, the circles provided many ME clients with a supportive bastion from the obstacles that lay ahead. Yet the absence of more critical assessments of business plans in the circles worried the ME staff. Throughout the borrowing stages, conflicts continued between the need for critical evaluation and concerns with maintaining circle bonds.

Circle-staff Tensions Interviews with the staff and clients revealed differing viewpoints on the program. Despite their strong efforts and commitment to show respect and concern for one another, each group felt extra-local pressures impinging on its work in the organization. Among clients these were economic and family demands; among staff these were concerns about how the program would appear to board members and funding sources. As the first circles progressed toward borrowing, these tensions increasingly focused on issues of circle autonomy. A ME staff member spoke about the difficulties surrounding circle autonomy: "They give us lots of feedback on everything that is wrong with the program. They are making decisions, but sometimes it all gets a bit out of hand" (Eve). Other conflicts between the circles and staff centered on the implementation of loan policies, perceived staff inadequacies, and continuing tensions between the circles' evaluative and support functions. The clients continued to identify inconsistencies between program policies and practices; some believed that certain staff were ineffective and/or disrespectful to them.

The concerns about lending practices centered on changes in loan amounts and the expediency with which loans would be granted and disseminated. Many of these problems stemmed from ambiguities in the ongoing development of program procedures during the first year of operations. Several clients expected that loans would be made immediately and did not understand that there would be a certification period and a lengthy loan-application review process. They were unaware of the eighteen-month repayment process that was required before getting additional loans. One client said, "They should have let people know about the length of the course and the circle period. Now we have to spend two years together" (Alan). Simultaneous to these internal tensions, the staff faced external pressure from the bank that served as the lending source for the first ME loans. Upon seeing the list and brief descriptions of the types of businesses planned by ME borrowers, the bank officer in charge balked at making the first loans. A ME staff member described his reaction:

It is the midnight hour, the loans are supposed to go out, and Arthur says they are not going to loan us the money. He thought their business ideas were just crazy. I could not imagine how I was going to tell the clients who have already waited longer for these loans than they think they should have. I called Fred [board member and officer at another bank]. . . . He said *his* bank could loan us the money. I called Arthur [CDB officer] back and told him [about arrangements to borrow from another bank]. Then he said. "Well, wait, I think we can work things out to loan you the money." (Karen)

Although the loans were secured after this incident, the ME staff decided to seek additional information from clients that had not been originally requested on the loan applications. Unaware that the loans had almost been canceled by the hesitant banker, clients became angry about the delays and requests for further information (e.g., a description of how loan funds would be used and repaid).

The greatest problems occurred when, several weeks after circles were formed, the ME staff informed clients that due to some miscalculation on the part of ME staff and bank lenders, the maximum loan amounts would be $1,200, not the promised $1,500. Members strongly objected to changes in lending amounts after the circle stage had begun. They said that the ME staff had not properly informed them about the conditions of the lending process. One client said, "No one is quibbling over $300. Really. What people didn't like is that the unity was broken. If during the 14 weeks, with the rapport that was there [they could have said], 'There's been some changes . . . and we know you might not be happy with that, we wanted to let you know right now this is what it is—where we thought we had 15 and there's only 12.' That would have been better accepted" (Rashad).

Although others shared this viewpoint, most clients were used to confronting financial disappointments and quickly accommodated decreasing loan amounts. A client who was already in business said, "I think if you want to sell your program you should stick with what you say. If you say you're going to [offer] $1,500, it should stay $1,500. . . . I had budgeted for $1,500 and I budgeted for the amount that had to go into the kitty. But that's okay, I could cut something to get by" (Jane).

Clients verified the perceived rule inconsistencies by carefully examining ME's Procedural Handbook. For example, the handbook referenced credit checks even though clients had been told that none would be required. One circle member said, "The policy of the program, that red book, and it's kind of significant that the color is red, because it put the credibility of the program in debt. That book was full of contradictions—how did that book even get printed? No one edited it?" (Ben).

Sometimes staff personalities caused problems. ME's circle facilitator was a source of tension both among circle members and between clients and staff. When the circles began meeting, the facilitator was not fully trained and his career in business framed his relations with circle members. He was unfamiliar with much of the program's philosophy and lending process. For example, he attempted to introduce paperwork and rules associated with traditional banking into the ME circle lending process, and he often lectured clients about their business responsibilities in ways that clients described as offensive and condescending. One angry circle member described him as being "a typical red liner . . . who had previously denied us credit" (Alan). In one meeting, the facilitator tried to encourage the male circle president to sit at the head of the table. The president objected to such hierarchical seating arrangements saying, " I have fought against . . . that kind of mentality all my life" (Ben). The facilitator also gave members some incorrect information about the lending process. One member said, "The groups feel—facilitate, don't dictate. If you don't know the answer, don't come off the hip and make one up. . . . In the circles, the facilitator just came off as the establishment, and it didn't fly. When the groups said, 'This is not what we were told,' instead of saying 'Let me check on that,' he defended the statement. So that's the root of the antagonism" (Rashad).

There were also staff-client tensions surrounding circle autonomy. Although ME planned for the circles to be self-governing and autonomous, the staff quickly decided that more guidance was necessary for the circles than had been originally planned. The staff were concerned that some circles had not strictly enforced their by-laws, and gave too little critical feedback to fellow circle members. In contrast, the clients argued that the staff tried to exert too much control over the circles and treated them like children. One member said, "Like I told you, ME needs to realize who they're dealing with. They're dealing with adults and as far as I know some of them didn't escape from a mental institution. They still have their faculties. . . . They just needed a helping hand and counseling. They each have character, they're willing to pay back, but when it comes to the control, it makes hostility" (Marge).

Circle-staff tensions sometimes converged with intracircle conflicts. In one case, disagreements over the circle attendance policy took on a gendered tone. The women felt that their male circle president had sided with the male facilitator in a dispute. The women described this as "the men sticking together." The president said that he had to "handle the women's dynamic personalities." One female member described the situation: "Before the meeting is over, . . . the facilitator says 'call me' [to the male president], or 'I want to talk to you after class.' We [female members] go into our little huddle and say, 'What's so important that they have to talk after class? How come he can't talk to all of us?' . . . We ladies say he [the president] talks out both sides of his mouth. One time he said he's in our corner and . . . next time he did the opposite" (Setera).

Resentment toward a Latino circle facilitator was seen by some circle members to be related to racial, ethnic, and gender differences. Several women (all Latinas) were supportive of the facilitator, but commented that he intervened too much in circle management and often sided with and related better to the men in their circles. In contrast, African American members, especially women with lower incomes and less education, were more openly hostile. Some of these clients accused the Latino facilitator of elitism, of forging closer ties with circle members who were Latino, more educated, and male. One African American woman said, "He would sit to the front . . . like a dictator. You know, it was like, now I thought it was supposed to be us who determined, and he was only there to facilitate. . . . He was like he thought we were *his clients*. . . . It was like, this man gonna be funky, I'm gonna be funky with him" (Betty).

The ME staff members described the tensions between circle members and the facilitator as "an example of conflicting cultures"—Hispanic [sic] and African American. For one staff member, "cultural differences" meant that African American clients "are more likely to directly confront the situation" and Hispanics either were "less likely to raise issues, or when they do, they do it more quietly." Despite its stereotyping, this staff comment pointed to the explicit and implicit racial tensions among the clients and between the clients and staff. These tensions were linked to the larger social context that included a history of both U.S. national and Southville local tensions among whites, blacks, and Latino/as.

Resistance by Circle Members Circle client strategies for dealing with ME-related problems typically took the form of individual protests or complaints. Over time, however, some circles became more organized in their resistance to rules and interventions that they perceived as unjust. Two circles called separate meetings that excluded the staff facilitator. The meetings were sometimes spontaneous, but over time became more planned. Two circles made their lending decisions privately and then reported the results to the facilitator: "It's kind of hard to talk with someone that's not in it with you. . . . We're in with all four of us. . . . With Manny [the facilitator], there, it's like we got this other person, who has nothing to do with us, listening in. Well, that's the reason we have conference calls and we discuss [in advance of the meeting] what we are going to discuss [in the meeting]. That's the reason our meetings after the first two have been more quiet" (Setera).

Client concerns about lending delays led the clients to organize and challenge ME to fund at least one person by early July and to fund three more members who showed equal need within the following month. When their request was denied, the circle contemplated several innovations for distributing the loans more quickly to their circle, including having two participants share one loan and drafting a proposal to ME staff requesting that all three get loans at the same time.

One circle organized and threatened ME with negative publicity from a local TV problem-solving program. They met with the ME staff to demand changes regarding each circle's autonomy to decide the timing of loans. Another circle's objections to both the facilitator and lending process led members to demand a private meeting with the executive director and a representative of the board of directors. Members said that after the discussion, the facilitator allowed the circle president to conduct meetings with fewer interventions: "Probably the third meeting maybe . . . where the president just took his stand and said, "This is our agenda, and this is what we're going to go over," and he ran the class like he was supposed to" (Betty). Clients also requested an increased presence by clients, alumni, low-income businesspeople, and racial and ethnic minorities on the ME staff and board of directors. In response, the board added a client member and tried to recruit more board members who were people of color.

Although many continued with ME and tried to promote change both in their own situation and in the program, some clients dropped out. They complained that the ME loans were simply too small to make a difference. In a follow-up interview, an African American client who dropped out of the program before borrowing said, "You have this big program and you look at the staff, look at the board members . . . they are all pretty much white, middle class people. How many poor minority people are on that board—not many, not enough. Those on the board and the staff do not understand our problems. They may try, but it won't be the same until that composition changes. You pay all those salaries. And the loans, after all the training that we have to go through . . . they are so tiny; they don't do anything to help start a business—they just put you in debt is all" (Mary). These dynamics shed light on the information about the low ratio of borrowers to nonborrowers in the national MDP studies described in chapters 2 and 3. Small business loans may simply be much less meaningful in the context of the United States than in the southern hemisphere.

Although the preloan period entailed many problems for circles, the greatest challenge of all came in keeping the circles together after first loans were issued. During the repayment phase, circles became increasingly fragmented.

Loan Repayment Phase: Circle Fragmentation and Breakdown

The repayment phase began in the weeks after loans were issued to the first two recipients of each circle. This phase included the distribution of the loans to other circle members, bi-weekly circle meetings, extended educational opportunities, and peer support. Despite the many problems during this phase, at least one-half the clients continued to view circle membership as beneficial. They supplemented one another's business skills and knowledge. For example, in one circle, two male members with experience in bill collections helped a female member strategize collections for her business services. Another client, a single mother, struggled to find clientele for her business. Her circle helped her develop methods for locating customers.

Circles comprising members who believed that they had had choice in selecting fellow circle members reported the most favorable assessments. One of these individuals, a woman who perhaps best conformed to the original vision of ME clients (see the introduction) said, "I'm real flattered; I like the fact that we're one of the first groups. That way I can say we began this program" (Carmen). Moreover, even some members who severely criticized ME during the lending phase of the program remained active during the repayment phase. They identified the opportunity to establish or rebuild credit as their main incentive for remaining. Some clients wanted to improve the program for future ME clients. One of them said, "It's a bad situation for the first class right now . . . because there are a lot of shortcomings and obstacles that have come up. . . . I think it is a good program and it has the greatest potential to be successful" (Ben).

Circle relationships improved with the departure of the bank-identified circle facilitator, who returned to private industry. The new facilitator was an African American woman whose past experience had been more in the social service area: she had worked in low-income housing. She was more readily accepted by African American clients and had a more relaxed and less interventionist style than had her predecessor. Although some clients and ME staff were concerned about her lack of attention to managerial and organizational details, staff-circle interactions became more peaceful.

Despite these positive aspects, the repayment phase was troublesome for staff and circle members. Overall, client attitudes were negative during this phase; almost one-half of the circle members indicated that they planned to leave the program as soon as their first loans were repaid. Much of this dissatisfaction stemmed from problems with the lending process. On a client satisfaction follow-up survey, items about the borrowing process received the lowest satisfaction ratings of any ME services (only 46–55 percent satisfied or very satisfied). The lowest satisfaction rating (46 percent) was associated with the timing of the loan. Still, 55 percent of the respondents reported being satisfied with the interest rate, repayment process, amount of the loan, and terms of borrowing.

In most circles, attendance and repayment were maintained until all circle members received loans. After this point, all the circles to varying degrees experienced more absences, diminished communications, and a breakdown in peer support and peer pressure. The ME circles' problems were similar to those reported by the providers in chapter 3: circles varied in their viability. Many problems were carried over from the early stages of the lending process. Clients who were disenchanted with the previous phases attended meetings the most sporadically. One client said, "We're working people. We are tired. I had arranged it so that I could be off on Tuesday [for class]. Now, on my day off, I'm down there [for circle meetings]. And because of my transportation situation, that's a whole day [on the city bus]" (Marge).

Several meetings were attended by the facilitator, researchers, and only one or two circle members. Several meetings became monologues by the circle facilitator. Although the circle presidents continued to maintain contact with circle members, the poor attendance decreased peer group effectiveness as a source of support and a mechanism for encouraging loan repayment. Despite the efforts of some clients to improve coordination and change meetings to times that all could attend, the presidents gradually relinquished more and more control over planning and conducting circle meetings to the facilitator.

The ME staff wanted to develop an alumni association to strengthen the training, support, and networking opportunities available to ME clients; however, attendance at alumni meetings was erratic at best. The clients said that the sessions were a waste of time or that they were too busy trying to start their businesses to attend more meetings. A few clients formed a subcommittee to help the staff and board members improve the alumni meetings. They challenged the ME staff and board to "cut the umbilical cord" and allow them to plan the meetings. One board member described the interaction: "They were adamant about, 'We want to do this ourselves,' and I thought to myself, 'Let them do this.' They are making it only too plain, and for what we want the alumni to do, . . . they can do that. I think our part is to . . . oversee it. Be there as support and watch them fly" (Joan). Two clients volunteered to solicit donations for refreshments from local businesses and to enlist other circle members to notify all attendees of the training sessions. The client committee's enthusiasm was short-lived. By the following week, they had not met to plan the alumni meeting. They said they were too busy with their new businesses to meet and abdicated planning to the ME staff.

Client lives were filled with jobs, family, and transportation problems as well as attempts to maintain their businesses. As in earlier program stages, women and very-low-income clients faced the greatest hurdles. Most clients continued to work at wage jobs while trying to establish their businesses. Individuals with full-time jobs and start-up businesses reported the most difficulties with attending circle meetings and alumni activities. Some clients were frustrated because, given such barriers, they needed circle support more than ever during the business start-up phase. One man who worked full time and helped raise his young children had put his education on hold to start his business. His circle became fragmented during the repayment phase and offered little support: "If you're going to be with people for a year, it's got to be more than, 'Hey Jim, how you doin', how's the wife?' There should be something more going . . . we should talk about our businesses . . . this is my problem. Then someone may say, I have someone who can help. . . . How can you get help if we don't talk about it" (Jim). Thus, the extra-local conditions that often explained why clients did not remain active in circles also challenged their business survival both with and without circle support.

ME Client Businesses Interviews with and observations of the circles during this phase indicate the importance of economic and social context on microenterprise start-up and operations. First, ME clients faced problems typical of small business start-up—identifying their market, distinguishing and pricing their product, balancing costs and revenues, maintaining cash flow, gaining a sufficient but manageable number of clients, and competing with larger, more established businesses. They struggled to get their businesses going and, once operating, to keep it from stagnating or growing too quickly. The regulatory problems associated with formalizing informal ventures, hiring employees, keeping books, and paying taxes were time consuming and frustrating for most clients. Many had to maintain full-time jobs while they struggled to establish their businesses. Some envisioned their businesses as supplemental income, but full-time work made it difficult to establish even viable part-time ventures. In sum, the ME borrowers experienced problems that are common among very small and home-based businesses, problems such as business instability, self-exploitation, the assumption of undesirable work just to get by, and conflicts between paid work and unpaid family or leisure responsibilities (Jurik 1998). In addition, the ME clients described confrontations with barriers associated with their race, gender, and class positions (e.g., access to resources).

Perhaps most salient were simply the competitive disadvantages they faced in running small businesses in the U.S. corporate-dominated economy. Several clients started businesses with their loans and discovered that they could not compete with larger established businesses. Ben, who tried to start a janitorial-supply company, never got his business off the ground because of intense competition from larger firms. Some clients realized quickly that their plans would not work and revised their business concepts in line with staff recommendations. One woman started cooking classes when staff advised her that starting a restaurant right away would be too costly. However, staff advice did not always help clients. One client had planned to open a photography business but was encouraged to open a craft gallery instead: "I wanted to work on my photography, and the [ME] counselors moved me toward the gallery. . . . That did not work . . . and I had to go back and work on the photography business" (Jane).

Many clients worked long hours, combining paid employment, entrepreneurial operations, and family responsibilities. Sometimes, family members and friends helped out. One man who was in the midst of a divorce got his mother to watch his baby. Some women traded child care with other mothers. In some cases, family responsibilities required that the business be put on hold or changed to accommodate new, unexpected family responsibilities. For example, Carmen was running a promising clothing manufacturing business. When her father became ill and came to live with her, she shifted to a home child-care business so that she could stay home with him. Informally, staff were very sensitive to women's competing family and work demands and assisted Carmen in her new venture. Yet formal discussions of such issues and strategies for women (or for men who were single parents) were never systematically incorporated into the training or alumni meeting agendas.

Some ME clients believed that they had experienced business barriers related to their race, ethnicity, or gender. Yet ME programming rarely addressed these concerns. For example, ME notified clients about opportunities for subcontracting relationships with local corporations or procurement contracts with government entities; however, clients were often ill-prepared for the discrimination or unfair competitive practices that they might face in such contract bids. One prospective client, an

African American woman, who attended the ME orientation and a few training sessions said, "I need some help in competing with the big companies who are going after the same contracts that I want. I did not see anything in their classes that even begins to help me deal with this. I am learning on my own what to bid for and how I can compete, but it would be nice to have had some help, to know more about my rights and any special programs for minority-owned businesses. How do I know if I am being discriminated against on a contract? Things like that. . . . It would have saved me a lot of time, and my business would be in better shape" (Shelly).

Borrowers from the first cohort ($n = 18$) included individuals at three stages of business formation. The most established group of borrowers ($n = 5$) had been operating businesses for six months or more at the time of their first loans. They hoped to use their loans to expand the businesses. The second and largest group ($n = 7$) had been running businesses on a more informal basis than the first group and for a shorter time period (less than six months). They hoped to use the ME loan to formalize their businesses. The third group of borrowers ($n = 6$) were in the business conceptualization and planning stages. They hoped to use the loans to start-up operations.

The first cohort of ME clients experienced the largest rate of repayment problems. One-half of these first 18 to receive first loans were either more than 120 days delinquent or defaulted on the loan entirely. It was not surprising that repayment patterns varied considerably across the three stages of business development. Twenty percent of the more established borrowers, 43 percent of the formalization group, and 83 percent of the start-up group were either delinquent or in default on their first loans. Although these numbers are small, our findings are consistent with reports by staff in the 50-program sample and with that of other research (e.g., Edgcomb, Klein, and Clark 1996; Servon and Bates 1998), suggesting that start-up or young businesses run a much higher risk for loan default. Interestingly, however, clients in the formalization stage of business development were generally those most positive about the ME program, those most persistent in soliciting guidance from ME staff, those who most visibly applied ME resources to revise their business plans and operations, and those who remained in the circles for the longest time period. They were also the group most likely to identify ME services as making a significant difference in their business efforts.

Four of the first cohort took out second loans from ME. Three of these borrowers were in the established category, and one was in the formalization category. The one second loan that went to a formalizing business was the sole default from this batch of loans.

The ME staff were sensitive to the many problems confronted by the first cohort of clients. They listened to client concerns and developed strategies for improving the program. However, within a few months after first loans were issued, the staff observed an emerging pattern of late payments. The struggles and loan delinquency in this first cohort alarmed the ME staff and reinforced their views and those of board members that significant programmatic changes should be made.

CONCLUSION

Community support, able leadership, and an enthusiastic group of clients got the ME program off to an exciting beginning. ME planners sought to locate supportive spaces for their innovative programming.[11] They consulted with well-known U.S. MDP practitioners to design their program. They self-consciously promoted legitimacy by recruiting a "balanced board membership" that included both community elites and grassroots professionals. The community elites facilitated the acceptance of innovative program components by funding sources, and the grassroots leaders and agency professionals helped with the recruitment of ME's clients.

This context of opportunities also raised limitations for planners. Early in the process, local funding sources exerted considerable influence over program design and encouraged modifications such as narrowing the program scope, scaling up target clients, and adopting a gender-neutral program name. These changes were similar to those reported by MDPs in the national sample: several programs hoped to increase their appeal to funders by expanding their target populations to include men and moderate-income clients, concentrating their energies on self-employment training and lending and avoiding extensive client support services such as child care and transportation. The ME board and staff members resisted pressures to avoid welfare-level clients altogether, to lend only to established businesses, and to deny circles the power to approve loans. Accordingly, ME remained committed to peer lending and circle autonomy over lending decisions and persevered in its efforts to obtain asset-restriction waivers for welfare clients.

In keeping with program modifications, the initial cohort of ME clients included a sizable percentage of men in addition to women. Clients also brought with them a range of disadvantages that marginalized them economically and socially. Chronic unemployment, low-wage jobs, poor health and disability, and family responsibilities challenged program participants. Still, clients were hopeful about ME's ability to help them begin and expand businesses that would promote their self-sufficiency and sense of accomplishment. The clients had creative ideas for businesses that were responsive to needs generated in the new economy; their plans included child care, low-cost children's clothes, diversity counseling, and massage enterprises.

The ME program promised to conduct its operations in a manner that was consistent with new privatization pressures for cost-effective, efficient social service programs. As a nonprofit, community-based provider, ME offered a break from welfare and other costly government services. The staff and board members were anxious to assist the ME clients to "help themselves." Still, the staff and clients each had to contend with extra-local conditions outside the program. Staff had to work with funders and bankers whose demands did not always fit the program vision (e.g., bankers required the loans to be secured because of their unease with the ME clients). On the other side, the low-income clients consistently had to negotiate the realities of their everyday lives (e.g., paid employment obligations and family demands) and their desire to be self-employed. Transportation, child-care, and financial problems made it difficult for the clients to muster the human and financial resources to start, much less expand, microenterprises.

Indeed, ME's first client group faced many difficulties in meeting the requirements to coordinate training and advance to the lending stages. Once at the lending stages, they were disappointed in how little funding was available for business loans. In the United States, operating even small microenterprises takes some investment of capital and massive amounts of human resources for these typically labor-intensive ventures. The ME staff tried to extend as much support to the clients as possible, but, as was true for programs in the national sample, cost-effectiveness demands sometimes meant that the ME services were insufficient to counter the problems confronted by disadvantaged entrepreneurs. Thus, ideological and financial support for microenterprise development produces persistent pressures to lower service costs while the lives of disadvantaged clients produce a contradictory pressure for increased service expenditures.

At times, the clients and staff became angry and frustrated. Despite such tensions, both groups struggled and developed creative strategies for making the program work. Although only approximately one-third of the first cohort clients were actually living in poverty when they entered the program, the ME staff associated the cohort's problems with the difficulties of serving poverty-level and welfare clients. These internal organizational struggles among clients and between clients and staff quickly led to further modifications in the ME training and lending procedures and in overall program goals.

CHAPTER 5

MATURATION OF A MICROENTERPRISE PROGRAM:
CASE STUDY PART II

I don't think we're a social service program. . . . That implies,
you know, that we're there to . . . give you . . . all things social.
I think that was part of the problem with some of our first class.
What came through is that they thought of it more in terms of an
entitlement and social service rather than a business assistance
program. I personally think there's a perfect place for
welfare . . . but that is not what we are here for.
—ME STAFF MEMBER

This program is an impression, not a real help. The loan amounts
do not make a difference; they just make you in debt. There needs
to be a program that will give enough to make a difference.
—ME CLIENT

During its first year of operation, the ME program struggled to balance its
goals of offering business training and lending services to poor entrepreneurs with concerns about organizational sustainability. In its second year,
the program made significant changes. The statements at the beginning of
this chapter illustrate both the transformation in the ME program's orientation and the gap between the program's services and client business
needs. Changes were made in concert with the concerns and demands of
funding sources and in response to internal organizational struggles. Experiences with the first client cohort, which included a number of poverty-
level and former welfare clients, convinced the ME staff and board
member that such clients were not right for the program. ME also recon-
sidered key elements of its organizational structure. From the outset, ME
was a kind of hybrid organization that contained a participatory peer-
lending component. Following the Grameen model, the board designed
the program to encourage circle self-governance and lending decisions.

But tensions among clients and between clients and staff during the first year undermined ME's commitment to this level of client participation. The maturing ME practice evidenced changes that were similar to those reported by practitioners in the national study (chap. 3).

This chapter examines ME's expansion and transformation after its first client cohort up through its eighth fiscal year of operations (through June 2002). It also considers changes in ME's service population over time and follow-up studies of client perceptions about the program and its impact. Over these eight years of ME operations, the first client cohort was a constant reference point for redefining goals and strategies.

EXPANSION AND FORMALIZATION: YEARS TWO THROUGH FIVE

The national and local opportunities for microenterprise development continued to offer both opportunities and challenges for ME's growth and success in Southville. The changes that accompanied ME's maturation included expansion and increased professionalization, specialization, formalization, and centralization. The first five years are generally considered the most formative period for new MDPs (see Edgcomb, Klein, and Clark 1999), and ME was no exception. Years two through five were characterized by rapid and often dramatic change.

Ongoing Context

After beginning its first classes in January 1995, the ME program expanded quickly in terms of the number of clients served, staff size, and geographical regions covered. The Southville area was receptive to small business development, and its low-wage economy made microenterprise an attractive alternative or, at minimum, supplement to employment income. A staff member described the perceived link between the economy and interest in the program: "Our calls for information and orientation attendance figures are up. Every time the unemployment rate goes up a lot, people start contacting us" (Karla). Strengthening the CRA further encouraged banking industry support for MDPs in areas such as Southville. With their ability to administer and even guarantee all or part of small-business loans to poor and low-income individuals, and with the positive publicity surrounding their efforts, MDPs such as ME were an attractive investment for large banks and other philanthropic-minded corporations.

As noted in chapter 2, the Clinton administration's interest in microenterprise development, AEO's activism, and criticism of the SBA for neglecting microenterprises stimulated additional federal support for microenterprise development (e.g., from SBA and HUD) (Riley 1995; Clinton and Gore, 1995). ME staff and board worked to publicize the program and take advantage of these new funding opportunities. As a result, ME received numerous donations and grants from local and national governments and private corporations. ME offered three four-week and three ten-week classes during its first year of operation. By its second year of operation, ME had expanded and offered training and lending in two of Southville's suburbs. ME's number of classes doubled during the second year. The program also obtained funding to conduct classes in Spanish. ME began to receive local and state-level recognition and later received several national awards for service quality.

Professionalization of the Staff and Board

Over the next several years, both the ME staff and board of directors expanded and professionalized. By the fifth year, the staff had grown to eleven full-time employees and three to five part-time positions.[1] The staff expansion was facilitated by funding from grants and corporate donations. Hiring more staff was seen as essential to program expansion. The newer staff members saw expansion as a means to increase their employment security and salaries. As one staff member said, "We want the program to get bigger and more successful with more secure and long-term funding. With more resources, we can get paid better, because otherwise a lot of us will leave" (Kevin). The staff's vested interest in program growth was logical given the insecurity associated with employment in nonprofits and in the new economy generally; however, it sometimes conflicted with the board's desires for more managed and cautious program growth. Expansion also increased the demands on the ME staff and board to secure additional funds, and the pursuit of funding opportunities took staff time away from other tasks such as client recruitment and improvements in program quality. Like the respondents in the national sample, the ME staff described how funding-related demands took time away from program basics: "But to go from having two completely full classes that were actually over-booked, to not even filling one class, which is what we're going to do in September, . . . there's something seriously wrong there that we need to work on. But we haven't got time to because of the grants that we're working on and the changes that are going on in the office. . . . We just need to sit down and have a staff meeting about it or something. But it's hard for us to take the time out to do that" (Avery).

As the program grew, the board of directors also expanded and shifted its composition to include fewer social service agency professionals and more members from the business community. On the advice of funders, several more bankers were added, as well as representatives of other firms that made large donations to ME.

With expansion, the board and staff became much more racially and ethnically diverse as both attempted to better reflect the composition of ME's client population. Some of the increase in board diversity was due to the banks' delegation of CRA officers as their representatives to the ME board (most CRA officers were minorities). Nevertheless, the board's class composition continued to be removed from the lives of poor and low-income ME clients.

ME's expansion and professionalization also brought greater specialization. Some of the staff focused strictly on lending issues, whereas others focused on training. The staff assumed duties that had been performed by volunteers and board members. ME's board worked through narrowly focused committees, and board management became a committee unto itself. Decision-making power became concentrated in the hands of ME's executive director and a five-member executive board of directors; the daily operations were managed by the ME staff members, who framed the parameters for board decision making. Full board meetings morphed into informational and brainstorming discussions rather than significant planning or decision-making sessions. Board involvement in the daily activities of ME decreased over time.

The increased divisions of labor and specialization heightened the distance between the staff and clients. The staff members could now use clerical assistants to screen their calls from clients more often, and their specialized duties often meant that they only knew the clients in their particular capacity. The remaining ME volunteers also became highly specialized. Board member attendance at client events (e.g., training graduations, and circle meetings) declined dramatically after the first year.

Prior research suggests that professionalized nonprofits gain respect and funding opportunities in the community at the loss of grassroots appeal (Smith and Lipsky, 1993), and ME exemplified this tendency. ME's growth, professionalization, and specialization were also consistent with patterns in the national MDP sample (chap. 3). The advantages of an elite, professional board facilitate program success and survival, but this often comes at the expense of losing touch with the very community (i.e., clients) that the program was designed to serve.

Increased Formalization: Records and Rules

ME's maturation also entailed greater formalization. Of course, some degree of formalization was essential to ME's establishment as a nonprofit organization. But the problems raised by the first cohort convinced both the staff and board that even more established and consistent policies were essential to smooth operations. Success in securing funding further promoted formalization through grant-reporting requirements. These entailed developing procedures to compile information on client businesses, loan repayments, and other matters.

Committees were developed to manage various program components: funding, marketing, programs, and lending. Lending was an issue of special concern, and, late in the second year of operations, the program established a loan policy committee comprising board members and staff to oversee lending issues. The power of this committee grew as ME centralized its lending decisions. Also important was the finance committee that supervised ME's bookkeeping and budgeting work and helped manage the external audit that was mandated for ME as a federally recognized nonprofit organization. Board members with extensive business, legal, and nonprofit management experience headed these committees. Like the practitioners in the national MDP sample, the ME staff found that bureaucratization was time consuming and sometimes distracted from basic services. For example, after ME received its first SBA grant, a staff member said: "We have so many new reporting requirements. SBA demands that we use its reporting software. We have to overhaul our entire record-keeping system to conform to their requirements. That is taking a lot of time from client services" (Tanya).

As ME formalized and bureaucratized, its operations grew more businesslike. The business orientation of the board members and nonprofit status requirements provided models for ME management in this regard. Nationwide, nonprofits have been moving toward corporate practices, in part because of fund-raising scandals but also because of economic downturns that increase competition for funding (Hammack and Young 1993; Ritzer 2000, 147–49; Steckner, 2003). But as noted in the introduction, this trend is also reflective of the new privatization ideology that regards business sector-practices as superior to government and nonprofit operations (Blau 1999; see also Jurik 2004). ME's operational shift was consistent with these national trends. For example, a management consultant hired by ME to help with its organizational evaluation commented that as nonprofits mature part of their maturity was to recognize the need to become more businesslike. The adoption of this business model changed the staff's orientation to clients in important ways.

CHANGES IN ME POLICIES AND PRACTICES: YEARS TWO THROUGH FIVE

Although the staff members were responsive to complaints and suggestions from the first cohort, their struggles with this client group led the ME staff and board to rethink program methodology, target population, and objectives. Several modifications were made in program practice and policies that (1) reframed the program's image, (2) redefined the types of clients that ME aimed to attract, (3) increased staff evaluation and screening of clients, and (4) increased staff control over the lending process, thereby diminishing circle power and autonomy.

Reframing the Program: From Social Service to Business, from Lending to Training

After the struggles with the first cohort over lending and loan repayment procedures, the staff worried that clients and funders regarded ME as "too much like a social service program" (Avery). The staff believed some clients viewed ME loans as "entitlements" rather than as business loans and associated this attitude with late payments and loan defaults. They feared that the first cohort's delinquency and default rates were so high that funding sources might regard ME as being reminiscent of welfare programs and thus as a bad investment.

During the second year of operations, the staff members decided to promote the business aspects of the program. They decided that all those using ME services would be referred to as "business owners" rather than as clients. This reference even applied to clients who had not yet received funding or started a business. The staff redefined ME as a business development rather than a social service or welfare-related program and developed brief sound bites for media interviews to communicate this image. One staff member explained: "We have to communicate to our funding sources and clients that ME is a *business* program. These loans are *not* entitlements. They are *business* loans that must be repaid" (Karen). Another staff member distinguished ME's objectives from those of welfare programs: "There are good social welfare programs, some educate people, help them get a job. . . . We educate them and help them run their own business, so they don't have to worry about standing in a line somewhere to get a check" (Sheryl). One staff member described ME's orientation toward clients: "We are not here to judge clients or to try to change or resocialize them. That is what welfare programs do. Our loans are business transactions. And we cannot do it for them. They have to be able to help themselves. If they can't help themselves, that is what welfare is for" (Karen).

This shift toward a business orientation was consistent with reports from the national sample of MDP providers (chap. 3) and with the increased formalization and business influence that characterized ME's board and staff composition. In discussing ME's management trends, a staff member said, "We have to set an example for our participants by running ME in a good business-like manner" (Karen).

Staff plans to communicate their businesslike intentions to clients included a reliance on traditional collection methods to pursue loan-delinquent clients. Staff tried to renegotiate payments when possible, but, if they decided that clients were avoiding calls or declining to reach an alternative payment agreement, they turned the account over to a collection agency and pursued the matter in small claims courts. A staff member described the effect of these actions: "We have some clients who think that these are grants, but once they see that we are serious about collecting and will pursue them aggressively, they realize that these are business loans, not grants" (Karla).

In addition to reframing ME as a business program, the staff and board decided that they should reframe ME as a training rather than lending program. They worried that they had made too many loans too quickly in the first cohort. They sought to reduce clients' expectations about loans by emphasizing the training aspects of ME. A board member explained, "We need to de-emphasize lending to our business owners. We must communicate to them in our orientations and all our literature that ME is, first and foremost, a *training* program. Lending is not our main activity. That is the carrot that gets them here, but once they're here, our focus has got to be on training, not lending. We have to be more careful about emphasizing lending, especially in light of our problems with this first class" (Patrice). Along with this program reframing, the ME board urged the staff to slow the recruitment of new clients and any additional lending. An executive board member said, "We don't want to expand much in our second year. We want to get our house in order" (Kate). First ME reassessed the target population for its programs.

Redefining the Target Population

Although they sought to distinguish themselves from social service providers, the ME staff shared with social service program workers the responsibility and discretion for allocating scarce services to a large group of potential beneficiaries. They developed strategies for identifying "appropriate" and "deserving" clients for the program and, consequently eliminating those they deemed inappropriate or undeserving.[2] During the second year, the staff began to aggressively screen clients (see Cowgill and Jurik In press). The ME staff performed these tasks using varied, ambiguous, and sometimes contradictory criteria. One staff member described her approach toward recruiting new clients:

> As much as you want to help everybody, you have to be really careful about who you allow to participate. . . . For a program like this to work, the participants have got to be motivated. . . . We have to be open, but it's a waste of resources to spend time with somebody who's not really serious and committed to the program. . . . It's not just the quantity, but the quality too. [ME is] still at the point where they're trying to get the right number of people [and] the right type of person not only based on gender, race and income, but attitude and motivation. ME needs people who are ready to make a change in their lives, not just somebody who wants a source of money. (Sheryl)

After the first cohort, most of the board and staff members concluded that the program would not work for poorly educated, poverty-level, and welfare-to-work clients. Even though most of the clients in the first cohort had never been on welfare and did not live at or below the poverty line, the ME staff and board came to associate "problematic" client attitudes and behaviors with having too many poverty-level and poorly educated individuals in the program. A staff member said, "We don't have a lot of people on welfare in the program now, and I think part of the reason for that is entrepreneurship requires a certain mentality in order to be successful at it. That you're outgoing, that you've got aspirations that you're trying to work toward something. And I think a lot of people on welfare get bogged down in their current situation and have troubles looking forward to things, which makes it hard to start a business. And I think that we should be helping people like that, but at the same time, a lot of those people don't have ideas for starting their own business" (Karen).

One board member argued that the program should never have included any poverty-level clients. A female entrepreneur from a poor background argued that the board needed to recognize that the poor have many problems that prevent their business success: "The people we have been targeting have a unique set of circumstances that they work with on a daily basis, and it cannot be overlooked. While we're trying to help them with self-confidence and help them grow with their business and help them become self-sufficient, we also cannot forget that there are things pulling, holding them back. . . . We have to be careful about serving folks who are really on the edge" (Kim).

Long after the first cohort, ME staff and board members invoked that group as an example of the wrong type of clients for ME. A board member said: "We know that a lot of those in the first class were not right for the program" (Kate). Another board member agreed and referenced information about the national field: "We need to find clients who are right for us, who understand our mission and can make the most with what we have to offer. We know a lot now about the people that we should *not* try to serve. . . . We do not have the resources for the very poor client. We now know that our market has got to be the "working poor," people who have at least some education, people who are not just coming off of welfare. . . . They have too much baggage, and we are not set up for them. I think that nationally, most microenterprise programs are having the same experience" (Patrice).

Thus, like many of the staff in the national MDP sample, the ME staff and board members decided that working with poorer and less-educated clients would be difficult without lowering the presumed educational level of the training and adding more social services. The ME practitioners remained committed to serving HUD low-income women and minorities, but planned to be more open to moderate-income clients.[3] The ME staff members also adapted, formalized, and polished their training curriculum. During this process, the staff decided to direct the training to individuals with at least a high school education.

Screening for Successful Clients

The staff increased client screening starting with outreach and continuing through the lending phases. First, staff members modified their community outreach by reducing activities that recruited poorer individuals. For example, they stopped holding orientations in churches and other inner-city locations and began to hold larger orientations in more centralized community centers in Southville and in two suburban locations. This change had an immediate impact on the client composition.

A comparison of the demographics of those attending orientations prior to the first classes (at program inception) with those attending orientation during the second year is shown in table 5.1.[4] The data reveal declines in the percentages of poverty-level (from 26 to 23 percent) and

TABLE 5.1

Demographics of ME participants at orientation for years 1994 and 1995 $(n = 130)^a$

	1994		1995	
Demographic characteristic	Number	Percentage	Number	Percentage
Gender				
Female	29	58	57	71
Male	21	42	23	29
Race/ethnicity[b]				
African American	25	50	44	55
White	6	12	24	30
Hispanic/Latino/a	14	28	5	6
American Indian	3	6	2	3
Mixed or other races	2	4	3	4
Don't know	0	0	2	3
Highest education level				
High school or voc/tech school	25	50	42	53
Some college or beyond	20	40	38	48
Don't know	5	10	0	0
Household income[c]				
Federal poverty level or below	13	26	18	23
Met HUD low-income level	31	62	42	53
Above HUD low-income level	4	8	17	21
Other/don't know	2	4	3	4
Start-up business[d]	34	68	41	51
Total	50		80	

[a]*Due to rounding, some percentages do not total 100.*
[b]*The difference between the percentages of 1994 and 1995 participants who were minority versus white was statistically significant at the* $p < .05$ *level.*
[c]*The difference between the percentages of 1994 and 1995 participants who fell into a combined poverty-low-income category was statistically significant at the* $p < .05$ *level.*
[d]*The difference between the percentages of 1994 and 1995 participants who were starting businesses was of borderline statistical significance at the* $p < .06$ *level.*

low-income clients (from 62 to 53 percent) and increases in the percentages of moderate-income clients (from 8 to 21 percent). The percentage of start-up businesses declined from 68 to 51 percent during this period. The percentage of white clients increased from 12 to 30 percent; the percentages of women clients increased from 58 to 71 percent. At the urging of board members, the ME staff tried to develop profiles of the "right clients" for the program.

Because of their concerns about loan delinquency and default rates, the board and staff increased their screening of clients moving from training to the lending stages. They eliminated the rules that allowed clients to advance automatically on completion of the ten-week class to a borrower's circle. A staff member explained, "There are people in the borrowing circles now [from the first cohort] that we wish weren't. We just didn't think they were ready to take that step, but we didn't feel we had presented the program well enough to say at the last minute, 'Well you can't do this'" (Avery). The completion of ME's training courses was no longer a guarantee of admission to the lending program. The staff members intensified their scrutiny of client business plans and commitment. Staff approval of the business plan became a formal requirement for joining a circle.

In deciding who would be admitted to the circles, staff members developed informal profiles or typifications of clients whom they believed would be the most likely to repay loans and develop successful businesses. The criteria for identifying clients as "right" for borrowing stages focused on clients who were (1) practical, (2) professional, and (3) productive in the program (see Cowgill and Jurik In press). Although the intent was to treat clients in a businesslike manner devoid of the moral judgments associated with welfare (see Fobes and Quadagno 1995), such assessments crept into the ME typifications of the "right client." ME staff profile themes were similar to those described by the fifty-program sample of practitioners discussed in chapter 3.

Practical Clients To move into circles, the staff required a completed business plan. Staff members were willing to help the clients complete their plans as long as both they and the clients had faith in the idea. The ME staff believed first and foremost that successful clients needed to have a practical business idea. This orientation entailed a realistic outlook toward business, understanding the need for start-up capital, profitability, cost projections, and marketing. The staff believed that businesses should be based on an existing skill and should be compatible with other demands in the clients' lives. For example, one client was dismissed as a dreamer because her idea of selling environmentally safe laundry disks was incompatible with her prior work experience (waitressing) and because she had no prior manufacturing or business experience.

Although this criterion seems reasonable, it significantly limited the options for women. Given the gender-segregation patterns that shape most women's work and business experiences, it tended to trap women in gender-stereotyped work roles. Women MDP clients are already more likely than are men to operate businesses in the traditionally feminine personal service industries of child care and clerical-related concerns (see Ehlers and Main 1998). Men are more likely to operate businesses in traditionally masculine fields, such as the construction trades (see Servon and Bates 1998). Because extant research suggests that businesses in stereotypically women's fields tend to offer lower incomes and less growth potential than those in stereotypically men's fields, it is likely that ME women business owners will be relegated to lower earnings and lower-growth businesses (Brush 1992; Carr 1995). Other case studies of microenterprise programs report this same tendency (Ehlers and Main 1998; Milgram 2001), and some of the Southville social program practitioners interviewed for ME's needs-assessment study warned about the limitations of encouraging women to begin "pink-collar" businesses (see chap. 4).

Professional Clients The second attribute of the "right client" was having a professional orientation. Increasingly, the staff and executive board members defined a professional orientation as a dedication to self-improvement, a focus more on training than borrowing, a professional demeanor, constructive problem-solving, and loyalty to the program (see Cowgill and Jurik In press). These notions of success and professionalism converged with popular constructions of the true entrepreneurial personality (see, for example, Brush 1992). One staff member described his view of true entrepreneurs as both professional and practical: "I believe if the people who come to us are sincere, committed, hardworking, and disciplined, and their . . . feelings toward what they do are really sincere, they are really committed to it, but they have to have a dream, a rational, practical dream" (Matt).

Once ME had been reframed by the board and staff as a training program, clients who in the opinion of staff had completed the training only to obtain loans were not taken seriously. According to the staff, professional clients were those who realized the value of the training process and demonstrated this realization by completing their homework assignments, making changes in their business as recommended by trainers and staff, and following ME rules and procedures. Clients who complained too much about the time it took to get a loan or about the size of the loan came to be viewed as suspect; they were devalued for "seeing loans as entitlements." One staff member described this entitlement seeker type:[5] "We have some that may have ulterior motives in the program. They're not really there for the spirit of the program like we want it. . . . [When] the program was new, staff had so much on their hands, that some of these people . . . slipped through, [who just wanted] the loans, [and they] didn't get into the spirit of the program which is educational" (Sheryl). After the first cohort, entitlement seekers were no longer viewed as desirable clients. A staff member said, "Is it the money and nothing else? Then they can't learn anything and have no interest. People like that are a waste of resources" (Karen).

The staff evaluated client "presentations of self" (Goffman 1959) including verbal and nonverbal communication. Client clothing, speech, and demeanor, as well as the quality of training homework assignments, were viewed as indicators of the clients' future business success. Clients were not expected to be "dressed up" for classes, but were expected to be "neat and tidy." As one staff member explained, clients should, "give an appearance that they have control over their life" (Avery).

This expectation posed barriers to clients who were poor, underemployed, or caring for small children—reasons that led them to a program such as ME. One client often was late for training sessions and program activities either because her car was undependable or one of her three children was sick. On nights when she could not locate a friend or family member to help with such problems, she missed these functions. Although the staff members tried to be sensitive, such issues made them doubt whether this woman could survive in a business. "I know she has got problems, but so do many of our clients, and they make it to meetings" (Avery). Although this is a reasonable observation, it again demonstrates the difficulty of serving disadvantaged MDP clients without providing additional services such as transportation and child care.

Clients were viewed as more professional if they were loyal to the program, negotiating organizational barriers and difficulties without public displays of anger or frustration. Clients who negotiated program hurdles such as training inconsistencies or delays in lending were preferred over clients who criticized ME to others outside the program. The threats of some members from a first cohort circle to report ME's lending delays to a TV consumer advocacy program angered the staff. In contrast, another client from the first cohort (Ben) challenged a ME policy, but did it within the rubric of the program (discussed in chap. 4). He asked for some class time to discuss the problem and propose solutions. His diplomacy led to a change in policy. One instructor described Ben's feedback as invaluable in improving subsequent classes: "A lot of the changes we made were due to Ben. Ben came in during the second session and he was all excited. He said, 'This is really great, Karen, but there are some things that you could do and you're not.' Boom, boom, and I was writing like a madwoman. And one of the things he said was we need to get people involved early on and so we did" (Karen).

Ben became a reference point for the client negotiating style that the staff favored. It is not surprising that staff members were also more open to criticism from clients whom they viewed as being successful in the program. A staff member described such a client from a later cohort, whom she compared to Ben: "She has done well in the classes, and when she has a problem, she always has suggestions about how to solve it . . . and, then there are those who want to tear down the program instead of fixing it, . . . or instead of asking what *they* might be doing wrong, causing themselves to fail" (Karla).

Clients who met the criteria of practicality and professionalism were admitted to the borrowers' stages and received at least one business loan. As the program matured, the timing and amount of the loans as well as the possibility of successive loans was increasingly determined by staff assessments of client productivity.

Productive Clients After the first cohort, clients were required to have their business plans approved by the staff before they joined circles. The completeness of the plan and clients' apparent readiness to start their businesses were factors that shaped the order and amount of their first loans. The staff gauged the clients' readiness for successive loans by assessing their productivity on several dimensions: (1) the client's timely repayment of the first loan, (2) a good record of attendance and participation at borrowers' circle meetings, and (3) the production of timely and measurable business results.

The ME staff believed that it was essential for clients, especially those who had low self-esteem, to identify very modest (i.e., practical) business goals. They advised clients not to wait for "the big payoff," but instead to aim for small successes during the first few months of their businesses. Clients were told to start their businesses promptly and show small, quick returns. Clients who did not produce quick results from the first loan were viewed negatively by the staff and judged too risky for further lending. A staff member said, "We don't need a lot of procrastinators. . . . the way that we're getting rid of those people is we're basically going to start having them prove that they have done something in the six months of the first loan for a [new] business. . . . If they haven't done anything with their business in six months, I don't think we'll be dealing with them any further. We're talking certification, licensing, business cards, customer base, income statement" (Karen).

ME's ongoing fund-raising efforts were greatly enhanced by examples of demonstrable client business achievements. Because it gave the program successful outcomes to report and gave clients a sense of success, this strategy was very practical in the short run. Unfortunately, it was not as practical in the long run. The quick-success strategy pressured clients to start very small, undercapitalized, labor-intensive businesses that were highly unstable over time. It also excluded clients who might need more sizable financing to get their businesses off the ground and those who might not be able to handle the added financial burdens (e.g., taxes and liability) or meet the citizenship requirements for quickly formalizing their businesses. One former client reported on a follow-up survey, "I did not have the bucks to register and do everything above the table like staff wanted. That costs a lot of money and paying taxes on my little bitty business income was ridiculous. I felt pressure to do these things . . . at least if I wanted another loan. The loans weren't big enough to justify all the paper work to make my business legit" (Norma).

Despite business literature arguing that only a small percentage of labor-intensive microenterprises ever really become viable (e.g., Grosh and Somolekae 1996; Servon and Bates 1998; Ehlers and Main 1998), some ME staff thought that little business successes could lead to larger profitable client businesses. These staff members avoided the technical terms *microenterprise* and *microentrepreneur* because they believed that such terms demeaned clients. They emphasized that despite the size differences and other limitations confronting their clients' businesses, there was considerable continuity between microentrepreneurs and large-scale entrepreneurs. One instructor said, "An entrepreneur is just somebody who wants to take risks and doesn't necessarily need to have a steady paycheck all the time, . . . and on a micro-scale, we're just talking smaller dollars, but we're talking the same kind of risks psychologically" (Clara). Despite staff sensitivity to client status, the emphasis on these shared characteristics underestimated the barriers that confronted ME microentrepreneurs compared with those facing entrepreneurs in large businesses and corporations (Goss 1991; Van Auken 1999; Kuratko, Hornsby, and Naffziger 1999).

Some ME staff and board members wanted to shift the program toward more experienced clients in growth-oriented businesses. A board member said, "We need to identify the kinds of businesses that can really have an impact, you know, ones that will provide jobs for others. Then when someone asks about the impact of our program we can point to the numbers of jobs created, or the growth in business receipts of the businesses that we helped create. Right now in looking at ME's businesses, I'm not seeing much impact, not enough that it would make me as a funder want to give to the program" (Tammy). This approach is consistent with the policy recommendations of some MDP experts (Servon and Bates 1998; Buckley 2002) that loans should be directed to businesses with significant growth potential. Despite this, at least one staff member disagreed. She argued that those most likely to show an interest in ME would not be starting growth-oriented businesses:

I see us helping people who are either having small hobbies or very small business dreams that they're trying to get a little bit further off their feet. But it's on such a small scale because of the loans, and most people go through the program to get the loans. That's why I really think those are the only kinds of businesses that we can target. I think that we should continue targeting those people who also have full-time jobs and are trying to start a business on the side. Again, it has to be on such a small-scale, home-based, one employee and maybe some family members working on it. They will be mostly service businesses because they have such low initial start-up costs rather than actually producing something and selling it. (Avery)

This emphasis on microenterprises as a source of supplemental income coincides with the Aspen Institute evaluation findings (e.g., Clark and Kays 1995). Low-growth labor-intensive businesses were those most closely associated with women, minority, and economically disadvantaged clients. Yet assistance to such clients often meant assisting businesses that were structurally doomed to remain at the economic margins. A statement from a client, who dropped out of the program after training, summarizes the dilemma in ME's client targeting and training: "The teachers [in the ME classes] kept talking about the need for that entrepreneurial spirit. But when I run up against these bigger companies bidding for the same job, I need more than some spirit. . . . I need information about how to find my own niche or how I can compete with the big guys. They were too busy telling us about that spirit, and how we just have to work harder. . . . I needed some strategies suited to my size and my level of capital in my business" (Shelly).

Nevertheless, the criteria of prompt loan repayment, good circle attendance, and quick (even if small) successes prevailed in staff definitions of serious and worthy clients. Such clients were more favorably considered for future loans. The staff discouraged individuals who failed to construct practical, professional, and productive client identities from continuing in the program.

The Typical Client

Tables 5.2 and 5.3 provide client demographic and business information drawn from client files for the first five and one-half years of the ME program (October 1994–June 2000). The demographic data were gathered from the clients at their ME orientation. Table 5.2 reveals that a majority of clients during this time were women and/or minorities who had had some college and met HUD low-income criteria. ME clients were more

TABLE 5.2

Demographics of ME participants served October 1994–June 2000 ($n = 970$)[a]

Demographic Characteristic	Number	Percentage
Gender		
Female	623	64
Male	327	34
Don't know	20	2
Race/ethnicity		
African American	357	37
White	303	31
American Indian	26	3
Hispanic/Latino/a	193	20
Asian American	11	1
Mixed race	12	1
Other	5	Neg[b]
Don't know	63	7
Highest education level (at orientation)		
Elementary school	12	1
High school	226	23
Vocational/technical school	55	6
Some college or associate's degree	484	50
Bachelor's degree	70	7
Graduate/law school or degree	42	4
Don't know	81	8
Household income level		
Federal poverty level or below	181	19
Above poverty but met HUD low-income criteria	525	54
Above HUD low-income level	202	21
Don't know	62	6
Source of participant income[c]		
Paid employment (wage labor)	577	59
Self-employment	276	28
Spouse	95	10
Public assistance	74	8
SSSI	49	5
Food stamps	31	3
Unemployment Compensation	27	3
Child support	25	3
Savings/investments	24	2
Social Security	23	2
AFDC	12	1
Other/missing	54	6
Number of children		
No children	334	34
1–2 children	362	37
3–4 children	134	14
5 or more children	24	3
Don't know	116	12
Self-employment status		
Full-time	176	18
Part-time	160	16

TABLE 5.2—cont.

Demographic Characteristic	Number	Percentage
Self-employment status—cont.		
Not self-employed	618	64
Don't know	16	2
Employment Status		
Full-time	427	44
Part-time or temporary	124	13
Not employed	178	18
Don't know	241	25
Prior business		
Yes	112	12
No	305	31
Don't know	553	57

[a]The demographic information in this table was drawn from participants' orientation forms. Due to rounding, some percentages may not total 100 percent.
[b]Refers to a percentage of less than 0.5 percent.
[c]Because participants had multiple income sources, percentages do not total 100.

highly educated than the larger U.S. population of poverty-level and low-income individuals and even more highly educated than clients described in other MDP studies.[6] During these first five and one-half years, few of the ME clients were on or recently off welfare; most had two or fewer children. Fifty-seven percent was employed full or part-time and 34 percent was in business full or part-time. Table 5.3 shows that over 40 percent of the clients already in business operated out of their homes and held jobs. Over 60 percent worked their business without paid employees. Their businesses were predominantly located in the service and sales categories. Women's businesses (not shown) were predominantly personal services and clerical types. The modal business operated by ME women clients was child care ($n = 34$, not shown in the tables). These occupational data replicate other national findings about MDP clients (e.g., Clark et al. 1999).

Extra-Local Pressures and the "Right Client" Resource-Dependency Issues

Despite board and staff consensus that poverty-level clients were "not right for the program," many federal grants as well as charitable funds were earmarked for service to poor and welfare clients. In accordance with the national legislative trends described in chapter 2, ME was awarded an SBA grant in its third year. This grant included a designation

TABLE 5.3

Participant business information at orientation, October 1994–June 2000[a]

Business Information (n = 336)	Number	Percentage of Total
Participant has a home-based business		
Yes	152	45
No/no response	184	55
Participant is both in business and employed	140	42
Part-time	38	11
Full-time	102	30
Monthly sales		
$500 or less	41	12
$501–$1,000	20	6
$1,001–$2,000	19	6
$2,001–$5,000	21	6
$5,001 and above	5	1
Don't know	230	68
Participant has paid employees		
Yes	127	38
No	209	62
Hours spent on business (weekly)		
Under 10 hours	12	4
11–20 hours	20	6
21–30 hours	15	4
31–40 hours	12	4
41 or more hours	41	12
Varies/don't know	236	70
Business Information (n = 970)	**Number**	**Percentage of Total**
Type of business planned or operating		
Service	206	21
Sales	126	13
Art/crafts	17	2
Construction or manufacturing	5	1
Other	48	5
Missing or don't know	568	59

[a]There were 98 cases that were missing data on their year of orientation. Due to rounding, some percentages do not total 100. The information in this table was drawn from participants' orientation forms.

for the program to be an SBA Women's Business Development Center and also included a welfare-to-work component.

On learning of the award, some board members expressed concern about renewed promises to serve welfare clients. One board member said, "We have learned that we do best by targeting the working poor. This new SBA grant calls for a welfare-to-work component. That seems to contradict our experiences, experiences that have taught us what we do best"

(Midge). A staff member also expressed concern: "I am worried because I do not think our services are set up to serve women who are trying to come off of welfare, but we had to put in that piece to get this SBA grant. That grant means a lot of operations money to the program. . . . And operations money is something we always need more of" (Avery). Thus, this new service component did not square with ME's redefined target population. The tensions were partially resolved by a decision to partner with a community organization specifically geared to the welfare-to-work population and to offer ME orientations and training but not necessarily lending to welfare clients. A board member said, "To get this grant, we need this welfare program. . . . We will maintain our primary target clients as defined—the working poor. And we will try this welfare-to-work training on strictly an experimental basis. We will offer the training, but there may not be any borrowers' circles to ever come out of this component. We will acquaint the welfare-to-work women with self-employment as an option" (Leah).

The ME program began orientations for welfare-to-work clients. Few of the women who attended ever signed up for the ME training and, years later, no borrowers' circles had been formed from the group. A staff member said, "I feel dishonest when I do these orientations, like I'm misleading the women. Some of them seem excited about the idea of owning their own business, but ME isn't really interested in them as participants" (Janelle).

As part of the same grant, ME also offered several training sessions for laid-off workers in towns outside Southville. No borrowers' circles were formed from these sessions either. The orientations for the welfare-to-work groups continued, but the training in the two outside towns was scrapped after the grant ended. The ME board and staff were frequently torn between their own definitions of best practice and pressures from the funding sources to alter that course.

Increasing Staff Control over Circles and Lending

Staff notions of success extended to the evaluations of clients in the borrowers' circles and of the circles as a whole. Initially, the circles were given the power to determine the lending order, review business plans, and decide the amount of loans made to members. But the CDB that provided ME's lending dollars had expressed concerns about the nature of the businesses proposed by clients in the first cohort; it also objected to the circle approving loan applications without staff review and expressed additional concerns about the number of late payments and defaults by the cohort.

ME board members and staff became increasingly concerned about these issues. The staff feared that the ME circles were so supportive that members were not sufficiently critical of fellow circle members' business plans. A staff member said, "We had wanted them to have a family atmosphere. We found that's not really what we wanted. Because you know and I know that you let family run over you sometimes and do things that you would not let a person do in business. . . . We want them to look at it in a business manner always. A friendly, trustworthy, *business* atmosphere. So yeah, we will be stressing more about being critical" (Avery).

Staff members were especially concerned about the stance of the circles toward loan application review. Like the practitioners in the national sample, they developed strategies to socialize the circle members to be more critical of one another's applications. Successful circles were expected to implement parliamentary procedures, negotiate disputes, and be supportive yet critical of each member's business plan. A staff member described the concerns about circles: "I think [we] need to . . . insist that the circle looks critically at each other's business. I mean I think they just *like* each other. They were committed to each other. They supported each other, but I don't think they looked critically at each other . . . it may have been because they don't know how, so we need to teach them how" (Sheryl). Another staff member said, "The first group went into the circles with . . . unrealistic ideas. They had kind of romantic ideas of what it would be about. And so, I think we will have smaller, fewer numbers of borrowers, but I think we will have borrowers . . . who understand the process more" (Karen).

ME made several changes in the borrowers' circles. First, the staff expanded the length of the circle orientations from six to eight weeks. Next, the staff added a mock borrowers' circle demonstration, comprising board members and community volunteers. This mock circle meeting was conducted in front of all prospective circle members, and its purpose was to socialize ME borrowers to be more critical of one another's business plans. The mock circle reviewed a fictional business plan. One member played the role of the loan applicant who had developed the plan, and her fellow circle members questioned her about its weaknesses. (The plan had several intentional flaws, so it was a good candidate for the mock critique.) This training was sometimes accompanied by comments from mock-circle members (who were board members) about the dangers of approving uncritically a fellow circle member's plans. One board member said, "Both your reputation and your opportunities for future lending can be harmed if you approve another member's poor business plan" (Maddie).

The multiple and contradictory roles of the circles as evaluators and supporters proved difficult to maintain, and staff control over circle management and loan approval increased dramatically over time. The ME staff and executive board members instituted several lending changes. By year two, ME's board permanently lowered the maximum first loan for clients from $1,200 to $500. For individuals who could prove that they had been in business for at least six months (e.g., by producing a business license and sales receipts), the maximum first loan was $1,000.

Later in year two, ME added other, more traditional banking procedures to their lending process. They required client credit checks "for informational purposes." They gave ME's executive director and loan manager the final authority for approving all circle lending decisions, thereafter termed "circle lending *recommendations.*" By year three, ME instituted a staff loan committee that had to review and approve all loans (ME also added a board loan-policy committee, described earlier). These changes gave the staff veto power over loans, a trend also noted in the national practitioner sample (see chap. 3).

With regard to subsequent loans, ME made other changes. In year four, the board formalized the previously informal practice that required clients to produce documentation of business successes before subsequent loan approval (e.g., evidence that they had registered their business, obtained additional clients, hired employees, and paid business taxes). These requirements discouraged clients who operated informal and undocumented businesses from applying for larger loans. ME also instituted a policy that client businesses be inspected by a staff member or volunteer prior to the third loans; this well-business check was aimed at providing clients with critical but constructive feedback for improving their business.

Some clients objected to the reduced loan sizes, arguing that such small amounts were not meaningful assistance for their businesses. A client who dropped out of the four-week class after learning of the new lending requirements said, "Our instructor did a great job. But, it's very difficult to begin any business without capital. Initially, ME presented itself as a program in which individuals could borrow $1,500 and eventually up to $5,000 once the $1,500 had been paid off. Near the end of the course, this amount lowered itself to something like $500–$600. This low amount of money would work nicely in third-world countries, but would do little for most businesses in the United States. This program could work, training people to sell at flea markets . . . but for most businesses, this low amount of money does not fund a business" (Phoebe). In response to such objections, the staff reminded clients that ME's primary contribution was business training not lending. One staff member said, "It's true that the loans are so small that they can't do much with them. But they do help our business owners reestablish their credit records. . . . And our real contribution, the most important thing we do is the training. We are, first and foremost, a *training* program" (Sheryl).

The staff and board also feared that recipients might not use their loans for business purposes. The staff considered site visits to examine client loan purchases, but after considerable discussion, settled on a receipt requirement. In fact, there was *no* evidence that clients were misusing loan funds. The change appeared to be based on anticipated behaviors commonly associated with welfare recipients and impoverished MDP clients (see Fobes and Quadagno 1995; Goetz and Gupta 1996). The board member who came from a poor background said, "Family, children, car, these are real. . . . I know that all their money is not going for their business. Some of that money is going for paying rent, some of that money is going to pay for cars, some of that money is going for baby sitters. . . . But, I mean we can't follow them to see what they do. I want to have them produce receipts" (Kim). The well-business checks and receipt requirement facilitated increased staff control over clients who wanted to apply for second and third loans.

Amid these changes in the lending process, the ME staff also assumed more authority over circle operations. In its second year, ME's office expansion provided space for circle meetings, and the staff could more easily supervise circle meetings. In part as a response to clients' failures to follow-through on their agenda-setting responsibilities, the staff also assumed a larger role in managing these circle duties. They developed standardized by-laws and arranged for circle speakers. Consistent with businesslike practices, these additional controls ensured more consistency and predictability in the ME circles, making life easier for the staff and providing a sense of businesslike stability for the ME board and funding sources. Such measures also limited circle autonomy and institutionalized staff control over the circle meetings.

By the fifth year, the circle facilitators had taken control over much of the content of the circle meetings in order to monitor client businesses and, hence, loan repayment "more efficiently." A staff member described his endeavors to promote a "business-like atmosphere" in circle meetings: "I require that we go over someone's financials during every meeting. Gradually, we get around to each member. I have my agenda for them each week, things we have to get done. Then, I give them some time to discuss whatever they want, or if they want to have a guest speaker on some topic of interest to them. But I require that we spend at least half of each meeting dealing with the status of their business. I want to know how they are doing, if they are in trouble" (Matt). The staff regarded these moves as essential for making sure that circles operated "professionally" (i.e., more critically), that client businesses received the guidance needed to be successful, and that the clients understood that the loans were business transactions and not handouts. The staff member reported that not all circles were amenable to this level of intervention: "The older circles do not like to follow the facilitator's agenda. We have one circle that has gone through three facilitators. They like to control their own agenda. I am letting them do that for now. But, I need to be able to go over their financials with them every month. If they are getting in trouble, I need to know sooner rather than later. I might be able to help them before they lose their business. . . . Eventually, we want to have all the circles on track, even if we have to split some of them up" (Matt). The members of one circle were a close-knit group and believed that their circle was working well without additional staff interventions. A member said: "We have been together so long now as a circle. We really know each other and help each other. We don't need them to tell us what to do. We would like some speakers on some topics and if they would help us with that, fine. Otherwise, just let us do our thing" (Bev).

In year five (Spring 1999), ME's founding executive director retired and was replaced by a man with extensive nonprofit experience. The board charged him with institutionalizing ME's services and making them more cost effective. At this time, the staff began considering more dramatic restructuring of the circles. There had always been some rotation and recombination as old members left and circles had to be combined so they had enough members to continue. During year five, the staff decided to split up the circles and rotate members to new circles in order to better manage them. Recalcitrant circles, such as the one described earlier, were among the first to be reorganized.

During these changes in circle management, running ME "as a business and not as a social service program" was a recurrent theme. The staff often described the numerous changes in ME rules and procedures as a process of "tightening-up" program operations. This tightening-up process gave the staff greater control over every phase of the program. Yet, despite the ostensibly businesslike tone, explicit and implicit moral assessments of the clients continued. For example, the following comment was made by a staff member arguing that ME clients needed to take their obligations to the program more seriously: "They've got to understand this is their only opportunity. If they screw this up, you know ME will go after them [i.e., for loan collection], and they've got to understand if they goof this up, that'll be it . . . this is the agency of last resort. The reason they're with us is that most of them can't get loans anywhere else . . . we're the end of the road" (Tommy).

Another of the new director's projects was to develop a partnership with the Southville County Community College District to offer ME's training. ME's four- and ten-week training workshops were combined into a fourteen-week course that was offered for three units of college credit at several community colleges in Southville County. The cost of the training rose to $150 for the course, but this change provided a mechanism to institutionalize ME's business training in a manner that increased its consistency and availability while reducing the costs for ME.

ME staff members still struggled to locate sufficient numbers of clients for classes every semester, but they perceived that the quality of the offerings improved with the college takeover. One drawback was that because most ME clients were not students, they were unused to the procedures for registering and attending these classes. Also, clients whose lives were better suited to two courses that were shorter in length (i.e., the original ME model of a four-week and then ten-week course) had to adjust to a full-semester commitment. Financial aid was available, but the increased cost and the intimidating college format discouraged some poorer clients. In response, the staff tried to develop methods for streamlining student applications for financial aid.

Although most clients were positive about the community college training, follow-up surveys of circle clients in year six[7] revealed that the length of time to lending was still a sore point. One client said, "The loan process takes way too long. One of my main criticisms is that the whole thing could be really compacted into a much shorter period of time. The course should also be shortened" (Kelly).

In year five, ME received another SBA grant to add an individual lending program (ILP) for clients who had completed ME's training (or an equivalent training course), had an approved business plan, and could certify that they had been in business for at least two years. The grant also allowed ME to become a certified lending agency. It no longer had to offer loans through the CDB. ME's ILP offered up to $15,000 to approved borrowers, but required credit checks and collateral similar to those required by more traditional lending organizations. Circle participation was not required for ILP borrowers.

The staff and board hoped that the community college partnership course and ILP would reduce ME's operating costs and increase service delivery. The confluence of alterations made by ME effected significant changes in its service population.[8] A review of the service delivery data from ME's first orientation in October 1994 through June 2000 reveals several trends that appear closely associated with the program policy changes made during the first five years of operations.

ME's services to poverty-level and, to a lesser extent, low-income clients declined significantly. The percentage of clients with some college education increased during the same period. Although the percentages of white clients increased, ME maintained a high overall percentage of minority clients (from 50 to 88 percent). These data are shown in table 5.4. Declines in overall percentage of minority clients were a function of decreases in African American and Latino/a clients. Minority service data are shown in table 5.5. ME's service to women clients remained consistently high (i.e., from 58 to 76 percent) throughout the service study period.

Table 5.6 lists the number of clients at various program stages. From this table, it is clear that only 8 percent of the clients who attended an orientation received ME loans. For comparison, 21 percent of those who completed the ten-week class received loans. Table 5.7 shows the demographics of clients at different program stages. Clients who were in start-ups at the time of orientation constituted 64 percent of all ME clients at that stage but only 39 percent of all clients at the lending stage. This attrition is not surprising given that start-up clients are more likely to change their minds about starting a business before borrowing; however, the high dropout rate of start-up clients is also a likely outcome of ME's policy of increased client screening prior to lending (ME staff members increased their screening of clients for the feasibility and practicality of their business plans). Other clients did not seem to be disproportionately screened out of the lending stages due to gender, race/ethnicity, education, or income (when their proportionate representation at orientation is compared to later program stages).

Also reflecting ME's reorientation away from lending and toward training, the number of first loans issued by the program decreased significantly over time. Declines in the proportions of poverty-level and less-educated clients occurred at orientation rather than in later screening stages. These longitudinal shifts in ME's client population were consistent with the alterations in staff marketing and orientation strategies.

CRISIS AND REEVALUATION: YEARS SIX THROUGH EIGHT

As the ME organization matured and the staff assumed more program operations duties, both the staff and board entered into a comfortable routine.[9] However, in its sixth year of operations, ME entered a period of crisis and reevaluation that stemmed from internal and extra-local

TABLE 5.4

ME participant demographics for those served at orientation by calendar year[a]

Demographic Characteristic	1994	1995	1996	1997	1998	1999	2000
Women	58% (n = 29)	71% (n = 57)	64% (n = 85)	63% (n = 77)	67% (n = 144)	65% (n = 151)	76% (n = 28)
Minority[b]	88% (n = 44)	68% (n = 54)	70% (n = 93)	62% (n = 76)	50% (n = 109)	63% (n = 148)	78% (n = 29)
Some college	40% (n = 20)	48% (n = 38)	67% (n = 88)	75% (n = 92)	62% (n = 133)	65% (n = 151)	57% (n = 21)
Federal poverty-level or below[c]	26% (n = 13)	23% (n = 18)	27% (n = 35)	19% (n = 23)	18% (n = 39)	16% (n = 38)	5% (n = 2)
Met HUD low-income level[c]	62% (n = 31)	52% (n = 42)	56% (n = 74)	60% (n = 74)	46% (n = 99)	57% (n = 133)	54% (n = 20)
Above HUD low-income level	8% (n = 4)	21% (n = 17)	13% (n = 17)	15% (n = 19)	31% (n = 67)	23% (n = 53)	22% (n = 8)
Average annual income	$18,936	$22,831	$20,872	$23,975	$31,293	$28,091	$32,743
Start-up business	68% (n = 34)	51% (n = 41)	65% (n = 86)	59% (n = 73)	62% (n = 133)	59% (n = 137)	65% (n = 24)
Total per year[d]	50	80	132	123	216	234	37

[a]The demographic information in this table was drawn from participants' orientation forms. A total of 970 clients were served from October 1994 through June 2000. Ninety-eight client files were missing orientation dates. For this reason, client totals for orientation each year differ from the totals listed in table 5.7, which does not break down by year. The demographic categories were treated as dummy variables (1, 0) and logistic regression was used to test the relationship between year and each demographic characteristic. The levels of significance that are reported were derived from these logistic analyses. Missing data on income variables are approximately 10 percent. On other variables in this table, missing data typically do not exceed 6 percent.
[b]Wald statistic for logistic regression using year to predict minority race was negative and significant at p < .05 level.
[c]Wald statistic for logistic regression using year to predict if participant was poverty or low income was negative and significant at the p < .001 level.
[d]Due to missing data on income, the three income categories do not add up to the total numbers listed per year.

TABLE 5.5

Breakout of racial/ethnic groups at orientation over time[a]

Racial ethnic group	1994 Number	Percentage	1995 Number	Percentage	1996 Number	Percentage	1997 Number	Percentage	1998 Number	Percentage	1999 Number	Percentage	2000 Number	Percentage
African American	25	50	44	55	62	47	54	44	61	28	87	37	6	16
White	6	12	24	30	39	30	39	32	84	39	76	32	7	19
Latino/a	14	28	5	6	20	15	18	15	38	18	51	22	18	49
American Indian	3	6	2	3	6	5	4	3	5	2	4	2	0	0
Asian American	0	0	0	0	1	1	0	0	3	1	5	2	1	3
Mixed	2	4	3	4	2	2	0	0	0	0	0	0	4	11
Other	0	0	0	0	2	2	0	0	2	1	1	Neg.	0	0
Missing	0	0	2	3	0	0	8	7	23	11	10	4	1	3
Total	50		80		132		123		216		234		37	

[a]Due to rounding, some percentages do not total 100. Neg., percentage less than 0.4 percent.

TABLE 5.6

Participants by type of ME service received, October 1994–June 2000
$(n = 970)^a$

Service Type	Number	Percentage
Orientation	970	100
Attended 4-week class	805	83
Completed 4-week class	778	80
Attended 10-week class	493	51
Completed 10-week class	358	37
Joined circle	103	11
Received 1st loan	76	8
Received 2nd loan	20	2
Received 3rd loan	2	Neg.
Individual loan—ILP (available in late 1999)	2	Neg.
Attended alumni meeting	119	12
Received technical assistance	163	17

^{a}*Percentages are based on the total participant population of 970. Because participants may have used multiple services, percentages do not total 100. Neg., percentage less than 0.5 percent.*

organizational conditions. These included a combination of personnel problems, board turnover and funding issues.

ME's second executive director resigned in the spring of 2000, leaving grant-reporting and proposal deadlines unmet. He left behind a number of staff conflicts and much ill will among several ME funders and community partners. The resulting funding crisis and community credibility gap produced a crisis in the program during what had otherwise been an era of rapid expansion. A new executive director was chosen from the existing staff.

During the months before the second executive director's resignation, the board had developed a pattern of delegating considerable policymaking as well as routine operational duties to the staff.[10] The terms of most of the founding board members had expired, and the new board members accepted this hands-off policy. One of the board's major fund-raising and founding members had also retired from the board. Thus, at the time of the second executive director's departure, contributions to ME had dramatically decreased. Board members used corporate connections to raise the funds to enable ME to survive this budget crisis. Later that year, the board chair, also an important fund-raiser, resigned for family reasons, leaving a relatively inexperienced board member to take her place. The new board chair called on members to assist him in his new leadership role and to help ME out of its crisis.

TABLE 5.7
Participant demographics by services received[a]

Stage of Program	Number	Percentage of Stage Total
Orientation		
Women	623	64
Minorities	604	62
Federal poverty level or below	181	19
Above poverty but met HUD low-income level	525	54
Some college education or more	596	61
Participants *not* in business at orientation (start-ups)	618	64
Total participants at orientation, stage total = 970		
Four-week class		
Women	549	68
Minorities	537	67
Federal poverty level or below	155	19
Above poverty but met HUD low-income level	445	55
Some college education or more	499	62
Participants *not* in business at orientation (start-ups)	574	71
Total participants in four-week class, stage total = 805		
Ten-week class		
Women	316	64
Minorities	303	61
Federal poverty level or below	89	18
Above poverty but met HUD low-income level	277	56
Some college education or more	328	67
Participants *not* in business at orientation (start-ups)	275	56
Total participants in ten-week class, stage total = 493		
Joined circle		
Women	74	72
Minorities	68	66
Federal poverty level or below	18	17
Above poverty but met HUD low-income level	60	58
Some college education or more	59	57
Participants *not* in business at orientation (start-ups)	40	39
Total joining circles, stage total = 103		

[a]*The demographic information in this table was drawn from participants' orientation forms.*

Strategic Planning Review

The crisis fueled another reevaluation and reassessment of ME's mission and daily operations. The new chair and executive committee called for a revitalization of board involvement in the program. ME set up its second strategic planning retreat for the staff and board in fall 2000. In preparation for this retreat, the Strategic Planning Committee reviewed the service delivery data previously described. An executive summary of these data and other program information were provided to the board.

The planning retreat generated much discussion about ME's mission, target population, service population, and future program expansion. Moreover, the service delivery data after June 2000 indicated that the percentage of low-income clients (poverty-level and low-income together) had fallen to an all-time low of 51 percent. The staff and board were concerned about these figures.

In response to these reports, some board members again suggested that ME reduce its commitment to serving low-income populations. A board member argued, "If we are going to make a sufficient impact on growing businesses out there in our community, then we have to get more loans out there. It sounds like the costs of loaning to high risk poor and low income communities will not be affordable for our program. We may need to rethink our targeted population at this time. It may be that we should target more moderate income borrowers; we may be able to have a much more significant impact with them, in terms of jobs created, business growth, and so on" (Samantha).

Two board members who were officers at two of Southville's largest banks, disagreed, arguing that maintaining a majority of low-income and poor clients (at least 51 percent) was imperative for continuing ME's funding support from banks because the banks received credit under the CRA for donating to organizations that served low-income populations. A banker board member said, "Banks can get CRA credit for giving organizations like ME money even if the program serves a majority of clients who are above the low income category. However, it is more difficult for them to justify these donations as worthy of CRA credit, and it takes more of their time. I would not recommend that we go in that direction" (Tim). Several board members emphasized that they had joined the board because of ME's commitment to serving the disadvantaged, especially poor and low-income people. They successfully lobbied the board to adopt a goal of increasing ME's low-income service population to 75 percent by year eight.

This discussion generated a reconsideration of ME's conservative lending practices. The board reviewed the data on ME. Table 5.8 contains the information on loan numbers and table 5.9 contains the information on the loan amounts that the board reviewed. Table 5.8 reveals the declining number of loans issued from 1995 to 1999 (no loans were made during the period of observation in 2000). This trend was consistent with ME's policy shift toward a greater emphasis on training. Another banker suggested that ME relax its concern about maintaining a banking-level

TABLE 5.8
Number of loans by year, 1995–1999

Loans	1995	1996	1997	1998	1999	Totals
1st loans	20	17	14	9	9	69
2nd loans	1	6	8	2	3	20
3rd loans	0	0	0	1	1	2
ILP[a]	0	0	0	0	2	2
Total number of loans	21	23	22	12	15	93

[a]*Loans made to individuals through ME's ILP began in late 1999.*

default rate: "It strikes me that we are too worried about our default rate. We keep aiming for a two percent default rate. That is similar to the level of default that is acceptable for banks. ME is loaning to a much higher risk market. We need to argue, to the banks and others who fund us, that this higher risk population will mean a higher default rate. We need to get the money out on the streets. I think donors will accept a higher default rate if we make a good argument and justify it." (Guy). Arguments to loosen up the lending criteria were bolstered by references to the average default rate of 11 percent reported in the field (i.e., most recent SELP directory). These reevaluation discussions frequently referenced "trends in other microenterprise programs," indicating ME's board and staff members' increased awareness of the extra-local MDP field. A staff member also urged that the program expand its lending capacities: "Let us try to ease our restrictions a bit and see what happens. We can increase our monitoring of late payments and tighten up at the first sign of problems" (Matt).

Several long-term board members countered that the training emphasis should continue because of the data on loan defaults, shown in table 5.10. The largest number of defaults was associated with ME's first cohort of

TABLE 5.9
Total amount loaned by year, 1995–1999

	1995	1996	1997	1998	1999	Totals
1st loans	$23,769	$16,100	$10,500	$ 7,000	$ 6,500	$ 63,869
2nd loans	$ 3,000	$15,500	$20,500	$ 6,000	$ 9,000	$ 54,000
3rd loans	0	0	0	$ 5,000	$ 5,000	$ 10,000
ILP[a]	0	0	0	0	$10,000	$ 10,000
Total amount	$26,769	$31,600	$31,000	$18,000	$30,500	$137,869

[a]*Loans made to individuals through ME's ILP began in late 1999.*

TABLE 5.10

Loan default information, 1995–1999

Defaults for Stated Years	Defaults	Percentage of Total for Period	Percentage of Total (all years)
Number of defaults—loans made 1995–1996	9	20	10
Number of defaults—loans made 1997–1999	3	6	3
Number of defaults 1995–1999	12	13	13
Total amount of loans defaulted, 1995–1999	$15,100	11[a]	11[a]

[a]*This figure reflects the percentage of total dollars loaned ($137,869) from 1995 through 1999 that were in default.*

clients (1995–1996 period). The default rate was 20 percent for this group, compared to an average of 13 percent for the entire time period. This information suggested to some board members that the increased screening and stricter lending approach should continue. They remained concerned about increasing lending too quickly and urged caution.

Nevertheless, the board agreed to reexamine ME lending policies, reduce some lending restrictions, and increase loan volume. This resolution was accompanied by significant warnings against easing restrictions too dramatically or increasing loan volume too quickly. Again, the first cohort was a point of reference. One board member said, "With that first class, we got a lot of money out on the streets quickly, and it came back to haunt us. We need to be careful about trying to move too fast again" (Patrice).

After the meeting, a staff member commented that it was time for some of the older board members to step aside so that the program could grow.[11] Staff members desired the increased job security and pay they thought would be associated with a larger program and indicated their enthusiasm for both geographic and lending-program expansion. The new executive director outlined plans for a regional expansion of the program to new towns in the state. The board members tentatively endorsed some "preliminary explorations" into expansion opportunities.

New Funding Opportunities and Further Institutionalization

Extra-local funding pressures converged with some staff and board encouragement to redirect the ME program and revitalize its interest in lending.

In fiscal year seven (after the strategic planning session), ME received another SBA grant of several hundred thousand dollars that included both lending and operations (technical-assistance) monies; however, the receipt of these operations funds was tied to the amount of monies that ME loaned (larger loan amounts would increase the operations grants for technical assistance). Thus, in order to gain the desired increase in operations funds, ME had to increase its lending activity.

Several board members continued to voice concerns about such large and rapid increases in lending; however, the grant weakened their position considerably. The board and staff resolved to increase the total number of loans to fifty per year by the following fiscal year. They hoped that much of this increased volume would be accomplished through the new individual lending program.

Staff added an Accelerated Lending Assistance Workshop (ALA) to speed up the loan process for experienced entrepreneurs who wanted the larger individual loans. The ALA included a four-week expedited business plan and application assistance workshop for a charge of $100. Eligible clients were those in business who could provide two years of tax and financial records.

Thus, despite years of shifting toward a training focus, ME now reemphasized its lending role. This reorientation was accompanied by further routinization, including another tightening up of the borrowers' circles and a further elaboration of lending policies.

Also in year seven, ME circles became even more institutionalized. Problematic circles were disbanded and their members were reassigned to new circles. Meeting time and formats were assigned and prestructured by circle facilitators and other ME staff. New clients selected circles based not on member bonding but rather on the most convenient meeting time. When old members left circles, new members were rotated in. This method helped circles endure when members left, but it also meant that the circle composition and structure was more staff- than client-driven. It also loosened the bonds among the members in most circles.

Circle members' responsibility for one another's loan repayment was also redefined. Initially, when one circle member fell behind on payments, no other members could borrow until either the payments had been made or six months had passed. The delay sanctions were removed and ME simply took the money out of the circle loan loss reserve fund. Most clients favored the new policy because it reduced pressures and sources of hostility among circle members. Staff members said that it made their jobs easier and that circle standardization increased the number of peer loans that they could issue. On the other hand, the changes reinforced the difficulties of building responsibility among circle members for their peers and reduced circle cohesion (in addition to reducing collective forms of resistance to staff controls). One client said, "I enjoy the circles; they're very helpful . . . I do not really know the people very well. They seem nice. The facilitator mostly manages the meeting format" (Stacey).

Confronted with concerns about funding related to ME's low-income mission and the board's enhanced service goals in this realm, the staff strategized about methods for increasing the percentage of low-income clients. They returned to the churches and community centers in poverty-level and low-income areas to offer orientations.

ME also developed a partnership with Western State Disability Services to provide training to disabled clients starting businesses. Disability Services had its own loan pool, but wanted its clients to take ME's business training program and emerge with a business plan that could be used in an application for state loan funds. The state paid for their ME courses. But serving disabled clients within ME's existing course and service rubric proved to be difficult. For example, one man missed several classes because the cab sent by the state to transport him to class was late and he could not walk to the bus stop. Another man who had lost much of his short- and long-term memory in an accident was unable to get through the course without special assistance. Moreover, clients discovered that having a business plan was not sufficient to receive the Disability Services business loans. This program increased the representation of low-income clients in ME, but evidenced few successes in terms of business start-ups.

In addition, the staff also considered working with state agencies to provide business training for women prison inmates and negotiated with American Indians to offer services on tribal lands. Neither of these two efforts were realized.

The staff feared that the ILP and ALA components would exacerbate the decline in low-income clients because these two programs typically attracted significantly more moderate-income clients and fewer low-income clients. Staff members reported that approximately 48 percent of ILP clients were low income, 57 percent were women, and 43 percent were minorities.

By the end of year seven, the staff reported that their stepped-up orientation activities and disability and welfare-to-work partnerships had increased low-income client representation to approximately 65 percent. Minorities made up 69 percent and women made up 74 percent of the peer-lending-program population in years seven and eight.

Return of Financial Woes

In fiscal year eight, ME suffered increased financial woes due to declines in corporate giving after the September 11, 2001, attacks and the recessionary economy that preceded and followed them. ME lost its free office space (due to such corporate cutbacks), and federal cutbacks on the percentages of technical assistance funds that accompany SBA loans (from 25 to 15 percent) further decreased the support of ME operations, including assistance to clients. The board had to approve staff layoffs.

Due to the loss of several of its most successful fund-raisers, the responsibility for fund-raising fell to the board as a whole. ME's executive board called on board members to increase their donations to the program and to take a larger role in fund-raising responsibilities. Staff and board members formed a fund-raising committee to develop a revenue-generating project and intensified staff grant-writing activities. Although a large grant from a private foundation early in year eight eased ME's financial problems, fund-raising during the rest of the year was severely hampered by the national economic recession.

During the frenzy of fund-raising activity, staff located a call for proposals from a U.S. Department of Health and Human Services (HHS) funding program. The grant was expressly designed to allocate TANF monies for programs that offered services to poverty-level clients and provided jobs to individuals who might otherwise be on welfare. ME submitted a grant proposal that promised to expand its services to poverty-level clients. Several board and staff members maintained their belief that ME worked best for low-income rather than poor or welfare clients, but as one staff member said, "I agree that we are most relevant for the working poor rather than people at the poverty level. But it seems like every call for grant proposals that comes across our desk calls for a welfare-to-work component. That is where the money is now" (Callie).

Although the HHS grant was not funded, ME's application for it and the continuing involvement of U.S. MDPs in welfare-to-work programs further illustrates the contradictory pressures on these organizations (see Greenberg 1999; Alisultanov, Klein, and Zandniapour 2002; FIELD 2002). Faced with demands to show client loan repayment and quick business successes, practitioners recognized that more moderate-income populations experience the most success in microenterprises (see Servon and Bates 1998). Yet the declining availability of operations monies and demands for success indicators in the form of number of businesses and number of new jobs created made it difficult for ME staff and board to know where and how to turn. TANF-related programs provided much-needed sources of program support.

Client Follow-ups and Program Framing to Funders

As funding demands added varied and conflicting program goals, they also distracted from more effective planning and assessment of ME's long-term impact on client welfare. Still, ME attempted to conduct periodic client follow-ups. These studies provided insights into the types of clients most likely to remain in the program and the ways in which they believed that ME services helped them.

ME conducted one study of drop-outs in year six: they compared individuals who had attended an orientation and joined the program with those who had attended but declined to enroll in classes. The findings of this study are summarized in table 5.11. The data suggest that women, minorities, and economically better-off individuals from households with more than one adult were more likely to move from orientation into ME classes. Reasons given for dropping out included scheduling conflicts, transportation issues, lack of need for the training, financial problems, and the small loan size. This study offers insights into the type of clients that are best served by MDPs—the better-off of the low-income group. These findings also reinforce the observations made by practitioners in other MDPs described in chapter 3.

Other follow-up studies included periodic telephone and mail surveys and focus-group discussions. These studies generally reported considerable

TABLE 5.11

Comparison of dropout study sample with continuing participants, spring 2000

Demographic Characteristic	Dropout, $n = 56$		Continuing, $n = 30$	
	Number	Percentage	Number	Percentage
Women	31	55	23	77
Minority	29	52	23	77
Starting business	39	70	21	70
Only adult in household	22	39	7	23
Average number of children living with adult	1.2		1.5	
Average household annual income	$29,534		$31,380	
Median household annual income	$24,000		$27,600	
Average personal annual income	$21,542		$24,228	
Median personal annual income	$20,400		$21,996	

client satisfaction with ME services and a significant number of respondents who credited business successes to their participation. Although the data are of limited generalizability, they provide important glimpses into the ways in which the ME program impacted the lives of some clients. One story came from a man who was a highly educated and skilled professional who had immigrated to the United States about seventeen years earlier. Over the previous seven years, he had been plagued by layoffs. He said, "I moved to work in this country. After several years, I was laid off. I moved to this town and worked a few years, but then they laid me off too. I almost lost my home. Then, I started my import and consulting business. I had a lot of good ideas. But without ME, I could never have turned those into a solid business. ME taught me how to make a business plan and through them I met a lot of contacts. My ME business mentor helped me so much. I am expanding my business. This is a wonderful program and a wonderful country" (Elario). A woman who manufactured a household item that she had designed said, "The money I received from ME put me in a position to actually become a real business. I had all the project plans, had everything laid out. I knew what I was going to do. . . . Without my loan I wouldn't be as highly paid now. It's increased my bottom line each month. . . . It was a small loan in comparison, but it paid for the equipment I needed. . . . [T]he loan opened up a bunch of doors and a bunch of dominoes started falling" (Luellen).

Despite their successes, even ideal clients described the fragile nature of their businesses. One man described his hard luck and the staff's efforts to work with him through the difficult period: "ME has been extremely compassionate with me. . . . [W]e had only been up and going for a month, and a cousin—[she was] like my sister—died, and I had to leave for that funeral and come back . . . We opened in September of 2001, and business was deader than a doornail for a year, because mine is a luxury business. . . . Then my partner got very ill and I lost a third of my income. ME has been wonderful working with me." (Gray).

Clients who participated in the ILP program and received larger loans also experienced instability and limited incomes. They often supplemented their businesses with resources from other sources (e.g., savings or their spouse) (see Jurik 1998). When asked how participation in ME had impacted her income, a woman in a professional computer-related business said, "My income has *decreased* since ME. My husband is the one who takes care of the household and I'm only with the business. Yes, I get money to do my nails and buy me some clothes and things like that. . . . I pay my car payment . . . things like that. ME has helped me improve my business, but I'm not at that point yet, so my household income has not increased, no" (Bettina). Clients who reported decreased or unstable incomes did not blame ME. They blamed the economic climate and the difficulties faced by small businesses in it. One client described the effects of the World Trade Center attack on her business: "I can't say if the program helped me because we started our business right after 9–11. That was such a horrific impact on my business that the loan wouldn't have made any difference. . . . I still would have gone through money" (Laura Jean). Two other clients described the disadvantages of small businesses: "One of the major challenges for an entrepreneur is they work a lot by themselves. That's all they have to rely on. And that's a major disadvantage compared to corporations" (Celina) and "I have to constantly figure out how I can provide something that a big company does not provide. Because I cannot compete with a corporation, it will always undersell me" (Joni).

Although they provided interesting stories about clients' lives and many stories about how MDP services helped, ME's follow-up studies were plagued by low response rates and the disproportionate representation of better-off clients. Of course, the problems with missing data were not noted in funding appeals and are seldom emphasized in MDP evaluations more generally. Funding appeals supplemented brief quantitative reports with a series of inspiring success stories from model clients who had done exceptionally well in their businesses and credited their success to ME. The stories of model clients were prominently featured in program literature and in media coverage of the program.

ME's lack of methodologically sound follow-up evaluations is not unique. The national MDP sample in chapter 3 indicates that such limited data are routinely used to justify the increased and continued funding of MDPs around the United States. Some programs devote far less energy to evaluative monitoring than did ME. More valid and representative studies are costly for small nonprofits to undertake. As noted earlier, even more expensive and rigorous national-level evaluations (e.g., Clark et al. 1999; Himes and Servon 1998; Charles Stewart Mott Foundation 1990, 1993, 1994; Raheim 1997) tend to lack adequate control comparison groups and proper differentiation of the types and amounts of services received (see Schreiner 1999a, 1999b, 1999c; Morduch 1999, 2000). It is difficult for programs and evaluators to track clients who become disillusioned or fail, and adequate comparison groups are difficult to locate and equally difficult to track in longitudinal follow-ups. Still, the absence of quality ongoing evaluation and the continued funding crises converge to make it extremely difficult for ME and organizations like it to identify clear, consistent goals and the paths to reach them.

Because many other economic development programs in Southville County had folded or were unable to show even these indications of success, ME understandably became a favorite program among Southville city and county officials. The ME program and staff received numerous local and state awards for community service and economic development, and, somewhat ironically, two national awards for achievements in the welfare-to-work realm.

In year eight, ME continued to fall short of its SBA lending goals, although it came closer to the mark than in year seven. ME's improved performance in the realm of lending volume was partially due to a loosening of the criteria for ILP eligibility (i.e., businesses had to show one year rather than two years of receipts and tax payments). The additional ILP loans were accompanied by heightened staff and board anxieties, however, and so other requirements for that program were tightened up. Even one ILP default (because the loans were much larger than peer loans) would significantly increase ME's default rates. Although tighter qualifications were viewed as reducing the likelihood of defaults, they also reduced the number of individual loans made.

The staff also struggled to meet the board's expanded goals for serving low-income clients. They were anxious about the impact of pending federal requirements that clients submit tax records to verify low-income eligibility. (Until that time clients were allowed to self-report.) Corporate donations and grant funding continued to lag behind program needs. ME staff constantly searched for new grant opportunities and other fundraising ideas.

ME continues its struggle to balance outreach with sustainability goals. Ironically, the new economy, which gave rise to programs like ME, is a constant impediment to successful new small businesses and also to funding for MDPs. Renewed threats of reductions in SBA funding for technical assistance have increased pressure to lend mostly to clients who do not need extensive support services. Also in jeopardy are funding allocations to older SBA Women's Business Centers. The rationale for these cuts is that programs must become locally self-supporting. Thus, as MDPs proliferate, so do the challenges to survival faced by mature programs like ME.

CONCLUSION

The experiences of the ME program elaborate the dynamic and embedded nature of microenterprise development. The IE approach focuses on how the activities within this local MDP were structured and shaped by institutional and social relations beyond it. Extra-local organizations and relationships, especially those related to anticipated and actual funding sources converged with problematic client relations to produce important changes in the ME program during the eight-year study.

To gain continued program funding, the board and staff perceived the need to produce client business successes and high rates of loan repayment. To increase the likelihood of such positive outcomes, they formalized their organization, increased its businesslike image, scaled up their targeted clientele, increased screening prior to the lending stages, and emphasized training over lending. These changes replicated findings from the national MDP data described in chapter 3 and other research on screening in social service programs (e.g., Fobes and Quadagno 1995; Holstein and Miller 1996; K. Grahame 1998a). They also illustrate new privatization ideologies that emphasize business practices as a model for government and nonprofit organizations. ME's changes led to a decreased emphasis on assisting welfare and poverty-level clients and to an increased assessment of client culture capital (i.e., commitment, attitude, and professional demeanor) and human capital (i.e., skills and experience) as prerequisites for lending. Increasing staff control over lending not only diminished the percentage of clients allowed to receive loans, it also decreased the autonomy and bonds of the client borrowers' circles. The weakening of the borrowers' circles reinforced the individualization of U.S. peer-lending models. The staff developed typifications of clients to help describe and justify practices that they deemed essential to organizational survival. Their activities were articulated to an understanding of what funders might be willing to support. But, in addition, these activities limited services to those disadvantaged clients whom ME and other MDPs have, either explicitly or implicitly, promised to serve.

It was ironic that just as ME became confident in targeting a more moderate-income clientele and emphasizing training over lending, extra-local funding opportunities produced a countervailing pressure to revitalize services to low-income clients, extend services to welfare and disabled clients, and dramatically increase lending activities. Through individual loans and accelerated training, ME tried to increase its loan volume and balance risks by more rigorous screening and lending criteria; however, these strategies produced new contradictions as the program struggled to meet new lending volume requirements. Clients who were acceptable risks often had other, more traditional lending options, and even the experienced and better-resourced clients that ME hoped to attract experienced tremendous amounts of instability in the new economy and consequent loan defaults.

Even model clients who professed the greatest appreciation and admiration for the program's contribution to their business success often reported diminishing and precarious incomes. They did not blame these problems on ME but, instead, attributed them to the perils of the economy and small business's place in it. These structural concerns are not and cannot be addressed by small nonprofit programs such as ME regardless of the commitment from their clients, staff, and volunteers.

CHAPTER 6

CONCLUSION: *MICROENTERPRISE DEVELOPMENT CONTEXT, CONTRADICTION, AND PRACTICE*

> People always made the mistake of thinking that starting
> a business was simple and then found that there were all sorts
> of hidden problems and unforeseen demands. She had heard of people
> opening businesses that lasted four or five weeks before they ran
> out of money or stock, or both. It was always more difficult
> than you thought it would be.
> —SMITH, 1998

This statement, drawn from the novel, *The No. 1 Ladies' Detective Agency,* aptly warns about the difficulties found in operating small businesses. MDPs aim to encourage economically and socially marginalized individuals to form microenterprises. In the past, these individuals were rarely seen as entrepreneurs, and helping them to become successful entrepreneurs is not as simple as proponent rhetoric makes it seem.

This book has examined microenterprise development as a socially embedded and emergent process. Using an IE approach, I have examined the experiences of MDP practitioners and clients, and mapped the connections between program practice and the larger society. These extra-local societal arrangements explain the popularity of microenterprise development as a method for poverty alleviation, but they also give rise to contradictions for practitioners and clients trying to achieve program successes.

The impetus to define poor and other marginalized individuals as entrepreneurs stems from a social context of increasing insecurity and declining state responsibility for social welfare. The new economy has fostered expanding rates of poverty and underemployment. Accompanying neoliberal ideologies justify decreased government spending for social investment programs and increased individual responsibility for economic and social welfare (see Rubin 1996; Quadagno 1999). These ideologies accentuate market-based solutions for social problems. International development specialists and social service practitioners attuned to neoliberal agendas advanced microenterprise development as a low-cost, locally driven mechanism for easing economic insecurities. MDPs would integrate disadvantaged individuals into the new economy by assisting small, flexible, self-employment ventures. These microenterprises would then substitute for and supplement low-paying, insecure, and inflexible wage employment activities.

Neoliberalism includes a new privatization agenda that encourages government and nonprofit social service organizations to operate in ways that are consistent with the management of for-profit firms (Jurik 2004). The justification for new privatization is the belief that emulating business models increases nonprofit and government-sector efficiency and effectiveness. Accordingly, advocates promise that MDPs will operate more like business than welfare programs and offset their costs with revenue from training and lending services. The possibilities that MDPs could promote not only client but program self-sufficiency attract the support of state policymakers and foundation funding sources. For clients, MDPs offer the hope of fulfilling long-standing American dreams of individual entrepreneurship. Even grassroots activists support MDPs in hopes that they can promote a multitude of small businesses or a "greening" of global capitalism. Thus, the context of economic restructuring, neoliberalism and new privatization presents opportunities for MDP establishment and expansion.

Despite its wide-ranging appeal, microenterprise development is problematic in practice. Fostering successful microenterprises takes more than a brief training course and small-business loan when clients are poor or otherwise highly disadvantaged. MDP funding demands for sustainability and outreach do not take the reality of client lives into account—the routine and institutional barriers that disadvantaged clients face in meeting program requirements and operating successful businesses. An IE approach focused on the concrete experiences of both practitioners and clients in MDPs reveals this disjuncture between prevailing MDP logic and client needs and the contradictions that ensue.

The figure maps the links among the three primary components of my analysis: (1) context, (2) contradiction, and (3) practice. It illustrates key elements of the extra-local context that produce contradictions that the staff, board, and clients attempt to resolve in practice. These strategies often produced further program contradictions. This chapter draws together findings from the review of MDP history, national sample interviews, and longitudinal case study to provide an overview of how MDP

CONTEXT

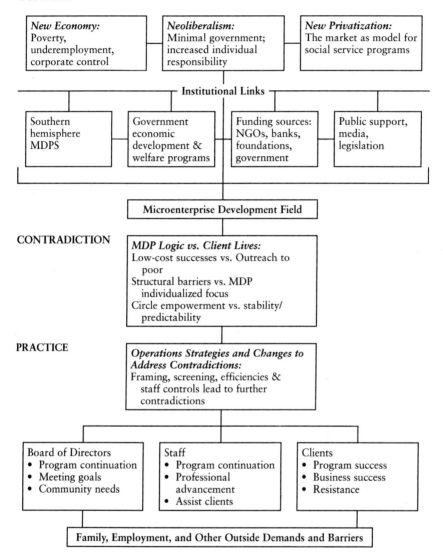

Figure: Mapping microenterprise development as an embedded and emerging process (the absence of arrows signifies the nonlinear nature of the process)

context and contradiction shape practice. The brief review facilitates an overall assessment of the conceptual and practical significance of U.S. microenterprise development for struggles to reduce inequality.

CONTEXT: INTERNATIONAL AND UNITED STATES

Throughout this book, I have emphasized how global, national, and local contexts of the new economy, neoliberalism, and new privatization shape the field of microenterprise development. The figure maps the links between MDPs and other institutions, including funding sources, government programs, national associations, and international MDPs.

U.S. programs drew on MDP models pioneered in southern hemisphere nations. Programs like the Grameen Bank emerged in the midst of tight-money policies, high unemployment, and an increasing polarization in the distributions of wealth and work opportunities. Because many of these same problems came to characterize life in the United States, it was not surprising that this country was also fertile ground for microenterprise development (Dennis 1998). Reports of poverty alleviation and self-sufficiency were especially attractive given the growing rates of poverty and structural unemployment in the United States and declining government expenditures and legitimacy in the social service arena (Jurik and Cowgill 1999). U.S. and other northern hemisphere-dominated aid agencies and NGOs were instrumental in shaping and diffusing southern models internationally as a low cost, locally managed poverty-alleviation mechanism (Tinker 1999; Poster and Salime 2002).

When these southern MDP models were adopted, they were reshaped through the influence of other institutions in the U.S. cultural context. The historical review in chapter 2 explains that many U.S. MDPs began as components of larger economic development or welfare-to-work programs. Although some programs adopted a place-based focus that was consistent with economic development programs, most U.S. MDPs assumed a more individualized focus that reflected welfare service models. But, instead of job training and other welfare services, they focused on the "technology" of self-employment development. The holistic focus and collective empowerment goals associated with prominent southern MDPs were greatly diminished. U.S. practitioners and their funders believed that nonbusiness and broader community-focused agendas were too costly. U.S. MDPs tended to favor individual rather than peer lending and blamed the difficulties that they and their clients encountered with borrowers' circles on the individualism of U.S. culture (Taub 1998). This transformation is not surprising: scholars have noted similar modifications when other programs are imported to the United States (e.g., Merry 1982). Clearly, the U.S. cultural context informed funder, practitioner, and client perceptions and, thus, the diffusion of MDP innovations (see Strang and Meyer 1993; Boyle 2002). This social context shaped the logic of microenterprise development, a logic that promoted assistance to disadvantaged entrepreneurs but also minimal program expenditures.

CONTRADICTION: MDP LOGIC VERSUS CLIENT NEEDS

Microenterprise development entailed the balancing of often-conflicting organizational goals and extra-local demands (see Bhatt 2002). On the one hand MDPs promised to alleviate poverty by extending self-employment opportunities to poor, welfare, and otherwise marginalized clients and, in some cases, to empower them through participation in lending and other program decision making. On the other hand, funders expected MDPs to provide services to large numbers of clients, show business successes, and keep loan loss rates and operating costs to a minimum (see Bates 1997). These concerns informed MDP practice and presented contradictions for program builders (i.e., board, staff, and clients) in the areas of client outreach and circle empowerment (see figure).

Disadvantaged clients faced problems with housing, transportation, and child care not only in operating businesses but in completing microenterprise program requirements. The limited business training and start-up capital were insufficient to overcome the barriers that these practical problems posed to client business futures. Even when successfully completed, the narrowly focused training and lending programs failed to address the embedded disadvantages of racism, sexism, and corporatism in U.S. business culture.

Like the ME program, many MDPs set out to include poor and welfare clients. Over time, however, most staff members concluded that poor individuals, especially former welfare recipients, had insufficient resources—financial or social—to run successful businesses without substantial additional expenditures for training and support services. They also feared that these clients would be unable to repay MDP loans. Increasing the training to serve highly disadvantaged clients might help increase their repayment and success rates, but it would also raise operations costs and undermine sustainability efforts. In order to appeal to funding sources, MDPs needed to document program successes according to emerging industry standards of best practice (Christen and Drake

2002). These findings highlight the contradiction between MDP sustainability pressures and outreach to the poor (also see Morduch 2000; Bhatt et al. 2002).

The logic and practice of peer lending also produced contradictions. Borrowers' circles were the very components that MDPs cited as sources of client empowerment and self-help (Woolcock 1998, 1999), but practitioners encountered problems in administering peer lending models. The circles were innovative but time consuming, and clients often had difficulties in meeting attendance requirements and developing rapport with peers. The circles' supportive roles sometimes conflicted with their evaluative functions (also see Montgomery 1996). Circle autonomy and client participation in lending and other program decisions also increased the complexity and uncertainty of the lending process. When there were problems within the circles, peer lending consumed considerable staff time. Practitioners searched for ways to increase the stability and predictability of circles (Ashe 2000).

PRACTICE: STRATEGIES TO MEET ORGANIZATIONAL CHALLENGES

MDP builders were forced to make difficult decisions about and trade-offs among program goals, client selection, and staff control over program management and lending decisions. Staff members developed some common but often quite innovative strategies to address these dilemmas (see figure). Despite these best efforts, the strategies often led to further contradictions.

Program Framing: New Privatization Discourses

There was much cross-fertilization and fluidity in MDP design. Practitioners were well aware of the different MDP models and this variety allowed programs such as ME to create their own hybrid organizational forms. MDPs also shifted the framing of their program to clients, funders, and the public. The framing of program goals and operations changed in response to program practice (i.e., successes and failures) and in anticipation of the desires of potential funding sources. The ME case study demonstrates the unfolding of these many changes also described in the national MDP sample.

Although MDPs were frequently presented as a mechanism for poverty alleviation and an alternative to welfare and other government social service programs, many practitioners distinguished their programs from welfare service models. As they matured, programs adopted discourses that were consistent with new privatization ideologies wherein government and nonprofit organizations strive to emulate for-profit organizations. Practitioners spoke of their program's maturation as entailing a shift away from social service terminology and analogies and toward business language and models of operation. They hoped this business frame would communicate to clients and funders that the loans were not grants and were to be repaid. Such changes are typical of any maturing organization (see Powell and Friedkin 1987), but they also reflect a larger societal tendency to romanticize market efficiency as a solution to all social problems (Blau 1999; Ritzer 2000; Jurik 2004).[1]

Screening and Stratification

Limited resources and high accountability to funders encouraged practitioners to develop strategies for increasing program successes. Most MDPs developed techniques for selecting appropriate clients. Target populations were selected with funding levels and requirements in mind. Practitioners recommended that MDPs avoid more highly disadvantaged clients, particularly welfare and poverty-level service objectives, unless there were specific initiatives such as state or federally funded welfare-to-work demonstration projects available. Even then, MDPs often shifted away from these special poverty or welfare target populations whenever funding incentives ended.

Screening mechanisms were an important method for selecting the clients who would be most successful within existing program resources. Screening mechanisms included specific criteria for program entry and eligibility for various stages of a program (e.g., having a business plan), as well as more subtle interactional criteria whereby staff assessed clients' orientations and attitudes toward their businesses and the program. For example, ME staff looked for clients who fit profiles of practical, professional, and successful entrepreneurs, assessments that often entailed moral judgments of client worthiness. The procedures that ME staff developed reflected practices in the national sample; in this, MDPs also reflected some of the standard elements associated with social welfare and safety net programs as agents of cultural reproduction (see Fobes and Quadagno 1995). Programs stratified clients, selecting only some for advancement to later and riskier program stages (e.g., lending). Novice businesses and, in some programs, more disadvantaged clients were relegated to training services alone. For example, ME reduced its outreach to less-educated and poverty-level clients and screened start-up entrepreneurs carefully before the borrowing stages.

Staff stratification of clients for lending blended with client self-selection to account for the relatively high ratio of nonborrower to borrower clients reported here and in prior research (Servon 1999a). Despite the strong emphasis on microcredit that dominates much MDP publicity, screening and stratification mechanisms relegate lending to a small component of most programs, especially for poor and welfare clients.

Training and Lending Efficiencies and Increasing Staff Control

The staff sought to promote efficient, low-cost operations in both the training and lending realms. At times, efficiencies prompted them to assume increasing authority over operations.

Training was a central method for preparing and selecting clients for lending, a method that practitioners believed reduced default rates. Regardless of the avenue selected, offering the quality of training needed by disadvantaged clients entailed significant program costs. Most practitioners agreed that training was an essential component of U.S. microenterprise development because it was so complicated to do business in the United States. Like the ME program, most MDPs limited training to traditional business topics. Programs targeting poverty-level and welfare-to-work populations, however, usually added training to address nonbusiness issues such as self-esteem, and balancing work and family; a few partnered with other organizations to include transportation, housing, savings, and child-care services. Stories of ME clients' experiences illustrated the need of disadvantaged clients for such support services. A small number of MDPs in the national sample also sought to develop advocacy, group purchasing, or marketing programs to counter the disadvantages that small businesses routinely encountered. Such services were rare because most practitioners, including those at ME, regarded these matters as too expensive or outside the purview of their programs. Regardless of their beliefs in its importance and their best efforts to increase efficiency, MDP training offerings were limited by the availability of funding to support them. Practitioners located numerous organizations that wanted to provide dollars for lending but far fewer that were willing to provide the money for the training and auxiliary services that might increase the likelihood of businesses succeeding and loans being repaid by disadvantaged entrepreneurs.

Practitioners also sought to increase efficiency in the lending realm. Peer lending was a particular area of concern. The MDP literature suggests that the individualism and anonymity characteristic of U.S. culture make it difficult for peer-lending programs to function as effectively as in southern hemisphere countries (Taub 1998), but practical difficulties such as transportation and family responsibilities also made it difficult for clients to commit fully to borrowers' circles. The dual function of circles as support networks and pressure for loan repayment promoted difficulties in some peer-lending groups. U.S. practitioners believed that borrowers' circles were unstable and time consuming for staff. These concerns led some MDPs in the national sample to eliminate peer lending altogether. Despite funder opposition, ME and several MDPs in the national sample continued peer lending, but increased staff controls over circle operations and decision making.[2]

Strategies Produce Further Contradictions

Strategies to ease MDP dilemmas often produced additional contradictions in practice. Staff screening and controls increased the difficulties of recruiting clients and, on occasion, fueled client alienation and resistance. Screening strategies led to increased competition with other lending sources for the most desirable clients. Target populations with more education and business savvy had borrowing opportunities from other small-business lending programs or through personal loans from banks and credit cards. Commercial lines of credit were attractive to credit-worthy clients because they were devoid of time-consuming MDP training and circle attendance requirements. The staff of both ME and the programs in the national sample complained about shortages of applications from qualified clients for their higher-end individual lending programs. These loans were designed to be a source of profit for MDPs, a means for subsidizing training and peer-lending activities.

Allowing service populations to drift too high up the income ladder also posed problem when MDP funds came from sources that targeted low-income or poverty-level populations.[3] For example, bankers warned that too few low-income clients would make the ME program less attractive as a recipient for donations from banks seeking CRA credits. Also, there were always board and staff members who remained morally committed to the principle of serving poor and very-low-income clients. They looked for ways to experiment with services to these groups. Yet staff and board members had to balance these desires with their perceptions that poorer clients exhibited higher loan default rates, lower rates of business successes, and higher operating costs because those results were *also* scrutinized by funding sources.

Staff members assuming increased authority in circle selection and management entailed further contradictions. Staff and board members wanted their programs to reduce inequality, yet program discourse and interactions often replicated rather than challenged structural disadvantages. Despite staff desires to avoid moralizing judgments, their screening of clients often reproduced (unconsciously) existing class, race, and gender relations. Both at ME and in the national sample, staff members held notions of practical, realistic businesses that effectively reinforced women's segregation into pink-collar service occupations and minority men's relegation to labor-intensive low-level service careers. The absence of any systematic treatment of racism, sexism, and more general barriers to small businesses in the U.S. corporate-dominated economy was also problematic for MDP clients. When asked how ME prepared clients for the racism or sexism that they might encounter in doing business, a staff member replied: "We don't really deal with that in the training, but if it happens we just tell them to go do business with somebody else."

The disjuncture between program demands and client lives sometimes led to resistance. Interviews from the national sample offer glimpses of client challenges to program rules, disputes within circles, and requests for additional assistance with matters such as child care, housing, and transportation. The ME case study data provide even more insights into client resistance. There were moments of both individual and collective ME client resistance to staff assessments of them and their business ideas. At times, clients demanded input into rule changes and resisted attempts to curb circle autonomy. Resistance produced program changes, but not always in ways that promoted client empowerment. The beleaguered staff regarded resistance as a costly disruption that threatened program reputation and funding prospects. As staff assumed more control over the circles, group cohesion and resistance diminished. In both the national MDP sample and the ME program, the staff identified loyalty to the program as an important indicator of client prospects for success. ME staff members' control over the circles greatly increased their efficiency and smoothed interactions among members, but it also reduced client cohesion and input. Although perhaps typical of moves toward centralization of authority and control in most maturing organizations, these changes reduced the collective empowerment potential of MDPs (McCarthy and Zald 1973; Matthews 1994).

IMPLICATIONS FOR THEORY AND METHOD

This study explores one type of post-welfare social service alternative that aims to ease the insecurities that plague marginalized individuals in the new economy. MDPs claim to encourage individual self-help, group empowerment, and a business ethic in lieu of big government and welfare dependence. But my findings reveal that MDPs have difficulties meeting such promises and thereby provide a critique of the application of neoliberal and new privatization ideologies to the social services arena. The IE approach helps identify the contradictions that emerge when organizational logics informed by these ideologies collide with the real-life circumstances of disadvantaged clients.

IE directs attention to the material experiences and routine organizational practices of program builders; however, an IE analysis goes beyond everyday routines to ask what societal arrangements are reflected in these practices (Smith 1987). IE avoids the arbitrary distinctions between external and internal, and macro and micro organizational dynamics that often limit sociological analyses. For example, local, national, and global issues of underemployment, unemployment, and division of social welfare programs informed the emergence and diffusion of MDPs. Program designers routinely interacted with and responded to the suggestions of policymakers and funding sources. Clients, in turn, responded to program requirements but always within the context of the demands of their lives. Yet such structures did not determine board, staff, or client actions. The staff persisted in some program goals that were not completely satisfying to funding sources, and the clients struggled to meet program demands even when their lives made it difficult to do so. The multiple standpoints of MDP clients, staff, and board members are briefly summarized in the figure. The data presented here reveal individuals' engagement and struggle to overcome the contradictions that emerge from the prevailing social service logic of their day. Staff-client interactions, pressures, and conflicts produced organizational changes, changes influenced by the extra-local milieu.

This study of MDPs exemplifies some of the classic tendencies in the diffusion, institutionalization and homogenization of new program innovations (see DiMaggio and Powell 1983; Strang and Meyer 1993; Jenness and Grattet 2001). Staff and board members aimed to rationally promote organizational innovations and success among clients and also in their own personal lives (e.g., employment advancement and security) (FIELD 1999). Their rationality was informed by internal organizational dynamics and extra-local opportunities and pressures (i.e., in the larger society and within local and national organizational fields). For example, SBA funding and regulations escalated the homogenization of MDPs. This large-scale federal funding promoted stability, but also increased pressures for bigger, more cost-effective individual loans (Von Pischke 2002a). Life in MDPs reveals the interplay between rational, goal-oriented attempts at innovation and culturally embedded ideologies and pressures in organizational practice (Granovetter 1992; Galaskiewicz and Bielefeld 1998; see also Emirbayer and Mische 1998). But the grounding of this study in real-life experiences also leaves room for contradiction, resistance, and innovation. Social structures and institutions come alive through the everyday actions of real people.

This study also demonstrates the usefulness of the IE approach for developing a critical economic sociology. Although economic sociology aptly emphasizes the social embeddedness of economic phenomena, much research in this realm aims to formulate propositions about the ways in which ostensibly economic phenomena are culturally determined (Portes and Sensebrenner 1993; Krier 1999; Biggart 2002). Instead of generating universals, IE directs attention to the disjuncture between predominant organizational logics (economic and sociological) and the real-world experiences of people. In the case of MDPs, IE points to the disjuncture between client needs in the new economy and an organizational discourse heavily informed by neoliberalism and new privatization ideologies. The losses in microlending programs from the 1950s through 1970s, together with the increased hegemony of the market over social life, pressured MDPs to frame themselves and operate as businesslike organizations (Green 1993). This tendency is consistent with new privatization trends and the increasing pressures on ostensibly nonmarket organizations to adopt for-profit management models (Blau 1999; Ritzer 2000; Jurik 2004).

My data highlight the variety of nonprofit organizations, even among those focused on a similar service field (e.g., microenterprise development), and exemplify the connections and overlap among the nonprofit, government, and for-profit sectors. My findings suggest that nonprofits are not necessarily the innovative, independent third way that they are often portrayed (see Giddens 1998; Schreiner and Morduch 2002). Demands by for-profit and government funding sources shaped nonprofit MDP organizational structure and functions. New privatization ideologies that pressure nonprofits to mimic business standards further blur the boundaries among these organizational realms. Thus, nonprofit MDPs should not be viewed so readily as alternatives or correctives for the weaknesses of the for-profit and government sectors. Increasingly, nonprofit organizations (like neoliberal nation states) discipline themselves in accord with market ideals or risk being ostracized by their field and rejected by funders (Foucault 1979; Powell and DiMaggio 1991; Slaughter and Leslie 1997; McMichael 2000).

IMPLICATIONS FOR POLICY AND FURTHER RESEARCH

This study of microenterprise development as a dynamic and embedded process has important practical and ideological implications. Here, I address an agenda for both policy and future research.

By focusing on disadvantaged entrepreneurs, U.S. MDPs redressed some shortcomings of economic development programs of the past that delivered most of their financial support to middle- and high-income entrepreneurs. Many clients attest to the differences that MDPs and practitioners have made in their lives. Even so, MDPs must not be portrayed as an alternative to welfare or other safety net programs.

Policymakers should more carefully consider the contradictions of microenterprise development that I have documented. There are tremendous pressures on MDPs to scale up to clients who are well above the poverty level (see Servon and Bates 1998; Bhatt 2002). Even in ME and other U.S. MDPs where there is a genuine desire (as well as pressure) to help poverty level clients, there is a countervailing reality. Overcoming the many difficulties and disadvantages that poverty-level clients face is expensive and, consistent with new privatization ideologies, MDPs must be mindful of operating costs. Thus, if MDPs are going to serve poverty-level or very-low-income clients, they should not expect to be inexpensive to operate, much less self-sustaining. Alternatively, if MDPs plan to offer only business-related training and services, they should target moderate-income groups and avoid reliance on funding meant for poor and welfare clients (e.g., TANF funds). Despite new privatization ideologies that suggest social programs can have it all—that is, reduce social problems and perhaps even turn a profit—the MDP experience lends truth to the old adage that you get what you pay for.

Placing the poor in programs that are unlikely to markedly improve their circumstances is an example of what Paula Dressel, Vincent Carter, and Anand Balachandran (1995) call "second-order victim blaming." First, individuals are blamed for being poor and, second, blamed again for failing in the programs offered. My research demonstrates another aspect of victim blaming: typifications of the "right client" often were premised on character assessments that reproduced cultural stereotypes of the poor.

Although acknowledging that MDPs are not a panacea for poverty alleviation, some advocates continue to paint an overly rosy picture by comparing MDP benefits with the stereotypic problems of welfare programs. Such characterizations evoke popular U.S. cultural sentiments that the poor should just help themselves and need little more than minimal support to do so (i.e., some business training and small loans) (see Arnold 1941 [1937]). Success stories propagated by MDP advocates underplay the costs of providing sufficient programming to poor entrepreneurs. In reality, the poor learn to operate little more than meager, labor-intensive enterprises that can at best supplement other low-wage employment activities (Bates and Servon 1996; Ehlers and Main 1998; Clark et al. 1999). Proposing such income packaging as a solution for poor and low-income families reinforces expectations that the poor should simply work more and harder to overcome their disadvantages.

Working harder by adding self-employment to ongoing employment activities may be especially problematic for women seeking to balance paid work and family obligations (Jurik 1998). Perhaps by involving their children in self-employment ventures women can manage to do it all, but this may mean that children miss other important developmental activities or that parents are not as available for supervising and supporting children's educational and extracurricular pursuits. Although income packaging may promote family survival, it may not be the most effective program avenue for societal investment, particularly if MDPs channel women and minority men only into businesses that reflect their past employment experiences. More training is needed in nontraditional businesses for women and in industries in which the self-employed typically prosper (see Ehlers and Main 1998; S. Johnson 1998).[4]

MDPs have potential, but in order to promote social and economic equality we must recognize that individual entrepreneurs are embedded in a broader social context that shapes their lives and opportunities. For example, promoting gender equality and empowerment through microfinance means more than deciding that a program will serve women (Young 1987). Susan Johnson (1999) argues that MDPs must address the gender-based obstacles to women in microenterprises at the individual, household, wider community, and national levels (also see Brush 1992; Rogaly and Johnson 1997). Thus, an MDP might offer individual skill development, but must understand how these services affect or are affected by household dynamics. A few MDPs have developed partnerships with other organizations that provide support services such as child care, transportation, or family counseling (Servon 1999a). These strategies would better address the barriers to poor women entrepreneurs than self-esteem classes and loans for pink-collar businesses alone. Johnson refers to microfinance interventions that address the special problems faced by women as having a "gender-aware mind set" (Johnson 1999). Along the same lines, serving clients who are people of color might call for services informed by a race-aware mind-set.

Researchers (e.g., Anthony 1997) and practitioners (e.g., Ashe 2000) have stressed the social capital—the business contacts and networks—developed through MDPs. Insufficient attention, however, has been paid by U.S. programs to the potential of MDPs for promoting collective empowerment (Rankin 2002). My study has documented the dynamics that reinforce an individualized and technical approach to U.S. microenterprise development, but more research is needed to detail the structural barriers to microenterprises and effective collective empowerment strategies. Incorporation by MDPs of collective buying, marketing, and savings strategies might begin to empower low-income women, minorities, and disabled groups beyond the limited effects of brief training courses and small-business loans (see Creevey 1996). Participatory peer lending, savings, community development, buying cooperatives, and other community ownership and control strategies, which are more common in southern hemisphere MDPs, are rare in U.S. programs (S. Johnson 1998). Political empowerment through collectively organized networks of microentrepreneurs and their communities might challenge the power structures that promote social exclusion. Programs should stimulate and be a part of dialogues and action to change existing social norms, economic conditions, and legal frameworks that disadvantage marginalized entrepreneurs and the poor more generally.

To date, most MDP evaluations assume rather than question the limited scope of U.S. programs. They are also are methodologically flawed in ways that exaggerate program effectiveness (e.g., by lack of comparison groups, sample selection bias, and sample mortality for successive follow-ups). For example, a recent TANF-to-work demonstration project reports higher earnings among self-employed than non-self-employed TANF clients; however, the TANF clients who chose self-employment were more highly educated than other clients in the study (Alisultanov, Klein, and Zandniapour 2002). Despite such limitations, advocates continue to recommend that MDP services be included in TANF-related programming allocations and regulations. MDP advocates bolster such requests with these research studies and anecdotes of clients successes.

Without better evaluations, it is nearly impossible for policymakers and the public to make informed decisions about the success and viability of MDPs as a social service and economic development strategy. Yet rigorous experimental evaluations are costly to undertake and involve ethical concerns about client and nonclient privacy issues. They also fail to come to grips with the ways in which programs interface with clients' lives. We need more rigorous answers to questions such as the following: How many poverty-level and how many low-income clients are served by different MDP services (e.g., various training and lending types)? Do the programs increase incomes and create jobs? For whom do they work best and least? Perhaps most important, we need to know how programs work from the standpoint of those whom they are intended to serve.

IE offers a guiding framework for further research on MDPs and other poverty-alleviation programs that attends to the ways in which programs work and how they figure into clients' lives. The IE approach can map the everyday experiences of individual clients and practitioners, as well as the ways in which their routines are influenced by extra-local institutional arrangements. Clients, practitioners, and programs should be understood as being embedded in a larger web of social relations that informs both practice and the contradictions in it. If MDPs commit to serving poorer entrepreneurs, additional research should focus on how they work (or do not work) from the standpoint of these individuals. An IE approach directs attention to the everyday lives of poor clients as they attempt to manage employment, run businesses, manage their families, and participate in MDPs. It can also identify ways in which these routine activities are embedded within the larger societal arrangements of work, family, community, and society. An IE study of poor women trying to start and operate microenterprises might facilitate the gender-aware program mind-set suggested by Susan Johnson (1999). An IE perspective will yield information to guide program design and modifications to better suit client needs and experiences. The difficulties that practitioners encounter in balancing funder demands and client needs can be articulated to the funding sources and other policymakers. IE's emphasis on the connections among extra-local demands, program practice, and client lives is essential for any MDP evaluation.

Research should not presume that MDPs are the only or best solution to poverty alleviation. Thus, instead of starting with MDP clients, research should be informed by an IE approach that begins with the material experiences of poverty-level individuals and former TANF recipients to consider their need for training, lending and other forms of assistance (e.g., Ng 1996; K. Grahame, 1998a; also Edin 1991; Ehrenreich 2001).[5] With such research findings in hand, additional innovations and pilot programs would be in order rather than calls for best or more uniform MDP practice (Rogaly and Roche 1998; Rogaly, Fisher, and Mayo 1999, 140; FIELD n.d.). These experimental programs could compare various methods for meeting the many financial needs of the poor and other socially and economically marginalized groups. For example, recent research on microfinance in northern and southern countries suggests that offering low-cost banking and insurance services to the poor might do more to ease the burdens of poverty than does microlending to poor businesses (e.g., Carr and Tong 2002; Rogaly, Fisher, and Mayo 1999).

MDPs, practitioners, and clients are embedded in a context of growing economic insecurity and an almost-blind faith in market-centered solutions to the resulting problems. This context promotes tensions in microenterprise development practice. An examination of these program contradictions provides a starting point for challenging the increasing social inequalities and the absence of meaningful programs to address them. Rhetorical claims of poverty alleviation and empowerment sound good, but without more comprehensive agendas, the MDP movement merely attempts to absorb poor and low-income people into the market in ways that neither fundamentally improve their situation nor challenge the logic of the market. Anecdotal success stories told by MDPs do nothing more than help the public and policymakers feel better about the demise of the safety net. A critical economic sociology can and should provide systematic and grounded research and advocacy on these issues.

NOTES

INTRODUCTION

1. The empirical studies of nonprofit organizations by Smith and Lipsky (1993) and Galaskiewicz and Bielefeld (1998) challenge such unified images of nonprofit organizations and argue that nonprofits vary considerably across organizational types in community control, level of bureaucratization, and autonomy from the government.

2. The ideological categories by Goodin et al. (1999) include "classic liberals" (a category that corresponds to my right/economic conservative category). Goodin et al. (1999) also include a "corporatist welfare regime" category that stresses the integrative functions of social welfare and communitarian values. I consider this corporatist welfare category to be consistent with popular conceptions that define contemporary liberals.

3. This function attracts the support of conservatives, who believe that women's place is in the home, *and* liberals, who desire programmatic support for working women and women business owners (Prugl and Tinker 1997).

4. Edgcomb, Klein, and Clark (1996) find that 38 percent of MDP clients are poor, Anthony (1996) finds that 28 percent of Working Capital clients are poor, and Himes and Servon (1998) find that 13 percent of ACCION's U.S. clients are poor.

5. The author, three graduate students, and two undergraduate-student research apprentices conducted interviews with program staff, clients, board members, and funding sources. The author and one graduate assistant conducted participant-observation studies at Association for Enterprise Opportunity (AEO) meetings. The author and two graduate assistants conducted documentary analyses of AEO literature. The author and a graduate assistant conducted a media analysis of U.S. newspaper articles on MDPs from 1990–2000.

6. To be consistent with federal, state, city, and practitioner terminology and to avoid confusion, I use the terms *minority* and *minorities* throughout this book, despite other possible and perhaps preferred terminology, including *men and women of color* and *persons of color*. Whenever possible, I use more precise designations of the particular racial/ethnic group involved.

7. MicroEnterprise, Incorporated (ME) is a fictitious name. Due to human subjects approval requirements at the time of the study and also because some of the program administrators in the larger sample requested anonymity as a condition of their participation, the program, practitioner, and client names used are fictitious. Also, I believe that the issues and dilemmas that I identify in any one MDP are more reflective of societal-level constraints than they are the fault of any one individual program. Hence, I prefer to keep individual program and practitioner names from our interviews and case study data confidential.

1. THE INTERNATIONAL ROOTS OF MICROENTERPRISE DEVELOPMENT

1. There has been some debate about the use of the term *nongovernmental organization* (NGO) in development literature. My use of the term is informed by the work of Sonia Alvarez (1999, 185–87). She agrees that NGOs are typically intermediary organizations between large funding sources (usually foreign foundations or multilateral agencies) and grassroots social-movement groups comprising volunteers. NGOs typically comprise educated middle-class professionals and experts who share an agenda of helping others or influencing public policies in a region. But, in contrast to restrictive dichotomies between NGOs and grassroots (volunteer) groups, Alvarez also argues that some NGO professionals view themselves and their organization as integrally linked to and supporting social movement groups (e.g., in her case women's movements and women's movement groups).

2. Unless otherwise noted, dollar amounts refer to the equivalent in U.S. dollars.

2. THE EMERGENCE OF U.S. MICROENTERPRISE DEVELOPMENT

1. The MESBIC program was renamed the Specialized Small Business Investment Company (SSBIC) program in the 1990s (Bates 2000, 228).

2. It is my contention that practitioners from the emerging U.S. MDP organizational field founded a social movement (loosely defined) to support the diffusion and institutionalization of U.S. MDPs. Scholars disagree about how broadly the term *social movement* can be applied (Burstein 1999). Some might argue that the U.S. microenterprise movement was merely an interest group working on behalf of a new organizational field and not a true social movement. Although both social movements and interest groups are forms of collective action that promote social change, social movements are typically viewed as more marginalized and less institutionalized than interest groups or social service organizations. McAdam and Snow (1997) suggest that "true social movements" typically employ unconventional or disruptive tactics, whereas interest groups seek institutionalized methods of influence. U.S. MDP advocates certainly characterized their activities as a social movement, but, like interest groups, they sought to gain institutionalized access to decision-making authorities. Other scholars (Oliver 1983; Gagne 1996; Bernstein 1997) suggest that social movements shift between marginalized tactics and institutionalized strategies.

3. CfED is a national, nonprofit organization for economic development policy research, consulting, and demonstration projects. It focuses on enterprise development strategies.

4. More recent evaluations of the success of TANF clients in MDPs also report successes—with higher incomes for self-employed TANF clients than for employed counterparts. However, those who select MDPs and self-employment tend to be much more highly educated than their TANF counterparts (Alisultanov, Klein, and Zandniapour 2002).

5. There was also considerable interest in replicating the Grameen Bank experience in Canada, where the Calmeadow organization developed its first peer-lending program in Wkwemkin, Ontario, in 1987 (Coyle et al. 1994).

6. The study lacked an adequate comparison groups of nonclients, and follow-up interviews also suffered from declines in client interview participation over time. Recent research also suggests that many MDP evaluations are plagued by the clients' or interviewer's misreporting of key outcome measures (Harrison and Krause 2002).

3. CHARACTERISTICS OF U.S. MICROENTERPRISE PROGRAMS

1. Typically, we spoke with one practitioner per program, but in some larger programs we spoke with two practitioners, each specializing in a different service area. Respondents included executive directors, program managers, or lending officers from each program. Women constituted 66 percent of those interviewed. Interviews ranged from forty-five to ninety minutes in length.

2. We used purposive sampling techniques to select the programs in our study (Babbie 2003). We drew participants from the 1994 Aspen Institute *Directory of U.S. MDPs* and lists of 1996 AEO conference participants (Clark, Huston, and Meister 1994). Because peer-lending programs make up a small minority of U.S. MDPs and we wished to compare them with individual-lending programs, we selected all the peer programs listed and a systematic sample of non-peer-lending programs. We mailed surveys to the resulting list of programs, and we followed up the survey with taped telephone interviews. Fifty-nine programs agreed to participate, but we eliminated nine from our sample because they no longer offered microloans. (We considered microloans to be loans of $25,000 or less.) The final sample of fifty MDPs represents a 57 percent response rate of eligible programs. Despite our attempts to oversample peer-lending programs, a sizable majority of MDPs in our study (68%) offered only individual loans. The combined percentage of programs that offered peer lending or both loan types was 32 percent. When compared with the figure of 28 percent for peer and peer-individual programs reported in the 1996 AEO-Aspen national survey (Severens and Kays 1997), it was clear that our sample overrepresents peer programs, but not as much as intended.

3. Because we oversampled peer-lending programs, our percentages of program types are not representative of the entire U.S. MDP population. Given the emphasis on peer lending as a prototype for MDP methodology and our extensive case study of a peer-lending program, we wanted to be able to effectively compare these programs with those that used individual-lending approaches. Ideally, we would have preferred to compare peer-lending-only programs with those that offered both peer and individual loans. However, such subsetting would have left too few programs in each category for later statistical comparisons. (Seven peer-lending programs offered both peer and individual loans, and nine programs used peer-lending methods alone.)

4. M. Johnson (1998a) refers to such programs as empowerment-oriented; however, in interviewing practitioners from these programs, we found Johnson's empowerment concept to be a less useful distinction.

5. It is important to note some limitations of our analysis. Although we examined the demographics of clients served by our program sample, we had difficulty in this regard. The MDPs varied in their record-keeping of client demographics. Missing data on client demographics ranged from 28 to 38 percent. The numbers in parentheses throughout this chapter refer to the program IDs listed in table 3.2.

6. These findings are consistent with feminist organization research (e.g., Martin 1990; Bordt 1997a) that documents the blending of traditional and nontraditional organization forms. It is also consistent with organizational diffusion studies that argue that cultural context is key to the diffusion and transformation of organizational innovations (Strang and Meyer 1993; Boyle 2002).

7. Smith and Lipsky (1993) found that shifts in response to funding were frequent practices among nonprofits. This trend is also consistent with the literature on institutional isomorphism, particularly with descriptions of the homogenizing tendencies within organizational fields (DiMaggio and Powell 1983; Jenness and Grattet 2001).

8. This tendency is consistent with social movement and organizational literature findings that organizational maintenance demands often distract from an organization's stated goals (McCarthy and Zald 1973).

9. Typifications are constructs or shared understandings among social actors in a setting about what types of behavior fit under a specified category. David Sudnow (1965) discusses notions of "normal crimes" held by police. Jurik and Gregware (1992) describe typifications of the characteristics that constitute a "battered woman" among presentence investigators. Social service workers also develop such constructs, as described here, for MDP workers.

4. FORMING A MICROENTERPRISE PROGRAM: CASE STUDY PART I

1. Recall that the name Micro-Enterprise, Incorporated, and the acronym ME are fictitious, as are the names given to the individuals described in the chapter.

2. One of us (Jurik) was a member of the steering committee and a volunteer who also provided *gratis* research-consulting services for the program. The other (Cowgill) worked for the program as a student intern, volunteer, and briefly as an employee. We performed a number of evaluation studies and provided reports regarding the various services and programs provided by the MDP. Thus, we experienced the benefits *and* challenges of simultaneous roles as organizational insiders and outsiders (Zinn 1979; Naples 1996).

3. Over the first eight years of ME's operation, we gathered over 600 hours of observational data from program planning sessions, business workshops, circle meetings, and client alumni activities. We conducted individual interviews and informal conversations with board members, staff, clients, program partners, funders, and other local social service providers who worked with poor and low-income populations. We conducted three surveys of clients and two surveys of board members (response rates for board surveys ranged from 50 to 60% and for client surveys from 20 to 80%). We conducted seven client focus groups about experiences in business and in the ME program, and we reviewed program records on all clients through June 2000 ($n = 970$). We shared our findings and recommendations with ME at various stages of the research.

4. This study was part of the designing phase of the ME program and was separate from the later, national study of 50 MDPs described in chapter 3.

5. The sample of service providers in the area was drawn from a list of providers who served low-income populations in Southville, particularly those that provided economic assistance or job training and those who worked with targeted groups of interest to the task force (e.g., American Indian, Latino/a, Asian or African American, displaced-homemaker, welfare-to-work, and refugee populations). From this list, we took every tenth program yielding a sample of 25 programs. Seventeen programs agreed to the interview, yielding a response rate of 68 percent.

6. As a result of lobbying efforts by MDP practitioners and advocates across the United States, MDPs were eventually recognized nationally as economic development organizations by CDBG funding councils (see chap. 3).

7. This finding of a strong initial volunteer component and gradual professionalization over time is consistent with the literature on social movement organizations (McCarthy and Zald 1973; Staggenborg 1988).

8. As noted earlier, we gathered a variety of data on the program throughout the planning and first eight years of operation. The focus of the discussion here, however, is on program implementation, particularly the interactions surrounding the first program cohort (see Cowgill 1996). We administered course-evaluation surveys to clients in the first four- and ten-week sessions of the ME program. Eighty percent of the clients in each class completed

the evaluations. In addition to these quantitative evaluation measures, we also gathered observational and interview data from training classes. Cowgill regularly attended the classes in both the four- and ten-week sessions of the first client cohort, and Jurik attended classes on an occasional basis. During breaks and after classes, we engaged in informal conversations with instructors and over 75 percent of students in workshops.

9. See Castells and Portes (1989) for a discussion of the structural disadvantages that routinely confront very small businesses.

10. This rule was developed because other MDP practitioners reported that women's leadership and participation in the borrowers' circles declined in the presence of men.

11. This finding is consistent with the literature on organizational innovation and diffusion (see for example, Bordt 1997b; Jurik et al. 2000).

5. MATURATION OF A MICROENTERPRISE PROGRAM: CASE STUDY PART II

1. Prior to its fifth year, the ME staff members were predominantly women; however, in 1999, men staff members briefly outnumbered women. After the first executive director retired, she was replaced by a man. However, he stayed only a short time and was replaced by a long-term ME staff member who was a woman. As of the seventh and eighth years of program operations, the staff members were all women.

2. This is similar to the practices of staff in other welfare and social service programs (see also Lipsky 1980; Miller 1989; K. Grahame 1998a).

3. The CDBG grant from the City of Southville required that low-income clients receive top priority for ME training courses; when classes were not filled, then moderate-income clients could enroll.

4. I used the U.S. Department of Health and Human Services (HHS) Poverty Level Guidelines for each year of service delivery data to define poverty level and HUD guidelines to define low-income levels. As per the requirements of their CDBG funding, ME used the HUD guidelines (also issued annually) to identify individuals at the low-income level (see chap. 4, table 4.1). I drew on ME clients' self-reports at the time of their orientation to derive data on each person's household income and number of individuals in their household. I used their household incomes, household sizes, and year of orientation to categorize them in one of three income categories: (1) at or below the U.S. poverty level, (2) above U.S. poverty level, but at or below HUD low-income level, and (3) above poverty and low-income level. The missing data on client incomes were approximately 10 percent.

5. The *term entitlement seeker* is a shorthand term used by Cowgill and Jurik (In press) and was not used by ME staff and board members. They described individuals as "those who viewed or saw the loans as entitlements." The terms *right client, true entrepreneur,* and *professional clients/participants* were often used by the staff and board in discussions about clients.

6. Clark et al. (1999, 14) cite census data suggesting that among the general U.S. poverty level population, approximately 22 percent has had one or more years of college. In their study sample of poverty-level MDP clients, 44 percent has had one or more years of college. Among the ME respondents who reported poverty-level incomes, 65 percent reported having one or more years of college.

7. In fall 1997 (fiscal year four of the program), I administered a mailed follow-up survey to all past and active clients. This survey yielded a response rate of 21 percent ($n = 59$). In 1999 (year six), I participated in another follow-up survey conducted by ME to comply with SBA requirements, which yielded an even lower response rate. Two graduate students

and I conducted focus groups with and surveys of clients in circles in fall 2000 and spring 2001 (fiscal year seven); 70 percent of circle participants responded to the survey and we visited five of the seven circles and conducted focus group discussions with four of the seven circles.

8. We reviewed the program records for all clients through June of 2000 ($n = 970$). The files included information on the demographics of clients, their involvement in various ME programs, the dates of their participation, and information about their businesses plans or operations. The data come from the universe of 970 ME files. This number included past and ongoing clients in any or all stages of the program, including attending an orientation, starting or completing four- and/or ten-week classes, joining a borrowers' circle, and receiving and repaying ME loans (see table 5.2).

9. It is common that, once an innovation or policy has been institutionalized and clear policies established and refined, activity becomes more settled and routine and, thus, more homogenous across organizations (Jenness and Grattet 2001).

10. This pattern of decreasing board involvement is common in maturing organizations (see Smith and Lipsky 1993).

11. It is not unusual for nonprofit staff to advocate program expansion (Galaskiewicz and Bielefeld 1998).

6. CONCLUSION: MICROENTERPRISE DEVELOPMENT CONTEXT, CONTRADICTION, AND PRACTICE

1. I suggest that these standards are romanticized because nonprofits and government are pressured to embrace them without meaningful dialogue about situations in which they are ineffective, problematic, or corrupt (Sclar 2000; Cullen, Maakestad, and Cavender 1987; Coleman 2002; Jurik 2004).

2. Sociological studies of organizations often examine bureaucratization, centralization, and formalization as almost automatic tendencies of maturing organizations (see Powell and Friedkin 1987; Pfeffer and Salancik 1974; DiMaggio and Powell 1983). Such assumptions, however, distract from the complexity and contradictions of real-life MDPs.

3. These findings are consistent with arguments about goal displacement or slippage by Smith and Lipsky (1993), and also with discussions by Jenkins (1987) and Freudenburg (1994).

4. For example, the WomenVenture program described in chapter 2 offers women training in traditionally male vocations.

5. Although neither Edin's nor Ehrenreich's analyses expressly uses an IE approach, both illustrate the sort of insights that can be gained by starting with the experiences of the poor and examining the disjuncture between their needs and social policy/program practice (also see Naples 1997).

REFERENCES

ACCION International. 2003. "Our History" ACCION International [updated 2003], http://www.accion.org/about_our_history.asp (accessed 10 February 2004).

Acker, Joan. 1990. "Hierarchies, Jobs, and Bodies: A Theory of Gendered Organizations." *Gender & Society* 4: 139–58.

Adams, Dale W., and J. D. Von Pishke. 1992. "Microenterprise Credit Programs: Deja Vu." *World Development* 20: 1463–70.

Agadjanian, Victor. 2002. "Men Doing 'Women's Work': Masculinity and Gender Relations among Street Vendors in Maputo." *Journal of Men's Studies* 10: 329–42.

Albelda, Randy. 2002. "What's Wrong with Welfare-to-Work." In *Work, Welfare and Politics: Confronting Poverty in the Wake of Welfare Reform,* edited by Frances Fox Piven, Joan Acker, Margaret Hallock, and Sandra Morgen, 73–80. Eugene: University of Oregon Press.

Alisultanov, Ilgar, Joyce Klein, and Lily Zandniapour. 2002. *Microenterprise as a Welfare to Work Strategy: One Year Findings.* FIELD Research Report No. 2. Washington, D.C.: Fund for Innovation, Effectiveness, Learning and Dissemination (FIELD).

Alvarez, Sonia. 1999. "Advocating Feminism: The Latin American Feminist NGO 'Boom.'" *International Feminist Journal of Politics* 1: 181–209.

———. 2000. "Translating the Global Effects of Transnational Organizing on Local Feminist Discourses and Practices in Latin America." *Meridians: Feminism, Race Transnationalism* 1: 29–67.

Amin, Ruhul, Stan Becker, and Abdul Bayes. 1998. "NGO-promoted Microcredit Programs and Women's Empowerment in Bangladesh: Quantitative and Qualitative Evidence." *Journal of Developing Areas* 32: 221–36.

Amott, Teresa. 1990. "Black Women and AFDC: Making Entitlement out of Necessity." In *Women, the State and Welfare,* edited by Linda Gordon, 280–98. Madison: University of Wisconsin Press.

Anthony, Denise. 1996. *Working: A Report on the Impact of the Working Capital Program.* Cambridge, Mass.: Working Capital.

———. 1997. "Micro-lending Institutions: Using Social Networks to Create Productive Capabilities." *International Journal of Sociology and Social Policy* 17: 156–78.

Arnold, Thurman. 1941 [1937]. *The Folklore of Capitalism*. Garden City, N.J.: Blue Ribbon Books.

Aronowitz, Stanley. 2000. *The Knowledge Factory: Dismantling the Corporate University and Creating True Higher Learning*. Boston: Beacon Press.

Aronson, Robert L. 1991. *Self-employment: A Labor Market Perspective*. Ithaca: Cornell University Press.

Ashe, Jeffrey. 1985. *The PISCES II Experience: Local Efforts in Micro-enterprise Development*. Washington, D.C.: United States Agency for International Development.

———. 2000. "Microfinance in the United States: The Working Capital Experience—Ten Years of Lending and Learning." *Journal of Microfinance* 2: 22–60.

Association for Enterprise Opportunity (AEO). 1994. *Glossary of Microenterprise Terms*. Chicago: Association for Enterprise Opportunity.

———. 1997a. "AEO Policy Paper." May. Chicago: Association for Enterprise Opportunity.

———. 1997b. "AEO Recommendations for Federal Microenterprise Policy." Special Policy Issue. Chicago: Association for Enterprise Opportunity.

———. 1998. "Policy Advocacy Training and Microenterprise Days." *AEO Exchange: Association for Enterprise Opportunity Newsletter,* July/August: p. 1.

———. n.d. "Who We Are." Association for Enterprise Opportunity, http://www.microenterpriseworks.org/whoweare/ (accessed 10 February 2004).

Auwal, Mohammad A., and Arvind Singhal. 1992. "The Diffusion of the Grameen Bank in Bangladesh." *Knowledge* 14: 7–28.

———. 1996. "Promoting Microcapitalism in Service of the Poor: The Grameen Model and Its Cross-Cultural Adaptation." *Journal of Business Communication* 33: 27–49.

Babbie, Earl R. 2003. *The Practice of Social Research*. 10th ed. Belmont: Wadsworth Publishing.

Balkin, Steven. 1989. *Self-employment for Low Income People*. New York: Praeger.

———. 1993. "A Grameen Bank Replication: The Full Circle Fund of the Women's Self-Employment Project of Chicago." In *The Grameen Bank: Poverty Relief in Bangladesh,* edited by Abu N. M. Wahid, 235–66. Boulder: Westview Press.

Bates, Timothy. 1997. *Race, Self-Employment, and Upward Mobility: An Illusive American Dream*. Washington, D.C.: Woodrow Wilson Press.

———.2000. "Financing the Development of Urban Minority Communities: Lessons of History." *Economic Development Quarterly* 14: 227–41.

Bates, Timothy, and Lisa Servon. 1996. "Why Loans Won't Save the Poor." *Inc Magazine* 18 (April): 27.

Bennett, Michael, Cedric Herring, and Noah Jenkins. 1998. "Empowerment in Chicago: Grassroots Participation in Economic Development and Poverty Alleviation." In *Empowerment in Chicago,* edited by Cedric Herring, Michael

Bennett, Doug Gills, and Noah Temaner Jenkins, 1–13. Chicago: University of Illinois.

Berenbach, Shari, and Diego Guzman. 1994. "The Solidarity Group Experience Worldwide." In *The New World of Microenterprise Finance: Building Healthy Financial Institutions for the Poor,* edited by Maria Otero and Elisabeth Rhyne, 119–39. West Hartford: Kumarian Press.

Berger, Marguerite. 1989. "Giving Women Credit: The Strength and Limitations of Credit as a Tool for Alleviating Poverty." *World Development* 17: 1017–30.

Berger, Marguerite, and Mayra Buvinic. 1989. *Women's Ventures: Assistance to the Informal Sector in Latin America.* West Hartford: Kumarian Press Inc.

Bernstein, Jared. 2002. "Welfare Reform and the Low-Wage Labor Market." In *Work, Welfare and Politics: Confronting Poverty in the Wake of Welfare Reform,* edited by Frances Fox Piven, Joan Acker, Margaret Hallock, and Sandra Morgen, 115–28. Eugene: University of Oregon Press.

Bernstein, Mary. 1997. "Celebration and Suppression: The Strategic Uses of Identity by the Lesbian and Gay Movement." *American Journal of Sociology* 103: 531–65.

———. n.d. Social Movements, Law and the Politics of Opportunities: The Lesbian and Gay Movement and the Decriminalization of Sodomy. Manuscript, University of Connecticut, Department of Sociology, Storrs.

Bhatt, Ela. 1995. "Women and Development Alternatives: Micro- and Small-Scale Enterprises in India." In *Women in Micro- and Small-Scale Enterprise Development,* edited by Louise Dignard and Jose Havet, 85–100. Boulder: Westview Press.

Bhatt, Nitin. 2002. *Inner-city Entrepreneurship Development: The Microcredit Challenge.* Oakland: Institute for Contemporary Studies Press.

Bhatt, Nitin, Gary Painter, and Shui-Yan Tang. 2002. "The Challenges of Outreach and Sustainability for U.S. Microcredit Programs." In *Replicating Microfinance in the United States,* edited by James H. Carr and Zhong Yi Tong, 191–222. Washington, D.C.: Woodrow Wilson Center Press.

Biggart, Nicole Woolsey, ed. 2002. *Readings in Economic Sociology.* London: Basil Blackwell.

Blau, Joel. 1999. *Illusions of Prosperity: America's Working Families in an Age of Economic Insecurity.* New York: Oxford University Press.

Blumberg, Rae Lesser. 1995. "Gender Microenterprise, Performance and Power." In *Women in the Latin American Development Process,* edited by Christine Bose and Edna Acosta-Belen, 194–226. Philadelphia: Temple University Press.

———. 2001. "'We Are Family': Gender, Microenterprise, Family Work, and Well-being in Ecuador and the Dominican Republic with Comparative Data from Guatemala, Swaziland, and Guinea-Bissau." *The History of the Family* 6: 271–99.

Bordt, Rebecca. 1997a. "How Alternative Ideas Become Institutionalized: The Case of Feminist Collectives." *Nonprofit and Voluntary Sector Quarterly* 26: 132–55.

———. 1997b. *The Structure of Women's Nonprofit Organizations.* Bloomington: Indiana University Press.

Bornstein, David. 1996. *The Price of a Dream*. New York: Simon and Schuster.

Boyle, Elizabeth Heger. 2002. *Female Genital Cutting: Cultural Conflict in the Global Community*. Baltimore: Johns Hopkins University Press.

Breton, Margot. 1994. "On the Meaning of Empowerment and Empowerment-Oriented Social Work Practice." *Social Work with Groups* 17: 23–37.

Brill, Betsy. 1999. "The Power of Small Change." *San Francisco Examiner,* 2 May, pp. A1, A2.

Brokaw, Leslie. 1996. "Issue of the Week: In Defense of Microloans." *Inc. Online* [24 June 1996] http://www.inc.com/extra/stories/microloans.html (accessed 2 February 1999).

Brush, Candida G. 1992. "Research on Women Business Owners: Past Trends, a New Perspective and Future Directions." *Entrepreneurship Theory and Practice* 92: 5–30.

Buckley, Robert M. 2002. "Microfinance in Industries Countries." In *Replicating Microfinance in the United States,* edited by James H. Carr and Zhong Yi Tong, 113–37. Washington, D.C.: Woodrow Wilson Center Press.

Burstein, Paul. 1999. "Social Movements and Public Policy." In *How Social Movements Matter,* edited by Marco Giugni, Doug McAdam, and Charles Tilly, 3–21. Minneapolis: University of Minnesota Press.

Campbell, Marie, and Frances Gregor. 2002. *Mapping Social Relations: A Primer in Doing Institutional Ethnography*. Toronto: Garamond Press.

Carr, James H., and Zhong Yi Tong. 2002. "Introduction: Replicating Microfinance in the United States: An Overview." In *Replicating Microfinance in the United States,* edited by James H. Carr and Zhong Yi Tong, 1–18. Washington, D. C.: Woodrow Wilson Center Press.

Carr, Marilyn. 1995. "Women, Technology and Small Enterprise Development." In *Women in Micro- and Small-Scale Enterprise Development,* edited by Louise Dignard and Jose Havet, 217–28. Boulder: Westview Press.

Castells, Manuel, and Alejandro Portes. 1989. "World Underneath: The Origins, Dynamics, and Effects of the Informal Economy." In *The Informal Economy: Studies in Advanced and Less Developed Countries,* edited by Alejandro Portes, Manuel Castells, and Lauren A. Benton, 11–40. Baltimore: Johns Hopkins Press.

Charles Stewart Mott Foundation. 1990. *Small Steps toward Big Dreams*. Flint, Mich: Charles Stewart Mott Foundation.

———. 1993. *Small Steps toward Big Dreams: 1993 Update*. Flint, Mich: Charles Stewart Mott Foundation.

———. 1994. *Small Steps toward Big Dreams: 1994 Update*. Flint, Mich.: Charles Stewart Mott Foundation.

Christen, Robert P., with Deborah Drake. 2002. "Commercialization: The New Reality of Microfinance." In *The Commercialization of Microfinance,* edited by Deborah Drake and Elisabeth Rhyne, 2–21. Bloomfield, Conn.: Kumarian Press.

Christensen, Kathleen. 1988. *Women and Home-Based Work*. New York: Henry Holt.

Clark, Kenneth, and Jeannette Hopkins. 1969. *A Relevant War against Poverty: A Study of Community Action Programs and Observable Social Change.* New York: Harper & Row.

Clark, Margaret, and Tracy Huston. 1992. *1992 Directory of U.S. Microenterprise Programs.* Washington, D.C.: Aspen Institute.

Clark, Margaret, Tracy Huston, and Barbara Meister. 1994. *1994 Directory of U.S. Microenterprise Programs.* Washington, D.C.: Aspen Institute.

Clark, Peggy, and Amy Kays. 1995. *Enabling Entrepreneurship: Microenterprise Development in the U.S.* Washington, D.C: Aspen Institute.

Clark, Peggy, and Amy Kays, with Lily Zandiapour, Enrique Soto, and Karen Doyle. 1999. *Microenterprise and the Poor: Findings from the Self-Employment Learning Project Five Year Study of Microentrepreneurs.* Washington, D.C.: Aspen Institute.

Clinton, Hillary Rodham. 1999. "Transcript of Remarks by First Lady at Presidential Awards for Microenterprise Event." Washington, D.C.: White House Press Office, 5 February.

Clinton, William Jefferson. 1997. *The State of Small Business: A Report of the President.* Washington, D.C.: U.S. Government Printing Office.

Clinton, William Jefferson, and Al Gore. 1995. "The New SBA: Reinventing Service to the Small Business Community." http://www.sba.gov.library/reform/archive/reinventingservicetosmallbusinesscommunity (accessed 10 February 2004).

Coleman, James William. 2002. *The Criminal Elite: Understanding White Collar Crime,* 5th ed. New York: Worth Publishers.

Collins, Patricia Hill. 1990. *Black Feminist Thought.* New York: Routledge Press.

Counts, Alex. 1996. *Give Us Credit: How Muhammad Yunus's Micro-lending Revolution Is Empowering Women from Bangladesh to Chicago.* New York: Random House.

Cowgill, Julie. 1996. Empowerment in a Microenterprise Program: A Case Study. Master's thesis, Arizona State University, Tempe.

———. 1998a. Legislation Affecting Microenterprise Development. Manuscript, School of Justice Studies, Arizona State University, Tempe.

———. 1998b. Microenterprise as a Social Movement. Manuscript, School of Justice Studies, Arizona State University, Tempe.

Cowgill, Julie, and Nancy Jurik. In press. "The Construction of Client Identities in a Post-welfare Social Service Program: The Double Bind of Microenterprise Development." In *Deserving and Entitled,* edited by Anne Schneider and Helen Ingram. Albany: State University of New York Press.

Coyle, Mary, Mary Houghton, Connie Evans, and Julia Vindasius. 1994. *Going Forward: The Peer Group Lending Exchange November 2–4, 1993.* Toronto: CALMEADOW.

Creevey, Lucy. 1996. *Changing Women's Lives and Work: An Analysis of the Impacts of Eight Microenterprise Projects.* London: IT Press.

Cullen, Francis, William Maakestad, and Gray Cavender. 1987. *Corporate Crime under Attack: The Ford Pinto Case and Beyond.* Cincinnati: Anderson Publishing.

Daley-Harris, Sam, ed. 2002. *Pathways out of Poverty: Innovations in Microfinance for the Poorest Families.* Bloomfield, Conn.: Kumarian Press.

Dantico, Marilyn, and Nancy Jurik. 1986. "Where Have All the Good Jobs Gone: The Effect of Government Service Privatization on Women Workers." *Contemporary Crises* 10: 421–39.

De Janvry, Alain. 1981. *The Agrarian Question and Reformism in Latin America.* Baltimore: Johns Hopkins University Press.

Dennis, William. 1998. "Business Regulation as an Impediment to the Transition from Welfare to Self-Employment." *Journal of Labor Research* 19: 263–76.

DePass, Dee. 2000. "Banking on Women, . . . She Pulled Her Family out of Poverty by Building Business Skills." *Star Tribune,* 8 October, p. 11D.

Desai, Manisha. 2002. "Transnational Solidarity: Women's Agency, Structural Adjustment, and Globalization." In *Women's Activism and Globalization,* edited by Nancy Naples and Manisha Desai, 15–33. New York: Routledge.

Duetsch, Claudia. 2003. "The Revolution That Wasn't: 10 Years Later, Corporate Oversight Is Still Dismal." *New York Times,* 26 January, sec. 3, pp. 1, 12.

DeVault, Marjorie. 1999. *Liberating Method: Feminism and Social Research.* Philadelphia: Temple University Press.

DeVault, Marjorie, and Liza McCoy. 2002. "Institutional Ethnography: Using Interviews to Investigate Ruling Relations." In *Handbook of Interviewing,* edited by Jaber Gubrium and James Holstein, 751–76. Thousand Oaks, CA: Sage.

Dignard, Louise, and Jose Havet, eds. 1995. *Women in Micro- and Small-scale Enterprise Development.* Boulder: Westview Press.

Dillon, Sam. 2003. "Report Finds Deep Poverty Is on the Rise." New York Times, 30 April, p. A18.

DiMaggio, Paul, and Walter W. Powell. 1983. "The Iron Cage Revisited: Institutional Isomorphism and Collective Rationality in Organizational Fields." *American Sociological Review* 48: 147–60.

Dressel, Paula L., Vincent Carter, and Anand Balachandran. 1995. "Second-Order Victim-Blaming." *Journal of Sociology and Social Welfare* 21: 107–23.

Edgcomb, Elaine, Joyce Klein, and Peggy Clark. 1996. *The Practice of Microenterprise in the U.S.: Strategies, Costs and Effectiveness.* Washington, D.C.: Aspen Institute.

Edin, Kathryn. 1991. "Surviving the Welfare System: How AFDC Recipients Make Ends Meet in Chicago." *Social Problems* 38:4 62–73.

Ehlers, Tracy, and Karen Main. 1998. "Women and the False Promise of Microenterprise." *Gender & Society* 12: 424–40.

Ehrenreich, Barbara. 2001. *Nickel and Dimed: On (Not) Getting by in America.* New York: Metropolitan Books.

Eitzen, D. Stanley, and Maxine Baca Zinn. 2000. "The Missing Safety Net and Families." *Journal of Sociology and Social Welfare* 27: 53–72.

Else, John, and Salome Raheim. 1992. "AFDC Clients as Entrepreneurs." *Public Welfare* 50: 36–38.

Emirbayer, Mustafa, and Ann Mische. 1998. "What Is Agency?" *American Journal of Sociology* 103: 962–1023.

Escobar, Arturo. 1995. *Encountering Development: The Making and Unmaking of the Third World.* Princeton, N.J.: Princeton University Press.

Fernando, Jude. 1997. "Non-governmental Organizations, Micro-credit, and Empowerment of Women. *Annals of the American Academy of Political and Social Sciences* 554: 150–77.

Field for Innovation, Effectiveness, Learning and Dissemination (FIELD). 1999. *Designing Microenterprise Programs for Welfare Recipients.* FIELD Forum issue 3. Washington, D.C.: Aspen Institute.

———. 2002. "Improving the Climate for Self-Employment: Policy Recommendations for TANF Reauthorization." FIELD Research Brief no. 2. Washington, D.C: Aspen Institute.

———. n.d. "FIELD, a Program of the Aspen Institute: Microenterprise Field for Innovation, Effectiveness, Learning and Dissemination" [online] (Washington, D.C.: The Aspen Institute [cited 10 February 2004]). Available from http://www.fieldus.org.

Finder, Alan. 1998. "Evidence Is Scant that Workfare Leads to Full-time Jobs." *New York Times,* 12 April, pp. A1, A18.

Fligstein, Neil. 2002. "Agreements, Disagreements, and Opportunities in the 'New Sociology of Markets.'" In *The New Economic Sociology: Developments in an Emerging Field,* edited by Mauro Guillen, Randall Collins, Paula England, and Marshall Meyer, 61–78. New York: Russell Sage Foundation.

Fobes, Catherine, and Jill Quadagno. 1995. "The Welfare State and the Cultural Reproduction of Gender: Making Good Girls and Boys in the Job Corps." *Social Problems* 42: 171–90.

Foucault, Michel. 1979. *Discipline and Punish.* New York: Vintage Books.

Foundation for International Community Assistance (FINCA). n.d. "FINCA: Small Loans, Big Changes." Foundation for International Community Assistance http://www.villagebanking.org/ (Accessed on 10 February 2004).

Freedman, Michael P. 2000. "Challenges to Launching Grassroots Microlending Programs: A Case Study." *Journal of Developmental Entrepreneurship* 5: 235–47.

Freudenburg, William. 1994. "Bureaucratic Slippage and Failures of Agency Vigilance: The Case of the Environmental Studies Program." *Social Problems* 41: 214–19.

Gagne, Patricia. 1996. "Identity, Strategy, and Feminist Politics: Clemency for Battered Women Who Kill." *Social Problems* 43: 77–93.

Galaskiewicz, Joseph, and Wolfgang Bielefeld. 1998. *Nonprofit Organizations in an Age of Uncertainty: A Study of Organizational Change.* New York: Aldine De Gruyter.

Gibbs, Nancy. 1990. "Boosting Cottage Capitalism." *Newsweek,* 5 November, p. 36.

Giddens, Anthony. 1998. *The Third Way: The Renewal of Social Democracy.* Cambridge, UK: Polity Press.

Goetz, Anne Marie, and Rina Sen Gupta. 1996. "Who Takes the Credit? Gender, Power and Control over Loan Use in Rural Credit Programs in Bangladesh." *World Development* 24: 45–63.

Goffman, Erving. 1959. *The Presentation of Self in Everyday Life.* Garden City, N.Y.: Doubleday.

Gonzalez-Vega, Claudio, Mark Schreiner, Richard Meyer, Jorge Rodriguez, and Sergio Navajas. 1997. "The Challenge of Growth for Microfinance Organizations: The Case of Banco Solidario in Bolivia." In *Microfinance for the Poor?* edited by Hartmut Schneider, 129–70. London: Development Centre of the Organisation for Economic Co-operation and Development.

Good Faith Fund. n.d. "What's New at GFF?" Good Faith Fund http://www.good-faithfund.org/index.html (accessed 10 February 2004).

Goodin, Robert E., Bruce Heady, Ruud Muffels, and Henk-Jan Dirven. 1999. *The Real Worlds of Welfare Capitalism.* Cambridge, UK: Cambridge University Press.

Goss, David. 1991. *Small Business and Society.* London: Routledge.

Grahame, Kamini Maraj. 1998a. "Asian Women, Job Training, and the Social Organization of Immigrant Labor Markets." *Qualitative Sociology* 21:75–90.

———. 1998b. "Feminist Organizing and the Politics of Inclusion." *Human Studies* 21: 377–93.

Grahame, Peter R. 1998. "Ethnography, Institutions, and the Problematic of Everyday World." *Human Studies* 21: 347–60.

Grameen Bank. n.d. "Grameen: Banking for the Poor." http://www.grameen-info.org (accessed 10 February 2004).

Granovetter, Mark. 1992. "The Sociological Approaches to Labor Market Analysis: A Social Structural View." In *The Sociology of Economic Life,* edited by Mark Granovetter and Richard Swedberg, 233–64. Boulder: Westview Press.

Green, Cecilia. 1993. "Advanced Capitalist Hegemony and the Significance of Gramsci's Insights: A Restatement." *Social and Economic Studies* 42: 175–207.

Greenberg, Mark. 1999. *Developing Policies to Support Microenterprise in the TANF Structure: A Guide to the Law.* Washington, D.C.: Aspen Institute.

Greider, William, P. J. O'Rourke, Hunter S. Thompson, and Jann Wenner. 1992. "Interview with Bill Clinton." *Rolling Stone Magazine,* 17 September, pp. 40–49.

Grosh, Barbara, and Gloria Somolekae. 1996. "Mighty Oaks from Little Acorns: Can Microenterprise Serve as the Seedbed of Industrialization?" *World Development* 24: 1879–90.

Gugliotta, Guy. 1993. "Harvesting a Living from Seeds of Credit: Anti-poverty Strategy Called Microenterprise Is Growing in U.S." *Washington Post,* 6 May, p. A1.

Guillen, Mauro, Randall Collins, Paula England, and Marshall Meyer. 2002. "The Revival of Economic Sociology." In *The New Economic Sociology,* edited by Mauro Guillen, Randall Collins, Paula England, and Marshall Meyer, 1–34. New York: Russell Sage Foundation.

Gulli, Hege. 1998. *Microfinance and Poverty: Questioning the Conventional Wisdom.* Washington, D.C.: Inter-American Development Bank, Sustainable Development Department.

Hahn, Susan, and Mario Ganuzza. n.d. "Midterm Evaluation: Microenterprise Development Project No. 519–0318, Chemonics" (for USAID/El Salvador). Washington, D.C.: USAID.

Hales, David. 1995. "Reallocating Credit: An Economic Analysis of the New CRA Regulation." *Annual Review of Banking* 15: 571–82.

Hammack, David, and Dennis Young, eds. 1993. *Nonprofit Organizations in a Market Economy: Understanding New Roles, Issues, and Trends.* San Francisco: Josey-Bass.

Hammel, Paul. 1999. "Sargent Major's Small Business Birdhouse a Golden Egg: Microenterprises Are Rural Nebraska's New Lifeblood." *Omaha World Herald,* 25 February, p. 1.

Harrison, David, and Stefanie Krauss. 2002. "Interviewer Cheating: Implications for Research on Entrepreneurship in Africa." *Journal of Developmental Entrepreneurship* 7: 319–30

Hatch, John, and Marguerite Sakir Hatch. 1989. *Village Bank Manual for Community Leaders and Promoters.* 2nd ed. Phoenix: Foundation for International Community Assistance.

Heclo, Hugh. 1986. "General Welfare and Two Political Traditions." *Political Science Quarterly* 101: 179–95.

Herrold, Melinda. 2003. Cranes and Conflicts: NGO Programs to Improve People-park Relations in Russia and China. Ph.D. diss., University of California, Berkeley.

Himes, Cristina, with Lisa Servon. 1998. *Measuring Client Success: An Evaluation of ACCION's Impact on Microenterprises in the U.S.* Washington, D.C.: ACCION International.

Hirschmann, Nancy J., and Ulrike Liebert. 2001. "Introduction: Engendering Welfare, Degendering Care: Theoretical and Comparative Perspectives on the United States and Europe." In *Women and Welfare: Theory and Practice in the United States and Europe,* edited by Nancy J. Hirschmann and Ulrike Liebert, 1–22. Rutgers: Rutgers University Press.

Holcombe, Susan. 1995. *Managing to Empower: The Grameen Bank's Experience of Poverty Alleviation.* London: Zed Books.

Hollis, Aidan, and Arthur Sweetman. 1998a. "Microcredit: What Can We Learn from the Past?" *World Development* 26: 1875–91.

———. 1998b. "Microcredit in Prefamine Ireland." *Explorations in Economic History* 35:347–80.

Holstein, James, and Gale Miller. 1996. *Dispute Domains and Welfare Claims: Conflict and Law in Public Bureaucracies.* Greenwich, Conn.: Jai Press.

Holt, Sharon. 1994. "The Village Bank Methodology: Performance and Prospects." In *The New World of Microenterprise Finance: Building Healthy Financial Institutions for the Poor,* edited by Maria Otero and Elisabeth Rhyne, 156–84. West Hartford, Conn.: Kumarian Press.

House of Representatives. 1991. Freedom from Want Act. 102nd Congress, 1st session, H.R. 2258. Washington, D.C.: U.S. House of Representatives.

House Financial Services Committee. 1999. "The Committee." U.S. House of Representatives, http://financialservices.house.gov/ (accessed 1 May 2001).

House Select Committee on Hunger. 1991. *Hearing on New Perspectives on Urban Poverty and Microeconomic Development.* U.S. House Select Committee on Hunger, 102nd Congress, 1st session, H. Doc., pp. 102–9. Washington, D.C.: U.S. House of Representatives.

Howells, Louise. 2000. "The Dimensions of Microenterprise: A Critical Look at Microenterprise as a Tool to Alleviate Poverty." *Journal of Affordable Housing and Community Development* 9: 161–82.

Hulme, David, and Paul Mosley. 1996. *Finance against Poverty.* Vols. I and II. London: Routledge.

Hung, Chi-Kan Richard. 2002. "From South to North: A Comparative Study of Group-Based Microcredit Programs in Developing Countries and the United States." In *Replicating Microfinance in the United States,* edited by James H. Carr and Zhong Yi Tong, 223–56. Washington, D.C: Woodrow Wilson Center Press.

Jenkins, Craig. 1987. "Nonprofit Organization and Policy Advocacy." In *The Nonprofit Sector: A Research Handbook,* edited by Walter W. Powell, 296–320. New Haven:Yale University Press.

Jenness, Valerie, and Kendal Broad. 1994. "Antiviolence Activism and the (In)visibility of Gender in the Gay/Lesbian and Women's Movements." *Gender & Society* 8: 402–23.

Jenness, Valerie, and Ryken Grattet. 2001. *Making Hate a Crime: From Social Movement to Law Enforcement.* New York: Russell Sage Foundation Press.

Johnson, Margaret. 1998a. "Developing a Typology of Nonprofit Microenterprise Programs in the United States." *Journal of Developmental Entrepreneurship* 3: 165–84.

———. 1998b. "An Overview of Basic Issues Facing Microenterprise Practices in the United States." *Journal of Developmental Entrepreneurship* 3: 5–22.

Johnson, Susan. 1998. "Policy Arena: Microfinancing North and South: Contrasting Current Debates." *Journal of International Development* 10: 799–809.

———. 1999. "Gender and Microfinance: Guidelines for Good Practice." http://www.gdrc.org/icm/wind/gendersjonson.html (Accessed 10 February 2004).

Johnston, Van R., ed. 2000. *Entrepreneurial Management and Public Policy.* Huntington, N.Y.: Nova Science Publisher.

Jonakin, Jon, and Laura Enriquez. 1999. "The Non-traditional Financial Sector in Nicaragua: A Response to Rural Credit Market Exclusion." *Development Policy Review* 17: 141–69.

Jurik, Nancy C. 1998. "Getting away and Getting By: The Experiences of Self-Employed Homeworkers." *Work and Occupations* 25: 7–35.

———. 2004. "Imagining Justice: Challenging the Privatization of Public Life." *Social Problems* 51: 1–15.

Jurik, Nancy C., Joel Blumenthal, Brian Smith, and Edwardo Portillos. 2000. "Organizational Cooptation or Social Change?" *Journal of Contemporary Criminal Justice* 16 :293–320.

Jurik, Nancy, and Julie Cowgill. 1999. "Women and Microenterprise: Empowerment or Hegemony?" In *Women's Progress: Perspectives on the Past, Blueprint for the Future,* 321–24. Proceedings of the Fifth Women's Policy Research Conference. Washington, D.C.: Institute for Women's Policy Research.

Jurik, Nancy C., and Peter Gregware. 1992. "A Method for Murder: The Study of Homicides by Women." In *Perspectives on Social Problems V,* edited by James Holstein and Gale Miller, 179–201. Greenwich, Conn.: Jai Press.

Kaplan, Tammy Sproule. 2003. "WomenVenture Celebrates 25 Years of Changing Women's Lives." *Venture Ahead* [Spring 2003], http://www.womenventure.org/pdf/April_2003_Venture_Ahead.pdf (accessed 10 February 2004).

Katz, Donald. 1991. "Where Credit Is Due—Microloans: The Amounts May Be Small but Their Effects Are Enormous." *Investment Vision* (August/September): 48–57.

Khandker, Shahidur, Baqui Khalily, and Zahed Khan. 1995. *Grameen Bank: Performance and Sustainability.* Washington D.C.: World Bank Poverty and Social Policy Department.

Kidder, Thalia. 1998. Microfinance Experiences in Rural Central America: Issues of Food Security and Gender Relations. Paper presented at Latin American Studies Association meetings, Chicago, September.

Klein, Joyce. 1994. *The Status of the Microenterprise Field.* Washington, D.C.: Corporation for Enterprise Development.

———. 2002a. *FIELD Best Practice Guide,* Vol. I. *Entering the Relationship: Finding and Assessing Microenterprise Training Clients.* Washington, D.C.: The Aspen Institute.

———. 2002b. *Improving the Climate for Self-employment: Policy Recommendations for TANF Reauthorization.* FIELD Research Brief no. 2. Washington, D.C.: Aspen Institute.

Korten, David C. 2001. *When Corporations Rule the World.* Bloomfield, Conn.: Kumarian Press.

Krier, Dan. 1999. "Assessing the New Synthesis of Economics and Sociology: Promising Themes for Contemporary Analysts of Economic Life." *American Journal of Economics and Sociology* 58: 669–96.

Kuratko, Donald, Jeffrey S. Hornsby, and Douglas W. Naffziger. 1999. "The Adverse Impact of Public Policy on Microenteprise." *Journal of Developmental Entrepreneurship* 4: 81–93.

Laguerre, Michel. 1998. "Rotating Credit Associations and the Diasporic Economy." *Journal of Developmental Entrepreneurship* 3: 23–33.

Lang, Sabine. 1997. "The NGOiszation of Feminism: Institutionalization and Institution Building within the German Women's Movements." In *Transitions, Environments, Translations: Feminism in International Politics,* edited by Joan Wallace Scott, Cora Kaplan, and Debra Keates, 101–20. New York: Routledge.

Levine, Marc. 1989. "The Politics of Partnership: Urban Redevelopment since 1945." In *Unequal Partnerships: The Political Economy of Urban Political Development in Post War America,* edited by Gregory D. Squires, 12–34. New Brunswick, N. J.: Rutgers University Press.

Light, Ivan, and Edna Bonacich. 1988. *Immigrant Entrepreneurs: Koreans in Los Angeles.* Berkeley: University of California.

Light, Ivan, and Michelle Pham. 1998. "Beyond Credit-Worthy: Microcredit and Informal Credit in the U.S." *Journal of Developmental Entrepreneurship* 3: 35–51.

Light, Ivan, and Carolyn Rosenstein. 1995. *Race, Ethnicity, and Entrepreneurship in Urban America*. New York: Aldine De Gruyter.

Lipsky, Michael. 1980. *Street-Level Bureaucracy*. New York: Russell Sage.

Litzenberg, Jack. 1996. "Microenterprise and Poverty Policy: Litzenberg Keynote." *AEO Exchange* (June), p. 1.

Magill, John. 1994. "Credit Unions: A Formal-Sector Alternative for Financing Microenterprise Development." In *The New World of Microenterprise Finance: Building Healthy Financial Institutions for the Poor,* edited by Maria Otero and Elisabeth Rhyne, 140–55. West Hartford, Conn.: Kumarian Press.

Maroney, Michael. 1998. "Testimony before the U.S. House of Representatives Banking and Financial Service Committee (September 23, 1998)." U.S. House of Representatives, http://commdocs.house.gov/committees/bank/hba52105.000/hba51205_0HTM#58 (accessed 10 July 2000).

Marris, Peter, and Martin Reins. 1969. *Dilemmas of Social Reform: Poverty and Community Action in the United States*. New York: Atherton.

Martin, Patricia Yancey. 1990. "Rethinking Feminist Organizations." *Gender & Society* 4: 182–206.

Matthews, Nancy. 1994. *Confronting Rape: The Feminist Anti-rape Movement and the State*. New York: Routledge.

McAdam, Doug, and David Snow. 1997. "Introduction: Social Movements: Conceptual and Theoretical Issues." In *Social Movements,* edited by Doug McAdam and David Snow, xvii–xxvi. Los Angeles: Roxbury Press.

McCarthy, John, and Mayer Zald. 1973. *The Trend of Social Movements in America: Professionalization and Resource Mobilization*. Morristown, N.J.: General Learning Press.

McLenighan, Valjean, and Jean Pogge. 1991. *The Business of Self-Sufficiency: Microcredit Programs in the U.S.* Chicago: Woodstock Institute.

McMichael, Philip. 2000. *Development and Social Change: A Global Perspective*. 2nd ed. Thousand Oaks, Calif.: Pine Forge.

Merry, Sally Engle. 1982. "The Social Organization of Mediation in Nonindustrial Societies: Implications for Informal Community Justice in America." *Politics of Informal Justice* 2: 17–45.

Meyer, David, and Nancy Whittier. 1994. "Social Movement Spillover." *Social Problems* 41: 277–97.

MICRO Loan Fund. n.d. "CDFI/Loans." Portable, Practical Education Preparation Inc., http://www.ppep.org/loans/index.html (accessed 10 February 2004).

Microcredit Summit. 1997. *Declaration and Plan of Action*. http://www.microcreditsummit.org/declaration.htm (accessed 10 February 2004).

Milgram, B. Lynne. 2001. "Operationalizing Microfinance: Women and Craftwork in Ifugao, Upland Philippines." *Human Organization* 60: 212–24.

Miller, Gale. 1989. "Defining Proper Work Performance: Complaint-making and Negotiation in a Work Incentive Program." *Journal of Contemporary Ethnography* 18: 30–49.

Mizan, Ainon N. 1993. "Women's Decision-Making Power in Rural Bangladesh: A Study of the Grameen Bank." In *The Grameen Bank: Poverty Relief in Bangladesh,* edited by Abu Wahid, 127–54. Boulder: Westview Press.

Mondal, Wali, and Ruth A. Tune. 1993. "Replicating the Grameen Bank in North America: The Good Faith Experience." In *The Grameen Bank: Poverty Relief in Bangladesh,* edited by Abu Wahid, 223–34. Boulder: Westview Press.

Montgomery, Richard. 1996. "Disciplining or Protecting the Poor? Avoiding the Social Costs of Peer Pressure in Micro-credit Schemes." *Journal of International Development* 8: 289–305.

Morduch, Jonathan. 1999. "The Microfinance Promise." *Journal of Economic Literature* 37: 1569–614.

———. 2000. "The Microfinance Schism." *World Development* 28: 617–29.

Naidoo, Davaniamah. 1994. Women in Income Generating Projects and Empowerment: The Case of Zimbabwe. Ph.D. diss., Arizona State University, Tempe.

Naples, Nancy. 1996. "A Feminist Revisiting of the Insider/Outsider Debate: The 'Outsider Phenomenon' in Rural Iowa." *Qualitative Sociology* 19: 83–106.

———. 1997. "The 'New Consensus' on the Gendered 'Social Contract': The 1987–1988 U.S. Congressional Hearings on Welfare Reform." *Signs* 22:907–45.

———. 1998a. *Activist Mothering, Community Work, and the War on Poverty: Grassroots Warriors.* New York: Routledge.

———. 1998b. "From Maximum Feasible Participation to Disenfranchisement." *Social Justice* 25: 47–66.

Nelson, Candace. 2002. *FIELD Best Practice Guide,* vol. 2, *Building Skills for Self-employment: Basic Training for Microentrepreneurs.* Washington, D.C.: Aspen Institute.

Ng, Roxanna. 1996. *The Politics of Community Service: Immigrant Women, Class and State.* Halifax: Fernwood.

Oliver, Melvin, and Thomas Shapiro. 1995. *Black Wealth, Wealth.* New York: Routledge.

Oliver, Pamela. 1983. "The Mobilization of Paid and Volunteer Activists in the Neighborhood Movement." *Research in Social Movements, Conflicts and Change* 5: 133–70.

Omi, Michael, and Howard Winant. 1994. *Racial Formation in the United States.* 2nd ed.

Otero, Maria, and Elisabeth Rhyne. 1994. "Financial Services for Microenterprises: Principles and Institutions." In *The New World of Microenterprise Finance: Building Healthy Financial Institutions for the Poor,* edited by Maria Otero and Elisabeth Rhyne, 11–26. West Hartford, Conn.: Kumarian Press.

Parpart, Jane L. 1995. "Post-modernism, Gender and Development." In *Power of Development,* edited by Jonathan Crush, 253–65. London: Routledge.

Pate, Kim. 2000. "The State TANF-Microenterprise Initiative." *AEO Exchange: Association for Enterprise Opportunity Newsletter* (November/December), p.1.

Pear, Robert. 2003. "House Endorses Stricter Work Rules for Poor." *New York Times,* 14 February, sec. A, p. 25.

Pfeffer, Jeffrey, and Gerald Salancik. 1974. "Organizational Decision Making as a Political Process: The Case of a University Budget." *Administrative Science Quarterly* 19: 133–51.

Pitt, Mark, and Shahidur Khandker. 1998. "The Impact of Group-based Credit Programs on Poor Households in Bangladesh: Does the Gender of Participants Matter?" *Journal of Political Economy* 106: 958–96.

Piore, Michael J., and Charles F. Sabel. 1984. *The Second Industrial Divide: Possibilities for Prosperity.* New York: Basic Books.

Piven, Frances Fox. 2002. "Welfare Policy and American Politics." In *Work, Welfare and Politics: Confronting Poverty in the Wake of Welfare Reform,* edited by Frances Fox Piven, Joan Acker, Margaret Hallock, and Sandra Morgen, 19–34. Eugene: University of Oregon Press.

Piven, Frances, and Richard Cloward. 1978. *Poor People's Movements.* New York: Vintage.

———. 1991. "Collective Protest: A Critique of Resource Mobilization Theory." *International Journal of Politics, Culture, and Society* 4: 435–57.

Portes, Alejandro. 1997. "Neoliberalism and the Sociology of Development: Emerging Trends and Unanticipated Facts." *Population and Development Review* 23: 229–59.

Portes, Alejandro, and Robert Bach. 1985. *Latin Journey.* Berkeley: University of California Press.

Portes, Alejandro, and Saskia Sassen-Koob. 1987. "Making It Underground: Comparative Material on the Informal Sector in Western Market Economies." *American Journal of Sociology* 93: 30–61.

Portes Alejandro, and Julia Sensebrenner. 1993. "Embeddedness and Immigration: Notes on the Social Determination of Economic Action." *American Journal of Sociology* 98: 1320–50.

Poster, Winifred, and Zakia Salime. 2002. "The Limits of Microcredit: Transnational Feminism and USAID Activities in the United States and Morocco." In *Women's Activism and Globalization,* edited by Nancy Naples and Manisha Desai, 189–219. New York: Routledge.

Powell, Walter W., and Paul J. DiMaggio. 1991. "Introduction." In *The New Institutionalism in Organizational Analysis,* edited by Walter W. Powell and Paul J. DiMaggio, 1–38. Chicago: University of Chicago Press.

Powell, Walter W., and Rebecca Friedkin. 1987. "Organizational Change in Nonprofit Organizations." In *The Nonprofit Sector,* edited by Walter W. Powell, 180–94. New Haven: Yale University Press.

Prugl, Elisabeth. 1996. "Home-Based Producers in Development Discourse." In *Homeworkers in Global Perspective: Invisible No More,* edited by Eileen Borris and Elisabeth Prugl, 39–59. Lanham, Md.: Rowman & Littlefield.

Prugl, Elisabeth, and Irene Tinker. 1997. "Microentrepreneurs and Homeworkers: Convergent Categories." *World Development* 25: 1471–82.

Puls, Barbara. 1991. *Building Communities that Work: Community Economic Development.* Denver: National Conference of State Legislatures.

Quadagno, Jill. 1999. "Creating a Capital Investment Welfare State: The New American Exceptionalism." *American Sociological Review* 64: 1–11.

Raheim, Salome. 1997. "Problems and Prospects of Self-Employment as an Economic Independence Option for Welfare Recipients." *Social Work* 42: 44–53.

Raheim, Salome, and Catherine Alter. 1998. "Self-Employment as a Social and Economic Development Intervention for Recipients of AFDC." *Journal of Community Practice* 5: 41–61.

Raheim, Salome, and Jacquelyn Bolden. 1995. "Economic Empowerment of Low-income Women through Self-employment Programs." *Affilia* 10: 138–54.

Rahman, Aminur. 1994. "Women, Cultural Ideology and Change in Rural Bangladesh: Conflicting Patterns and Possibilities of Empowerment." *Peace Research* 26: 19–39.

Rahman Aminur, and Abu Wahid. 1992. "The Grameen Bank and the Changing Patron-Client Relationship in Bangladesh." *Journal of Contemporary Asia* 22: 303–21.

Rankin, Katharine N. 2002. "Social Capital, Microfinance, and the Politics of Development." *Feminist Economics* 8: 1–24.

Reed, Larry, and David R. Befus. 1994. "Transformation Lending: Helping Microenterprises Become Small Businesses." In *The New World of Microenterprise Finance: Building Healthy Financial Institutions for the Poor*, edited by Maria Otero and Elisabeth Rhyne, 185–204. West Hartford, Conn.: Kumarian Press.

Remenyi, Joe, and Benjamin Quiñones, Jr., eds. 2000. *Microfinance and Poverty Alleviation: Case Studies from Asia and the Pacific*. London: Pinter Press.

Rhyne, Elisabeth. 2001. *Mainstreaming Microfinance: How Lending to the Poor Began, Grew, and Came of Age in Bolivia*. West Hartford, Conn.: Kumarian Press.

Riley, Charles A. 1995. *Small Business, Big Politics: What Entrepreneurs Need to Know to Use their Growing Political Power*. Princeton: Peterson's Guides.

Ritzer, George. 2000. *The McDonaldization of Society*. 21st Century ed. Thousand Oaks, Calif.: Sage.

Roberts, Bryan. 1978. *Cities of Peasants: The Political Economy of Urbanization in the Third World*. Beverly Hills: Sage Publications.

Rodriguez, Cheryl Rene. 1995. *Women, Microenterprise, and the Politics of Self-Help*. New York: Garland.

Rogaly, Ben. 1996. "Micro-finance Evangelism, 'Destitute Women,' and the Hard Selling of a New Anti-poverty Formula." *Development in Practice* 6: 100–12.

Rogaly, Ben, Thomas Fisher, and Ed Mayo. 1999. *Poverty, Social Exclusion, and Microfinance in Britain*. Oxford: Oxfam.

Rogaly, Ben, and Susan Johnson. 1997. *Microfinance and Poverty Reduction*. Oxford: Oxfam.

Rogaly, Ben, and Chris Roche, eds. 1998. Learning from South-North Links in Microfinance. Oxfam Working Paper. Oxford: Oxfam.

Rogers-Dillon, Robin, and John David Skrentny. 1999. "Administering Success: The Legitimacy Imperative and the Implementation of Welfare Reform." *Social Problems* 46: 13–29.

Rose, Kalima. 1996. "SEWA: Women in Movement." In *The Women, Gender & Development Reader*, edited by Nalini Visvanathan, Lynn Duggan, Laurie Nisonoff, and Nan Wiegersma, 382–88. London: ZED Press.

Rose, Nancy. 1995. *Workfare or Fair Work: Women, Welfare, and Government Work Programs.* New York: Routledge.

Rosen, Ellen I. 2002. *Making Sweatshops: The Globalization of the U.S. Apparel Industry.* Berkeley: University of California Press.

Rubin, Beth. 1996. *Shifts in the Social Contract: Understanding Change in American Society.* Thousand Oaks, Calif.: Pine Forge Press.

Rubin, Herbert J. 1988. "Shoot Anything That Flies; Claim Anything That Falls: Conversations with Economic Development Practitioners." *Economic Development Quarterly* 2: 236–51.

Ryan, Michael. 1997. "A Recipe for Prosperity." *Parade Magazine,* 17 August, pp. 4–7.

Sabatier, Paul. 1986. "Top-Down and Bottom-Up Approaches to Implementation Research: A Critical Analysis and Suggested Synthesis." *Journal of Public Policy* 6: 21–48.

Sandoval, Daniel, and Thomas Hirschl. 2000. The Penalty for Existing Welfare: The Well-Being of Former Recipients in the New Economy. Paper presented at The Pacific Sociology Meeting, April, San Francisco.

Santiago, Nellie, Thomas Holyoke, and Ross Levi. 1998. "Turning David into Goliath into the Odd Couple: How the *New Community Reinvestment Act* Promotes Community Development Financial Institutions." *Journal of Law and Policy* 6: 571–651.

Schreiner, Mark. 1999a. Lessons for Microenterprise Programs from the Unemployment Insurance Self-employment Demonstration. Manuscript, Washington University, St. Louis.

———. 1999b. A Review of Evaluations of Microenterprise Programs in the U.S. Manuscript, Washington University, St. Louis.

———. 1999c "Self-Employment, Microenterprise and the Poorest of the Poor in the U.S." *Social Service Review* 73: 496–523.

Schreiner, Mark, and Jonathan Morduch. 2002. "Opportunities and Challenges for Microfinance in the United States." In *Replicating Microfinance in the United States,* edited by James H. Carr and Zhong Yi Tong, 19–64. Washington, D.C: Woodrow Wilson Center Press.

Schuman, Michael. 1993. "The Microlenders." *Forbes* 25 October, pp. 164–66.

Sclar, Elliot D. 2000. *You Don't Always Get What You Pay For: The Economics of Privatization.* Ithaca: Cornell University Press.

Self Employed Women's Association (SEWA). n.d. "Self Employed Women's Association Index." Self Employed Women's Association, http://www.sewa.org/search/index.htm (accessed 10 February 2004).

Senate Committee on Small Business. 1991. "Microloan Programs for New and Growing Small Business." U.S. Senate Hearing before the Committee on Small Business, 102d Congress, 1st session. Washington, D.C.: U.S. Senate Committee on Small Business.

———. 1994. "The Small Business Administration's Microloan Demonstration Program and Business Development Programs." Hearing before the U.S. Senate Committee on Small Business, 103rd Congress, 1st Session (Opening Statement of Honorable Dale Bumpers). Washington, D.C.: U.S. Senate Committee on Small Business.

Servon, Lisa. 1998a "Credit and Social Capital: The Community Development Potential of U.S. Microenterprise Programs." *Housing Policy Debate* 9: 115–49.

———. 1998b. "Helping Poor Women Achieve Self-Sufficiency through Self-Employment: The Potential of U.S. Microenterprise Programs." Working Paper Series 98–06. Washington, D.C.: Research Institute for Small & Emerging Business.

———. 1999a. *Bootstrap Capital: Microenterprises and the American Poor.* Washington, D.C.: Brookings Institution Press.

———. 1999b. "Executive Summary: Helping Poor Women Achieve Self-sufficiency through Self-employment: The Potential of U.S. Microenterprise Programs." Research Institute for Small & Emerging Business, http://www.riseb.org/eshelppoor.html (accessed June 2000).

Servon, Lisa, and Timothy Bates. 1998. "Microenterprise as an Exit Route from Poverty." *Journal of Urban Affairs* 20: 419–41.

Severens, C. Alexander, and Amy Kays. 1997. *1996 Directory of U.S. Microenterprise Programs.* Self-employment Learning Project. Washington, D.C.: Aspen Institute.

Sherraden, Michael. 1991. *Assets and the Poor.* Armonk, N.Y.: M.E. Sharpe.

Sidel, Ruth. 2000. "The Enemy within: The Demonization of Poor Women." *Journal of Sociology and Social Welfare* 27: 73–84.

Simanowitz, Anton, with Alice Walter. 2002. "Ensuring Impact: Reaching the Poorest while Building Financially Self-Sufficient Institutions, and Showing Improvement in the Lives of the Poorest Women and Their Families." In *Pathways Out of Poverty: Innovations in Microfinance for the Poorest Families,* edited by Gary S. Fields and Guy Pfeffermann, 1–73. Bloomfield, Conn.: Kumarian Press.

Singh, Kavaljit, and Daphne Wysham. 1997. "Micro-credit: Band-Aid or Wound?" *Ecologist* 27: 42–43.

Slaughter, Sheila, and Larry Leslie. 1997. *Academic Capitalism: Politics, Policies, and the Entrepreneurial University.* Baltimore: Johns Hopkins Press.

Small Business Administration (SBA). 1997. "Creating Opportunities for Small Business Success." SBA's Five Year Strategic Plan (FY 1998–FY 2002), September 30. Washington, D.C.: U.S. Small Business Administration.

Smith, Alexander M. 1998. *The No. 1 Ladies' Detective Agency.* London: Abacus Fiction.

Smith, Dorothy E. 1975. "The Statistics on Mental Illness: What They Will Not Tell Us about Women and Why." In *Women Look at Psychiatry,* edited by Dorothy E. Smith and Sarah David, 12–52. Vancouver: Press Gang.

———. 1987. *The Everyday World as Problematic: A Feminist Sociology.* Boston: Northeastern University Press.

———. 1990. *Texts, Facts, and Femininity: Exploring the Relations of Ruling.* New York: Routledge.

Smith, Steven R., and Michael Lipsky. 1993. *Nonprofits for Hire: The Welfare State in the Age of Contracting.* Cambridge, Mass.: Harvard University Press.

Smith, Vicki. 2001. *Crossing the Great Divide: Worker Risk and Opportunity in the New Economy.* Ithaca: Cornell University Press.

Snow, David, E., Burke Rochford, Jr., Steven Worden, and Robert Benford. 1986. "Frame Alignment Processes, Micromobilization, and Movement Participation." *American Sociological Review* 51: 464–81.

Solomon, Lewis. 1992. "Microenterprise: Human Reconstruction in America's Inner Cities." *Harvard Journal of Law and Public Policy* 15: 193–221.

Squires, Gregory D. 1989. "Pubic-Private Partnerships: Who Gets What and Why." In *Unequal Partnerships: The Political Economy of Urban Political Development in Post War America,* edited by Gregory D. Squires, 1–11. New Brunswick, N. J.: Rutgers University Press.

Staggenborg, Suzanne. 1988. "The Consequences of Professionalization and Formalization in the Pro-choice Movement." *American Sociological Review* 53: 585–606.

Steckner, Susie. 2003. "Getting down to Business: Non-profits Adopt Corporate Tactics." *Arizona Republic,* 30 April, pp. A1–A2.

Strang, David, and John Meyer. 1993. "Institutional Conditions for Diffusion." *Theory and Society* 22: 487–511.

Sudnow, David. 1965. "Normal Crimes: Sociological Features of the Penal Code." *Social Problems* 12: 255–76.

Taub, Richard. 1994. *Community Capitalism.* 2nd ed. Boston: Harvard Business School Press.

———. 1998. "Making the Adaptation across Cultures and Societies: A Report on an Attempt to Clone the Grameen Bank in southern Arkansas." *Journal of Developmental Entrepreneurship* 3: 53–69.

Teeple, Gary. 2000. *Globalization and The Decline of Social Reform: Into the Twenty-first Century.* Amherst: Humanity Books.

Thayer, Millie. 2001. "Joan Scott in the Sertao: Rural Brazilian Women and Transnational Feminism." *Ethnography* 2: 243–72.

Theodore, Nikolaus. 1998. "Jobs and Poverty Alleviation in Chicago's Empowerment Zones." In *Empowerment in Chicago,* edited by Cedric Herring, Michael Bennett, Doug Gills, and Noah Temaner Jenkins, 183–206. Chicago: University of Illinois Press.

Thomas, Paulette. 1997. "With a 'Microloan' for a Truck, Family Leaves Welfare." *Wall Street Journal,* 15 October, p. B1.

Tinker, Irene. 1989. "Credit for Poor Women: Necessary, but Not Always Sufficient for Change." *Journal of the Marga Institute* 10: 31–48.

———. 1999. "Nongovernmental Organizations: An Alternative Power Base for Women." In *Gender Politics in Global Governance,* edited by Mary K. Meyer and Elizabeth Prugl, 88–106. Lanham, Md.: Rowman and Littlefield.

Van Auken, Paul. 1999. "Obstacles to Business Launch." *Journal of Developmental Entrepreneurship* 4: 175–87.

Vartanian, Thomas, and Justice McNamara. 2000. "Work and Economic Outcome after Welfare." *Journal of Sociology and Social Welfare* 27: 41–77.

Vidal, Avis C. 1995. *Rebuilding Communities: A National Study of Urban Community Development Corporations.* New York: New School for Social

Research, Community Development Research Center of the Graduate School of Management and Urban Policy.

Vinelli, Andres. 2002. "Financial Sustainability in U.S. Microfinance Organizations: Lessons from Developing Countries." In *Replicating Microfinance in the United States,* edited by James H. Carr and Zhong Yi Tong, 137–65. Washington, D.C.: Woodrow Wilson Center Press.

Visvanthan, Nalini, Lynn Duggan, Laurie Nisonoff, and Nan Wiergersma, eds. 1997. *The Women, Gender and Development Reader.* London: ZED Books.

Von Pischke, J. D. 2002a. "Current Foundations of Microfinance Best Practices." In *Replicating Microfinance in the United States,* edited by James H. Carr and Zhong Yi Tong, 97–112. Washington D.C.: Woodrow Wilson Center Press.

———. 2002b. "Microfinance in Developing Countries." In *Replicating Microfinance in the United States,* edited by James H. Carr and Zhong Yi Tong, 65–96. Washington, D.C: Woodrow Wilson Center Press.

Wahid, Abu N. M. 1993a. *The Grameen Bank: Poverty Relief in Bangladesh.* Boulder: Westview Press.

———. 1993b. "The Growth and Progress of The Grameen Bank." In *The Grameen Bank: Poverty Relief in Bangladesh,* edited by A. N. M. Wahid, 33–48. Boulder: Westview Press.

———. 1993c. "The Socioeconomic Conditions of Bangladesh and the Evolution of The Grameen Bank." In The Grameen Bank: Poverty Relief in Bangladesh, edited by N. M. Wahid, 1–8. Boulder, Colo.: Westview Press.

———. 1994. "The Grameen Bank and Poverty Alleviation in Bangladesh." *The American Journal of Economics and Sociology* 53: 1–15.

Walker, Britton A., and Amy Kays Blair. 2002. *The 2002 Directory of U.S. Microenterprise Programs.* Washington, D.C.: Aspen Institute.

Wallace, Sherri Leronda. 1999. "Life on 'EZ' Street: Linking Community Economic Development to the Empowerment Zones and Enterprise Community Policy Goals." *Journal of the Community Development Society* 30: 154–77.

Williams, Rhys. 1995. "Constructing the Public Good: Social Movements and Cultural Resources." *Social Problems* 42: 124–44.

Wittrock, Björn, and Peter de Leon. 1986. "Policy as a Moving Target: A Call for Conceptual Realism." *Policy Studies Review* 6: 44–60.

Women's Self-Employment Project, n.d. "Women's Self-Employment Project Home Page." Women's Self-Employment Project, http://www.wsep.net (accessed 10 February 2004).

WomenVenture. n.d. "Your Guide to More Rewarding Work." http://www.womenventure.com/ (accessed 10 February 2004).

Wood, Geoffrey D., and Iffath A. Sharif, eds. 1997. *Who Needs Credit?: Poverty and Finance in Bangladesh.* London: Zed Books.

Woolcock, Michael. 1998. "Social Capital and Economic Development: Toward a Theoretical Synthesis and Policy Framework." *Theory and Society* 27: 151–208.

———. 1999. "Learning from Failures in Microfinance: What Unsuccessful Cases Tell Us about How Group-Based Programs Work." *American Journal of Economics and Sociology* 58: 17–42.

Working Capital. n.d. "Working Capital U.S.A." The Global Development Research Center, http://www.gdrc.org/icm/work-capital.html (accessed 10 February 2004).

Working Women's Forum (India). n.d. "Grassroots Organisations Operating Together in Sisterhood (South Asia)." Working Women's Forum (India), http://workingwomensforum.org/ (accessed 10 February 2004).

Young, Dennis R. 1987. "Executive Leadership in Nonprofit Organizations." In *The Nonprofit Sector: A Research Handbook,* edited by Walter W. Powell, 167–79. New Haven: Yale University Press.

Young, Iris Marion. 1994. "Punishment, Treatment, Empowerment: Three Approaches to Policy for Pregnant Addicts." *Feminist Studies* 20: 33–57.

Yunus, Muhammed. 1997. "The Grameen Bank Story: Microlending for Economic Development." *Dollars & Sense* 212: 27–29.

Zinn, Maxine Baca. 1979. "Field Research in Minority Communities: Ethical, Methodological and Political Observations by an Insider." *Social Problems* 27: 209–19.

INDEX

Tables are indicated by the letter *t*; figures are indicated by the letter *f*.

Nancy Jurik is a professor in the School of Justice and Social Inquiry at Arizona State University. She teaches courses on women and work and economic justice. Her publications focus on gender, work organizations, and small business. She has published *Doing Justice, Doing Gender: Women in Law and Criminal Justice Occupations* (Sage 1996) and numerous articles on gender and work issues. She is a past president of the Society for the Study of Social Problems.